D0002692

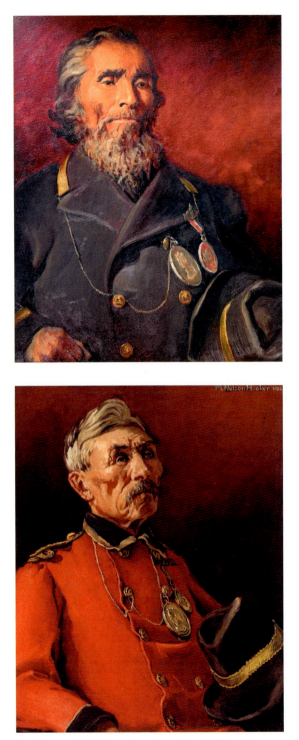

Jacob Berens, chief at Berens River 1875–1916, and William Berens, chief 1917–47. Portraits by Marion Nelson Hooker.

Memories
Myths
and Dreams

of an

Ojibwe Leader

William Berens, *as told to*
A. Irving Hallowell

EDITED WITH INTRODUCTIONS BY
JENNIFER S.H. BROWN AND SUSAN ELAINE GRAY

McGILL-QUEEN'S UNIVERSITY PRESS
MONTREAL & KINGSTON · LONDON · ITHACA

© McGill-Queen's University Press 2009

ISBN 978-0-7735-3586-2 (cloth)
ISBN 978-0-7735-3605-0 (paper)

Legal deposit third quarter 2009
Bibliothèque nationale du Québec

Printed in Canada on acid-free paper that is 100% ancient forest free (100% post-consumer recycled), processed chlorine free.

This book has been published with the help of a grant from the Canadian Federation for the Humanities and Social Sciences, through the Aid to Scholarly Publications Programme, using funds provided by the Social Sciences and Humanities Research Council of Canada.

McGill-Queen's University Press acknowledges the support of the Canada Council for the Arts for our publishing program. We also acknowledge the financial support of the Government of Canada through the Book Publishing Industry Development Program (BPIDP) for our publishing activities.

Library and Archives Canada Cataloguing in Publication

Berens, William, 1866–1947
Memories, myths and dreams of an Ojibwe leader / William Berens as told to A. Irving Hallowell ; edited with introductions by Jennifer S.H. Brown and Susan Elaine Gray.

(Rupert's Land Record Society series ; 10)
Includes bibliographical references and index.
ISBN 978-0-7735-3586-2 (bnd)
ISBN 978-0-7735-3605-0 (pbk)

1. Berens, William, 1866–1947. 2. Ojibwa Indians–Manitoba–Biography.
2. Ojibwa Indians–Manitoba–History. 4. Ojibwa mythology.
I. Hallowell, A. Irving (Alfred Irving), 1892–1974 II. Brown, Jennifer S.H.,
III. Gray, Susan Elaine IV. Title. V. Series: Rupert's Land Record Society series ; 10

E99.C6B47 2009   971.27'00497333092   C2009-901279-0

This book was designed and typeset by studio oneonone in Minion 11/14

Frontispiece:
Untitled (William Berens, chief of the Saulteaux), 1932. Oil on masonite, 67.8 x 56 cm, by Marion Nelson Hooker (1866–1946). Collection of The Winnipeg Art Gallery; gift of the artist; accession #G-36-129. Photo by Ernest Mayer, The Winnipeg Art Gallery

Jacob Berens. Nah-Wee-Kee-Sick-Quah-Yash. Chief of Saulteaux. Oil on canvas by Marion Nelson Hooker, 1909. Archives of Manitoba (N7644 CN 117)

Contents

PART III *Dibaajimowinan*, Stories and Dreams for Living

Illustrations and Maps

Illustrations

Maps

Preface

The origins of this book go back to several times and places. Its oldest roots lead back to the late 1700s, when Ojibwe people first moved westward to the Lake Winnipeg region. Some of the early newcomers moved back and forth along the waterways, but others stayed in the west, reaching as far as the Cumberland House area along the Saskatchewan River or settling along Lake Winnipeg. Trading with Scottish and Canadian fur traders based in Montreal and with the English-based Hudson's Bay Company, they and their descendants also sometimes intermarried with Crees and with members of the traders' Aboriginal families. These first generations included some of the ancestors and older relatives whose stories William Berens, chief of the Berens River band from 1917 to 1947, recounted to A. Irving Hallowell, the American anthropologist with whom he worked from 1930 to 1940.

Hallowell in turn preserved those stories and memories with care until his death in 1974, and his papers eventually passed to the safekeeping of the American Philosophical Society in Philadelphia. This book is rooted in the decade-long collaboration between these two men – Berens as a steward of his oral traditions and Hallowell as creator and guardian of their written versions. Together, they generated the texts presented in the following pages. Although Hallowell published extensively on the Ojibwe from the 1930s through the 1960s, most of the texts published here have not previously appeared in print. William Berens's reminiscences (Part II) survived only in Hallowell's handwriting, as did most of his stories and dream accounts (Part III), even though Hallowell quoted from some of them extensively in some of his publications. A number of Berens's myth texts (Part IV) were typed out for inclusion in Hallowell's projected book on Ojibwe myths and tales, which he never completed. Of the sixty myths he collected, about one third came from Berens. This volume accordingly presents much material that has rarely or never been cited or seen in print since it was first produced.

Ethnography into History

Most of the texts in this book are almost as fresh as field notes. Hallowell was evidently an excellent listener who took notes on the spot, often rather telegraphically, using numerous abbreviations. Although he did not edit or change them much after first writing them down, he commonly asked for clarifications of terms and concepts; his marginalia and small handwritten emendations often add significantly to understanding. Sometimes he wrote the stories out more fully after hearing them, recopying them by hand and elaborating on some detail or piece of information. The typed texts in his files appear to be a secretary's work as their typos reflect difficulty with unfamiliar names and terms; they can, however, generally be clarified by referring to Hallowell's other writings.

Hallowell began work with William Berens in 1930, at almost the same time the Nebraska poet John Neihardt was working with the Lakota holy man Black Elk in South Dakota. But Hallowell produced no equivalent to *Black Elk Speaks*, which is a good thing in some ways. The texts in this book are far less mediated than Neihardt's and have not required a Raymond DeMallie to seek out and retrieve transcripts closer to the original words.[1] As well, even as Hallowell never elevated Berens to the stature of a Black Elk, he rarely went to the other extreme of cloaking him in the anonymity that anthropologists often imposed on their "informants," whether they wanted it or not. Rather, he often credited and thanked the elderly chief warmly in his writings, recognizing his role and historical importance.

The present volume also has several roots in events and developments of the mid-1980s. In 1985–86, Susan Gray was completing a history thesis with Jennifer Brown in a joint master's program at the universities of Winnipeg and Manitoba. Looking at Methodist Indian day schools in four northern Manitoba communities from 1890 to 1925, she focused part of her research on schooling in the Ojibwe community of Berens River. Her studies led her to A. Irving Hallowell and other published and archival sources on the region, in the same period that Brown was returning to deeper study of the Hallowell works she had known as a graduate student. The American Philosophical Society in Philadelphia had received Hallowell's papers in 1983 and had just begun to make them available for use. Jennifer Brown was fortunate to be the first visiting researcher to work on them.

Brown had read much of Hallowell's published work during her doctoral studies at the University of Chicago in the early 1970s. Although she never met him, Hallowell was something of an intellectual grandfather figure for her, as two of her major professors, Raymond D. Fogelson and George W. Stocking, Jr., had studied with him at the University of Pennsylvania. When she arrived to teach at the University of Winnipeg in 1983, she looked forward to following up on the historical dimensions of Hallowell's work in Manitoba and on the story of his collaboration with William Berens. University of Winnipeg grants and funds from the Social Sciences and Humanities Research Council of Canada provided support for research in Hallowell's papers and between 1986 and 1992 she made several visits to the APS Library in Philadelphia.

Other doors began to open in the same period. In 1985–86 Maurice Berens, a grandson of William and an undergraduate history major at the University of Winnipeg, signed up for a couple of Brown's courses. Encouraged by Brown's interest in Berens River, he began to research family information that could be synthesized with archival and documentary sources. Brown's first discoveries among Hallowell's papers included the Berens reminiscences published here, and she and Maurice Berens undertook initial research on and transcription of this text, while he drew upon the memories of his father, John Berens, and other family members to research his course papers and add to our knowledge. In turn, other relatives became interested, leading to further links, friendships, and sharing of information.

At about that time, anthropologist James A. Clifton was planning a book of essays on historical personages he described as "culturally marginal," who functioned between Indian and white worlds and experienced complex issues of identity during their lives in these border areas. When he approached Brown about contributing a chapter for the book, she saw it as an opportunity to write a life of William Berens, pulling together the material already gathered, although she debated Clifton's positioning of such personages, seeing Berens as central to his Ojibwe world, not marginal. Her essay, "'A Place in Your Mind for Them All': Chief William Berens" is the rather distant ancestor of the introduction (Part I) of this book.[2]

Research in Hallowell's papers opened still other doors. Most strikingly, further exploration revealed the unpublished, almost final draft of an ethnography that Hallowell had prepared for the Holt Rinehart Winston series Case Studies in Anthropology, founded and edited by George and Louise Spindler. The original final manuscript had been lost in transit to the publishers in 1967 and Hallowell died in 1974 without being able to replace it. In November 1989, Brown met with the Spindlers (still the editors of the series) at the American Anthropological Association meetings in Washington, DC, and proposed reviving, editing, and updating the manuscript. They and the publisher were delighted and the result was *The Ojibwa of Berens River, Manitoba: Ethnography into History* (1992).

The preparation of that volume led to the mining of Hallowell's other manuscript materials for footnotes and emendations that would enhance his text and supply the referencing that he had not completed himself. It also led into the study of his remarkable collection of Berens River photographs, almost none of which had been published. Certain of his photographs, writings, and notes from Pauingassi and Poplar Hill, small Ojibwe communities on the upper Berens River, portrayed an old medicine man known as Fair Wind or Naamiwan, whose ceremonies Hallowell was privileged to attend and many of whose relatives he met. In 1990–91, Jennifer Brown talked with Winnipeg journalist Maureen Matthews about these materials and Matthews proposed to the Canadian Broadcasting Corporation (CBC) a radio show in the *Ideas* series that would focus on the story of Fair Wind and the origin and spread of the distinctive drum ceremony he founded. The field research for the show led Matthews and Brown to all the major Berens River communities Hallowell had visited, from the mouth of the river to Little Grand Rapids, Pauingassi, Poplar Hill, and Pikangikum, and in all those places they met people who remembered Hallowell, William Berens, and Fair Wind and his family. The two-hour show played in May 1992 with great success and led to continued research and further visits to the communities. The appearance of "The Search for Fair Wind's Drum" and of the Hallowell book, as well as the discovery of his photographs, led to memories and stories that immeasurably enriched our understanding of Hallowell's work and materials and of William Berens, his Moose clan relatives, and the other Ojibwe people whom Berens and Hallowell met along the Berens River.

While that work was going forward, Susan Gray was back at the University of Manitoba pursuing a doctoral degree with an emphasis on Ojibwe-missionary relations. Again working with Jennifer Brown, she completed her studies in 1996 with a dissertation entitled, "The Ojibwa World View and Encounters with Christianity along the Berens River, 1875–1940." In 2004, Jennifer Brown was awarded a Canada Research Chair (CRC) at the University of Winnipeg. This position provided funds for a post-doctoral research associate and Gray was the successful candidate. One of the major outcomes of her work in this position was the publication of her revised dissertation as a prize-winning book. *"I Will Fear No Evil": Ojibwa-Missionary Encounters along the Berens*

River, 1875–1940 appeared in 2006. The research support provided by the CRC enabled both Brown and Gray to return to work on Hallowell and Berens River and to create this book, which they had initially imagined as a possibility back in 1994.

This book appears in the Rupert's Land Record Society Series, which features edited volumes of documentary and oral material that would otherwise remain little known in archives or would fade from memory. In our efforts to preserve the voices of both Berens and Hallowell we have dealt lightly with the texts they generated. We have provided clarifying footnotes where necessary for amplification or understanding, but we have made every effort to preserve the personalities of the actors and the authenticity of the manuscripts. A case in point is William Berens's Reminiscences (Part II). While the text is unpolished (it was set down by Hallowell on the spot as Berens spoke), it brings us as close as we can get to Berens's voice. There is a genuine coup-tale quality to his narrations of his exploits, his adventures, the ways in which he dealt with difficult or dishonest people, and his successes in conquering difficulties in order to feed his family and chart his course in the best ways possible.

Another example, this time relating to the question of Hallowell's voice, comes in our treatment of the myths (Part IV). In the 1940s Hallowell intended to publish a book about Ojibwe myths and tales and their relationship to what he called the Ojibwe world view. We considered including some of his draft writing for that book here but decided that we could not determine just how Hallowell would have developed these materials into final form if he had been able. (Interested readers may consult these draft texts in his papers in the American Philosophical Society.) Here too, we have kept the focus on William Berens's voice and words, presenting them in the context of the rich information that Hallowell recorded about his friend and collaborator and about his people. We have, however, included as an appendix a short unpublished essay on Thunder Birds that Hallowell wrote in about 1935, fresh from his first two summers of fieldwork on the Berens River. The depth of his research and his close contact with William Berens and others are amply

reflected in this paper, which adds context and resonance for much of
the material in this book.

We hope that this volume will draw readers into the world – and
world view – of Chief Berens and will generate further rich interpretive
studies and reflections in the spirit of the long conversations that Berens
and Hallowell carried on throughout the 1930s. We both wish that it
could have appeared earlier; after all, most of the materials for it were
gathered by the early 1990s. But in the meantime, we have learned a
great deal more and our understandings have improved. Also, the researches and publications of others have added greatly to our contextual knowledge, as has the wealth of information and documentation
now available on the Internet. We can now situate and annotate these
texts much better than we could have done even five years ago.

Hallowell in Retrospect: Views from Academe

Hallowell's career does not need reviewing here, as other sources have
offered good coverage of his life and work.[3] Recently, however, a
few authors have approached his work and contributions from some
new and varied angles. In 2004, George W. Stocking, Jr., in his essay,
"A.I. Hallowell's Boasian Evolutionism: Human Ir/rationality in Cross-
Cultural, Evolutionary, and Personal Context" (2004), suggested some
links between Hallowell's scholarly interests and his personal life. Hallowell was one of Stocking's professors during his graduate studies at the
University of Pennsylvania in the late 1950s and had a strong interest
in the history of anthropology; he played a critical role in encouraging
Stocking towards that specialty.

Stocking has returned the favour by placing his mentor in historical
context, reviewing Hallowell's studies with the early major Algon-
quianist Frank Speck, the influences of Boas and other scholars on his
thinking, and his position in twentieth-century anthropology. But his
essay does more than that. Stocking considers how elements of tragedy
in Hallowell's family life, notably the recurring criminal and violent
activities of his adopted son, may have affected the trajectory of his

work. He then looks at how later generations have viewed and drawn upon Hallowell's scholarly legacies, a theme that is particularly relevant for this book, as we bring his Berens River work forward through the texts that he and William Berens put together.

Hallowell, after a brief career as a social worker, turned to anthropology in the 1920s, with the encouragement of his mentor, Frank Speck. But psychology, as Stocking observes, was also among the many fields in which he read widely. In the late 1930s, he drew some notice for his experiments with using Rorschach inkblot tests in his field work and also began to explore issues of fear, anxiety, and aggression in Ojibwe culture and personality structure; several publications from the late 1930s onward reflect these interests. Stocking states that one could argue that Hallowell's turn to these interests was intellectually grounded and "reflected a dynamic internal to his own research." But he also suggests that Hallowell's son's troubles surely had some effect on his intellectual trajectory: the themes and topics in human nature that he began to explore by the late 1930s "can be interpreted as reflecting anxieties or sensitivities that might have been aroused in the parent of a psychologically disturbed adoptive child."[4] Indeed it is hard to imagine that his son's problems did not have an impact on Hallowell, even though he was distanced from his former wife and his son by the early 1940s. At the least, his son's troubles with the law in the early summer of 1939 may have helped make it impossible for Hallowell to get to Berens River that summer; he did not return until 1940. On balance, his summers of extended fieldwork in the 1930s and his absorption in the work with William Berens must have offered respites or even an escape from deteriorating familial conditions and troubles at home.[5]

Stocking goes on to discuss Hallowell's influence on later scholars, referring especially to his studies of Ojibwe views of persons and the self, to his concept of behavioural environment, and to the fact that even after his death he continued to be much cited by Americanists, notably in the *Subarctic* volume of the *Handbook of North American Indians* (1981).[6] But Stocking sees Hallowell's influence as receding in the new century: "his students are passing and the students of his students have learned to speak a different discursive language, to which their students are now native, in a context of creeping disciplinary amnesia." He describes those who have continued to use Hallowell's work almost as survivors: "at the turn of the millennium there were still a number of Algonquianists who may be considered in one way or another 'Hallowellian'" (here Stocking lists Robert Brightman, Jennifer Brown, Mary Black-Rogers, Richard Preston, and a couple of others).[7] Hallowell's tendency to produce descriptive-theoretical articles rather than major books, along with an overall declining interest in Native American ethnography and "a changing disciplinary milieu" in the late twentieth century, have left him less prominent than other leading anthropologists of his day: "beyond the Algonquian lineage [and] the anthropology of the 'self'," for example, "Hallowell has only a limited place in the disciplinary consciousness of anthropology at the turn of the millennium." Yet Stocking admits that things could change. Scholars with an interest in "problems related to those that motivated Hallowell's research" may re-engage with and re-contextualize his works. And Stocking allows for the possibility, however remote, that Hallowell's "larger project of integrating behavioral environment and behavioral evolution – the relativist diversity of human cultures in the context of an evolving human nature – may again become a central anthropological concern."[8]

On that note, Stocking might have found cheer in the work of an anthropologist who has written of Hallowell's work with great enthusiasm. Tim Ingold's essay "A Circumpolar Night's Dream" (2000) expresses warm appreciation of Hallowell, presaging what Stocking thought might happen to bring his work back to prominence. For Ingold, Hallowell's essay "Ojibwa Ontology, Behavior, and World View" (1960) is "one of the great classics of northern circumpolar ethnography. I have turned to it over and over again for inspiration, and every reading has yielded some new insight." What particularly draws Ingold to Hallowell is his elucidation of the inclusive Ojibwe concept of "persons," which may include animals, birds, some stones, Thunder Birds, and other entities that, even if they appear commonplace, may be revealed through dreams and waking experiences to be animate and powerful. Further, those beings ("fellow participants in the same life-world") may change their form and, across species boundaries, be the kin of humans. As Ingold states, he has been "searching … for a way of understanding the continuity of the relations between human beings and all the other inhabitants of the earth which does not fall foul of the difficulties of … taking human powers of intellect as the measure of all things, that can only comprehend the evolution of species in nature by supposing an evolution of reason that takes [human beings] out of it" and "places them unequivocally at the top." Reading Hallowell, he finds that "the ontology of a non-Western people, the Ojibwa, points the way towards a solution."[9]

Another admirer of Hallowell, particularly of his style of ethnographic writing, is Regna Darnell, who highlights his contributions in chapter 7 of her *Invisible Genealogies: A History of American Anthropology* (2001). Finding his Berens River Ojibwe studies "canonical," she credits his ability "to convey the Native point of view." "Hallowell was meticulous in letting the Ojibwe speak for themselves," and "based [his] generalizations about Ojibwe worldview on consecutive narratives in Ojibwe voices, presenting them to the reader so as to make clear which words were his and which were those of Ojibwe persons."[10] Seen in that perspective, this book grows naturally from his efforts, as we aim for a fuller and richer representation of the voice of the Ojibwe person most central to his work, that of William Berens.

Other scholars have been revisiting Hallowell's work and finding it fruitful for their studies. In his *Animism: Respecting the Living World*, British professor of religious studies Graham Harvey cites a strong debt to Hallowell's work, not only for "his coining and use of the term 'other-than-human persons,'" but also for "the respect with which he engaged in ethnography and the clarity of his challenge to what is often taken for objectivity in academia."[11] It may be true that, as George Stocking says, Hallowell has slipped away from being a major ancestral figure in anthropology as a whole. But he has a special, enduring niche among Algonquianists and, thanks to Tim Ingold, also among some circumpolar scholars and others with broader interests. Meanwhile, he has also retained a niche in memory in his old fieldwork home.

Hallowell Remembered: Words from Berens River

The Ojibwe people who met Hallowell along the Berens River in the 1930s have remembered him warmly and well. In the summer of 1952, twelve years after Hallowell's last visit to Berens River, Stephen T. Boggs, a graduate student in anthropology, and his wife, JoAn, did fieldwork there for several weeks. William Berens had died five years earlier but his wife Nancy and other family members still occupied the two-story frame house, built for a former fish hatchery manager, that the chief and four-teen other members of his family were living in when Hallowell was there in the 1930s.[12]

JoAn Boggs recalls visiting the house just once. Talking with Nancy Berens, she mentioned that she and her husband were friends of Hal-lowell. Nancy "then took the initiative to say that she was still keeping the things he had entrusted to her and hoping he was going to come back for them. She took me to look into a drawer and showed me a small bundled up tent and an old camp cookstove. I told her Hallowell was disappointed he was unable to return, but we would give him news about the people here." On another occasion, JoAn was talking with Rosie Bittern, daughter of William and Nancy Berens. Rosie was the wife of Antoine Bittern who had accompanied Hallowell on his upriver trips. She "expressed pride in Antoine's connection with Hallowell, and that Antoine had been chosen to help on the trips."[13]

Forty years later, in November 1992, one of us, Jennifer Brown, along with Maureen Matthews who recorded the occasion, had the opportu-nity to meet Antoine Bittern in the company of his daughter Margaret Simmons, who translated what he recalled about those travels. Bittern went up the river three times with Hallowell. They went to Little Grand Rapids and Pauingassi, and he would tend the camp and cook while Berens and Hallowell went off every day to visit the old people. One summer when Hallowell arrived at Berens River, Bittern had already gotten hired to fish all summer. But as Margaret said, quoting from her father, "Hallowell wouldn't give in. He went to my dad's boss. Talked to the boss, and the boss said OK you can go. OK because he [Bittern] says the chief and Hallowell really liked him going along with him."

Hallowell paid Antoine Bittern well. Bittern also told us, through his daughter, "It was very important the work that he did. It was very, very important. It wasn't anything that was useless. What he did was for a good purpose." He remembered, as did others, that the people at Little Grand Rapids and Pauingassi called Hallowell *Midewigima* (*Mide* master) because he was so interested in *Midewiwin* ceremonial practices, "and he had learned so much from them."[14] Everyone got along very well with him. Bittern added that when Hallowell arrived from Winnipeg, he would bring "bundles and bundles of material to give to the women … cloth for dresses, sweaters." He talked to the women as well as the men, and he would bring gifts "if he wanted to learn about something about the way of life … That way it became worth something."[15]

On the same day that we met Antoine Bittern, we also talked with his brother-in-law, Gordon Berens, who as a young man travelled twice with Hallowell up to Little Grand Rapids. Speaking in English, Berens said Hallowell wanted to learn "the way the Indians lived before, like, their livelihood. That's what he was after to know. But he knew it all because my old dad interpret for him from the old people that he knew." Speaking of Hallowell's book, *The Ojibwa of Berens River*, which we showed him, Berens said Hallowell "understood the Indian ways and all that, their livelihood and how they made their living through trapping and fishing … He got so interested in it he went a long, long ways with it and that's why he made that book … He made it so plain. A white person could understand the ways of an Indian as soon as he reads this book." Then we asked if Hallowell danced in the ceremonies he attended. Berens's reply was animated: "Oh, he was in it! … He was crazy dancing at the Indian dance. He can do it too. He could do it good. Just as good as the Indians did. Oh, he sure enjoyed that."[16]

Another person with vivid memories of Hallowell and William Berens is Gordon Berens's brother Percy, born in 1912. He recalled having heard a number of the stories that Hallowell wrote down in his father's reminiscences (Part II). He said the relationship between his father and Hallowell was "like a partnership." As he recollected, William Berens offered Hallowell a room in his house while he was staying at Berens River. But Hallowell (no doubt mindful of the fact that, as he recorded, fifteen people already lived there) camped outside the house in the tent that was later carefully stored by Nancy Berens. There he had a table and books, and he and the chief would sit working together.[17]

In November 1994, we (Brown and Gray) shared some of William Berens's transcribed dream stories (Part III) with Percy Berens. He remembered hearing about some of the dreams, and we asked for his thoughts about putting them in a book. He replied that his father might not have wanted to tell some of the dreams to children or to other Indians on the reserve who might laugh at them. (Perhaps there was also an issue of church disapproval.) But he would tell these stories to Hallowell, because "there was *very high mutual respect* between the two of them, and because Hallowell would write them down and *understand* them" (Percy Berens's emphasis). And yes, Percy said, they should be in the book because his father wanted Hallowell to record and preserve them.[18]

In March 2008 Susan Gray and David McCrady visited Percy in the Fisher River Personal Care Home. Percy was delighted to learn of the book's progress, saying that it "is good that young Indians can learn about him [his father, William] and [about] being an Indian." Percy was adamant about the importance of young Aboriginal people learning about what he called their "genuine history"– something that he believes is all but forgotten in these times.[19] We rejoice that this book has finally come together, to bring the words of William Berens out of the archives and to fulfill the mandate that his son, Percy Berens, gave to us back in 1994 and renewed in 2008.

Ojibwe Words: Editorial Procedures

Working with the Ojibwe words in this book has presented some interesting challenges. In his writings, Hallowell used many Ojibwe words, rendering them in a distinctive orthography not currently in use. As well, especially in his handwritten research notes, he often spelled the same word in different ways, sometimes within the same document. Some of his handwritten texts were typed by a secretary not familiar with the words and symbols, and he did not always proofread them if they were not developed for publication. For consistency, we have silently adopted the spelling he most frequently used for each word. With the generous help of Roger Roulette, a fluent speaker and teacher of Ojibwe, and Rand Valentine, a scholar of Algonquian languages, we have, when possible, emended these usages with modern orthography in square brackets (a few words could not be identified) and have provided additional translations where needed. Any other emendations that we have added are in square brackets; Hallowell's own insertions remain in parentheses. For a full listing of Hallowell's Ojibwe vocabulary, see the "Glossary of Ojibwe Words" in Hallowell, in press. Hallowell also italicized Ojibwe words in his published works, but not in manuscripts. For consistency, we have silently italicized all Ojibwe words except for proper names, which, in accord with current usage, are in roman letters.

Finally, we should add a note regarding kin terms. Hallowell's translations do not reflect the fact that certain nouns in Ojibwe, notably kin terms, always have personal prefixes before their stems; in the phrasing of Nichols and Nyholm (1995), they are "obligatorily possessed." These class codes also indicate grammatical gender: *nad* for animate dependent nouns, and *nid* for inanimate dependent nouns. Thus, for example, Ojibwe-speakers do not refer to a person as "grandfather" or "sister" or "mother." They would say, "my/our grandfather," "my/our sister," or "my/our mother." Again, where appropriate, we have provided English translations of these possessive markers in square brackets.

Acknowledgments

Our first and warmest thanks go to William Berens and A. Irving Hallowell, who made this book possible through their work together. We and the readers of this book are immensely in their debt.

As some elements of this project began more than twenty years ago, these acknowledgments follow a more or less chronological path. The American Philosophical Society Library in Philadelphia began to organize the Hallowell papers after their acquisition in 1983, and Library staff members have been unfailingly helpful. Jennifer Brown thanks in particular Beth Carroll-Horrocks and Martin Levitt, who greatly aided her work during her visits in 1986–94. Charles B. Greifenstein, the current associate librarian and manuscripts librarian of the American Philosophical Society (APS), has strongly supported the project, and the APS has generously granted permission for us to publish the Berens and Hallowell materials presented in this book.

Over the years, a number of people who knew Hallowell or William Berens or both, have contributed much knowledge and many insights. On the Hallowell side, Raymond D. Fogelson, George W. Stocking, Jr., and Regna Darnell were his students to varying extents at the University of Pennsylvania and their lively memories and writings about him have helped us to know and appreciate him better. Stephen T. Boggs, while a graduate student, also knew Hallowell and was influenced by him to spend the summer of 1952 doing fieldwork at Berens River; there he had friendly relations with members of William Berens's family. He and his wife JoAn have shared their warm memories of the community, and in 1990–91, he arranged to deposit copies of his field notes in the Manitoba Archives in Winnipeg. In the same period, George and Louise Spindler, good friends and admirers of Hallowell, were facilitating Jennifer Brown's plan to publish his ethnography of Berens River, his final manuscript copy having been lost in 1967 in transit to the publisher. The collegial contributions and encouragement of all these good folk have assisted our work and sustained our enthusiasm.

On the Berens side, Maurice Berens, as a history student at the University of Winnipeg in the mid-1980s, contributed greatly to knowledge of his family through his own research and through conversations with his father, John Berens, and with others. Maurice also did a great deal of work on the initial transcription of his grandfather's reminiscences, and he and his father helped identify family members in Hallowell's photographs. At Berens River, Percy Earl Berens, William's eldest surviving son, was tremendously helpful with his vivid memories of both Hallowell and his father and their work together and in conveying his appreciation of their relationship and the importance of their work. Similarly, William's son, Gordon Berens, and his son-in-law, Antoine Bittern, who both accompanied Berens and Hallowell on some of their upriver trips, shared their memories of those travels and of how the chief and the anthropologist worked together; it was a blessing to be able to talk with each of them before their passing in 1993. Antoine Bittern's daughter, Margaret Simmons, was also part of this voyage of (re)discovery, as she too shared in and learned from these conversations. Darlene Overby has shared old family pictures with us and has been an enthusiast for the work. Darlene's grandfather, John James Everett, and his sister, Mary Jane, were raised by their grandparents, Jacob and Mary Berens (William Berens's parents) after their mother, Lizzie (Berens) Everett, died. (See the story of her passing and of her brother William's foreshadowing dream of her death in Part III, 25, this volume.)

Numerous others have contributed greatly to this work over the years. When Maureen Matthews undertook the making of the CBC *Ideas* program, "The Search for Fair Wind's Drum," she and Jennifer Brown had the privilege of traveling to the same communities in which Hallowell and Berens had worked – Berens River, Little Grand Rapids, Pauingassi, Poplar Hill, and Pikangikum. In the early 1990s, they were still able to meet and talk with people who remembered the visits of the chief and the anthropologist during which Chief Berens introduced his visitor to his Moose clan mates and their families. The conversations brought back many warm memories that provided invaluable context for understanding how Hallowell and Berens worked together, how they were perceived, and how Hallowell and his work were understood. Matthews's recordings and transcripts and her outstanding radio journalism provided important documentation of these conversations. As many of the upriver people spoke in Ojibwe, we relied immensely on the translation and interpretive work of Margaret Simmons and Roger Roulette and their invaluable linguistic skills to interpret and transcribe these conversations.

Other fellow researchers and relatives of Jennifer Brown have greatly assisted this work in various ways. Raymond Shirritt Beaumont of Frontier School Division, Winnipeg, has long been a keen and generous colleague, sharing the Berens River genealogies and family and community histories that he has worked on for years. Mary Black Rogers took great interest in the Hallowell/Berens materials and freely shared her archival notes and transcripts on Berens and McKay family histories and her transcripts from the HBC Berens River post journals. H. Egerton Young and Harcourt Brown, grandsons of the Reverend Egerton R. Young whom William Berens knew at Berens River in 1874–76, both shared and helped to assemble rich documentation and information on the Young family and their experiences there.

At the United Church Archives at the University of Winnipeg, Diane Haglund, archivist, has offered invaluable help over the years, assisting us to track information on the missions and missionaries around Lake Winnipeg. The Hudson's Bay Company Archives staff under the direction of Judith Hudson Beattie and, more recently, Maureen Dolyniuk, have been equally helpful. The biographical sketches of HBC employees posted on their website proved a remarkable resource as we struggled to identify all the people Berens met in his travels. Another wonderful resource for this sort of research is the Manitoba Historical Society website on which all past MHS publications are now searchable for names, whether of people, places, businesses, or fishing boats on Lake Winnipeg. Our warm thanks to Gordon Goldsborough, MHS webmaster, for creating and building this fine site.

In their student days some years ago, David McCrady and Lacey Sanders mined the archives to help trace the many people and travel and work details mentioned in William Berens's reminiscences. More recently, David McCrady has offered Susan Gray insights and perspectives that have enriched this book. Some years ago Victor Lytwyn prepared a map of Lake Winnipeg that located the numerous place names that Berens mentioned. Weldon Hiebert, cartographer at the University of Winnipeg, helped prepare the final version for publication. Anne Lindsay, assistant at the Centre for Rupert's Land Studies, has always been eager and ready to help with research queries and source materials. Wilson Brown helped greatly in preparing the photographic images that appear here.

Finally, our linguist colleagues, Roger Roulette and Rand Valentine, have generously shared their expertise and devoted much time to advising us on Ojibwe language issues; John Nichols has also advised most helpfully on names and orthography. At McGill-Queen's University Press, Joan McGilvray's editorial expertise and advice and Philip Cercone's support of the project (and of the Rupert's Land Record Society series in which this volume appears) have been of the greatest importance in bringing this book into being. Our thanks also go to Joan Eadie for her skill and commitment in preparing the index. We are deeply grateful for their contributions.

PART I

Introduction

A Conversation at Berens River, Dominion Day, 1930

On Tuesday, 1 July 1930, a small steamer, the S.S. *Keenora*, docked at Berens River, an Ojibwe community on the east shore of Lake Winnipeg, Manitoba. On board was an anthropologist from the University of Pennsylvania in Philadelphia, making his first trip to western Canada. A. Irving Hallowell was on his way to a summer of fieldwork in Cree communities north of Lake Winnipeg. As he travelled up the lake, he felt himself embarking into the unknown: "I had only the vaguest notions about the physiography and history of the region I was entering, or the location and ethnography of the Indian population." He described his moment of arrival at Berens River in his diary: "In sight of Berens River before 5 [pm]. Turned sharply to right and up the river – landing about 6:15 pm. Wharf near H.B. [Hudson's Bay Company] post. Indians – mostly Saulteaux. Took 3 photographs. Talked to chief – Wm. Berens. About 100 men in his band – [he is] very intelligent – excellent English."[1]

William Berens, chief of the Berens River band of Ojibwe, made a habit of being on hand when the *Keenora* made its brief weekly summer visits to his community on its way up or down Lake Winnipeg. When he and Hallowell had that first conversation, they covered a lot of ground – hunting territories, conservation issues, cross-cousin marriage, and conjuring – to judge by Hallowell's notes for that day. In August, Hallowell returned from his visits to Norway House, Cross Lake, and Island Lake and stayed for a week at Berens River. He spent a good many hours with Chief Berens. They walked to the cemetery to see the grave of Chief Jacob Berens, William's father, and Berens sold him some artifacts.[2]

As Hallowell later recalled of that visit, "as a result of long conversations, my interest in the Ojibwa people began to crystallize … I was particularly impressed by the fact that there were still unchristianized Indians 250 miles up the river in the Pikangikum Band. Besides this, Chief Berens said he would go with me if I wished to arrange a trip to Lake Pikangikum." Two years later, they made their first trip upriver together, leaving "what my friend Chief Berens called 'civilization' at the mouth of the river," to visit communities far less touched by immigration, missions, and Lake Winnipeg traffic and fisheries.[3]

The chief's offer of help, his knowledge and interest, and the unique opportunity that he presented led Hallowell to shift his fieldwork emphasis for the next decade, through 1940, from the Cree to the Ojibwe of Berens River and to focus his scholarly writing mainly on the Ojibwe for the rest of his life.[4] During the next several summers, with a couple of gaps, Berens and Hallowell travelled to Little Grand Rapids and Pauingassi, and sometimes reached Poplar Hill, Pikangikum, and other settlements on the upper Berens River. They also worked together at the chief's house in Berens River, the community at the mouth of the river. Hallowell never used a tape recorder, but he wrote hundreds of pages of research notes and drafted extensive manuscript analyses of his findings, on which he based his many publications on the Ojibwe.[5]

From Conversations to a Book

Through William Berens, Hallowell met numerous Ojibwe people from whom he learned a great deal. But the stories, memories, experiences, and observations that Berens himself shared with his visitor stand out for their quantity and the depth of the contextual knowledge that he was able to provide. In particular, one unpublished document, Berens's reminiscences of 1940, led us to see this book as a means of setting forth as fully as possible the voice of William Berens from the many oral texts that Hallowell recorded on paper. Accordingly the project grew to include not only the reminiscences (Part II) but also twenty-seven stories and dream experiences that Berens recounted to Hallowell at various times (Part III, "*Dibaajimowinan*, Stories and Dreams for Living") and seventeen myths that Hallowell wrote down as his mentor told them (Part IV, "*Aadizookaanag*, Myths").

In the summer of 1940, the two men must have spent many hours together as Chief Berens recounted his life story and Hallowell set down the closely written manuscript that resulted. At that, the text covered only the first four decades of Berens's seventy-five years – their time evidently ran out. But the manuscript provides our most complete record of Berens's childhood and younger years. For that reason, and because it presents the most continuous narrative we have from him, it comes first in this volume.

Berens also shared with Hallowell a large number of stories and myths, and Hallowell faithfully wrote them down, sometimes in slightly different versions as stories were repeated. Part III of this book presents the stories from William Berens's life that he told to Hallowell at various times from 1932 to 1940 (some are undated). These stories were not repeated in the reminiscences, possibly because Berens had already told them and Hallowell had written them down elsewhere. Also, many of them were of a different genre: they told of dreams and other epitomizing experiences distinct in quality from the more linear, secular telling of a life story. A few elements, however, do recur in both the stories and the reminiscences, and the latter text helps us to date and situate some of the stories, as the annotations indicate.

The stories are all quite short and may appear anecdotal in quality. Yet that appearance is deceptive because they all have much to teach. They provide insight into William Berens's mind and thinking, but they also deepen our understanding of Ojibwe perspectives and their frameworks of observation and interpretation, particularly as formed and guided through dreams, which are important elements in over half of them.

Part IV presents seventeen *aadizookaanag*, or myths, to use an inadequate English translation, that Hallowell recorded from William Berens (see 116–17, this volume, for a discussion of the translation issue). Hallowell hoped to include them in a book on Ojibwe myths and tales that he began in the 1940s, but never completed. As usual with his Berens River studies, he relied more on Chief Berens than on anyone else for the material he gathered. The myths complement Berens's shorter stories of "real life" while evoking some parallel themes; certain kinds of experiences recur both in Ojibwe dreams and in the legends.

Berens must have chosen those myths that he particularly wanted Hallowell to hear from a large repertoire. But he faced more than a problem of selection: within an Ojibwe framework of understanding, winter was the proper time for the telling of *aadizookaanag* and penalties awaited those who told them out of season. Because Hallowell was never able to visit in wintertime, Berens assumed those risks by telling the myths in summer. He, and probably others, told Hallowell of the Ojibwe belief that "if the taboo upon narrating myths in summer is broken, toads will come and crawl up one's clothes." Hallowell was camping with Berens one night when the chief saw a toad near at hand. On searching outside the tent he found a great many others, which clearly confirmed his anxieties. That night, and every time they set up camp thereafter, Berens was at pains to weigh down the edges of their canvas tent carefully with stones.[6]

While Berens would have believed that his Christian faith afforded protection from the bad medicine associated with toads, the fact that he saw their proliferation around the tent as a penalty for telling the myths reflects the complexity of his beliefs and his enduring Ojibwe worldview. Evidently, however, his belief in Hallowell's work was stronger than his fear of toads, reflecting the trust and mutual respect that had developed between them (see 112–13, this volume). William Berens welcomed the opportunity to assist the world, through Hallowell, to better understand his people's history and traditions, even if this understanding came at some cost to him. Among all the white men who travelled the Berens River during Berens's lifetime, Hallowell was surely his best student and his best listener.

William Berens and his Family

Taken together, the reminiscences, stories, and myths provide a rich and textured portrait of the man whom Hallowell described as "my interpreter, guide, and virtual collaborator," "whose genial companionship in camp and canoe, in fair weather and foul, never failed to enliven my task."[7] William Berens was a leader among his people and, through Hallowell's writings, indirectly became a mentor to a host of scholars and students in anthropology and ethnohistory. He belonged to an important Ojibwe family. The son of Jacob Berens (ca. 1832–1916), the first treaty chief of his community, he in turn served as chief from 1917 until his death in 1947. Working with Hallowell, he mediated the transmission and interpretation of his people's history, religion, and worldview to communities extending far beyond his own.

Along with these roles, he lived a life of many intersecting circles. He was born in 1866, the year before Canada's confederation as a dominion and four years before that new nation acquired title to Rupert's Land, as the Hudson's Bay Company territory (the Hudson Bay watershed) was known before it became part of Canada in 1870.[8] He vividly remembered his father's signing of Treaty No.5 in 1875 and the beginnings of the reserve and mission phase of his people's existence. His occupations ranged from hunting, trapping, fur trading, and commercial fishing jobs to guiding and interpreting for surveyors, Indian agents, and anthropologists. In his last years, he stirred some controversy for his pacifist leadership of his people during World War II.

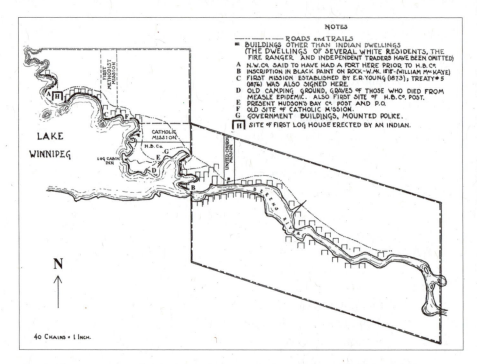

NOTES

---·---·--- ROADS and TRAILS
▪ BUILDINGS OTHER THAN INDIAN DWELLINGS
(THE DWELLINGS OF SEVERAL WHITE RESIDENTS, THE
FIRE RANGER AND INDEPENDENT TRADERS HAVE BEEN OMITTED)
A N.W.C° SAID TO HAVE HAD A FORT HERE PRIOR TO H.B.C°.
B INSCRIPTION IN BLACK PAINT ON ROCK-W.MK. IF IT-(WILLIAM M°KAYE)
C FIRST MISSION ESTABLISHED BY E.R.YOUNG (1873); TREATY #5
(1876) WAS ALSO SIGNED HERE.
D OLD CAMPING GROUND, GRAVES OF THOSE WHO DIED FROM
MEASLE EPIDEMIC. ALSO FIRST SITE OF H.B.C° POST.
E PRESENT HUDSON'S BAY C° POST AND P.O.
F OLD SITE OF CATHOLIC MISSION.
G GOVERNMENT BUILDINGS, MOUNTED POLICE.
[H] SITE OF FIRST LOG HOUSE ERECTED BY AN INDIAN.

LAKE
WINNIPEG

N

40 CHAINS = 1 INCH.

Mouth of Berens River and reserve, based on surveys of 1878 and 1910. "H" marks the log house built by Zhaawanaash (Cauwanas in Hallowell's spelling). From copy in United Church Archives, University of Winnipeg.

Chief Jacob Berens, seated, ca. 1910, Berens River, probably with band councillors and Indian agent (middle). The councillors at the time were James MacDonald and William Everett; the agent was C.C. Calverley. Postcard image kindly provided by Patricia Albers; photographer unknown.

The family of William Berens epitomized, Hallowell wrote, "the broader sweep of historical events in the Lake Winnipeg area and the consequences of the acculturation process." Through their paternal line, the men of the Berens family belonged to the Moose clan. Hallowell's genealogies of the 1930s identified three distinct Moose patrilineages with different regional origins. The Berens line traced its ancestry back to Yellow Legs (Ozaawashkogaad), William's great-grandfather, who was living on the west side of Lake Winnipeg in the late 1700s and died before 1830. Berens family tradition places Yellow Legs's origins in the Lake Superior area. Although we don't know his birthplace, he was one of the first Ojibwes to grow up west of Lake Winnipeg; most sources place the people's first major movements into this area in the 1780s and 1790s as they and their Montreal-based fur trade associates extended their ranges westward.[9]

Yellow Legs was remembered as a great leader of the *Midewiwin* or Grand Medicine Society and was possibly the first to introduce that ceremony into the Lake Winnipeg region. His wife, Mistamut, who lived long enough to know some of her great-grandchildren around Berens River, passed down the stories of his achievements. For instance, as a *manao* or curer who received medicines from the *memengwesiwag* (small dwellers in rock cliffs who possessed great powers), Yellow Legs once walked on water to a small island in Lake Winnipeg to obtain a special remedy. Another time, he sent two men to an island to bring him a certain stone he had described; it later exhibited its magical properties in the *Midewiwin* lodge.[10]

Yellow Legs's eldest son, Bear (known as Maskwa in Cree and Makwa in Ojibwe), born in about 1790, was William Berens's paternal grandfather. Bear married a woman named Amo (Bee), listed as Victoria in her burial record of 1890, of the Pelican clan; she was from the Cumberland House (Saskatchewan) area.[11] They and Bear's younger brother, Zhaawanaash (The One Who Flies with the South Wind), later moved to the east side of Lake Winnipeg and Bear brought with him his father's magical stone. Sometime around 1870, he and Zhaawanaash (William's great-uncle) conducted the last *Midewiwin* ceremonies recorded at the mouth of the Berens River, which William attended as a small boy. William's paternal grandparents and Zhaawanaash were strongly influential in bringing the boy up within Ojibwe culture and traditions.[12] William told Hallowell that Bear, in a traditional naming ceremony, gave him his Ojibwe name, Tabasigizikweas, "Sailing Low in the Air after Thunder."[13]

Berens River was not a static or homogeneous community. Hallowell remarked on the considerable mobility of the Ojibwe lineages whose genealogies he traced: various founders had reached the area from distant communities in every direction.[14] Ojibwe groups along the river had met and mingled with one another and, to a lesser extent, with Crees and with fur traders of British, French, and Algonquian ancestry. William's immediate kin exemplified such mingling, perhaps more clearly than any group that Hallowell recorded. Correspondingly, they adapted in different ways to life in a community that was both changing and diversifying.

Bear died at Berens River "about the time the first missionary came" (Egerton R. Young in 1874), but according to his grandson, "he never changed his beliefs."[15] At some point he adopted a European-style surname, Berens (borrowed ultimately from the names of two HBC governors and also applied to the river on which he lived[16]), which his son Jacob carried on. Bear's brother Zhaawanaash was baptized in 1877 by the Rev. John Semmens, the second Methodist missionary to serve at Berens River, and took the name of a respected Hudson's Bay Company chief factor, Roderick Ross.[17] The flexibility of Ojibwe surname adoption patterns in this period is illustrated by the names chosen by Zhaawanaash's offspring: one kept the name Ross, a second chose Mac-Donald, and a third took the surname Felix. The name Zhaawanaash, variously spelled as Souwanas, Sowanas, and Sawanash, also persisted as a surname around Berens River. These surname developments suggest that here, as in other Ojibwe communities, personal identities were also changing or diversifying in response to new situational needs.[18]

Jacob Berens or Naawigiizhigweyaash (Aloft in the Centre of the Sky), William's father, was born in about 1832 according to Hallowell's account. In 1861, during a visit to the Methodist mission at Norway

House at the north end of Lake Winnipeg, he became the first Berens River Ojibwe to convert to Christianity. There, he learned the Cree syllabic system that the Methodists were using to transcribe the scriptures and was baptized by the Reverend George McDougall.[19]

Jacob's crossing of this spiritual bridge may have been a quest for new powers comparable to those of his father and uncle. Or it may have been related to a development in his personal life, his marriage around that time to Mary McKay (1836–1908), whom the Berens River Ojibwe identified as "white." Her father, William McKay (1793–1887), was an HBC trader at Trout Lake in Ontario's Severn River drainage for much of his career; her mother, Julia Chalifoux (d. 1860), was of Cree and French Canadian descent. The Berens River Ojibwes' classification of Mary Berens as white would have been influenced by her evidently fair complexion, the fact that the Berens River people did not use racial terms such as "halfbreed" or Metis, their custom of classifying people by patrilineal descent, and, finally, her linguistic and cultural attributes (speaking English, drinking tea). In the 1930s, William Berens recalled that tea drinking was uncommon before his father's time. His mother remembered how his maternal grandmother, Julia Chalifoux McKay, "made her weekly cup a part of the Sabbath ritual."[20]

In one significant respect, William Berens's mixed parentage reversed the usual pattern in such families. Intermarriage had long been commonplace in the fur-trade setting of northern Canada,[21] but typically European social and cultural influences and fair complexions came through the fathers, while Native mothers transmitted the Aboriginal languages, values, and knowledge they had grown up with. Ties with Aboriginal kin and communities were usually maternal ties. As Euro-Canadian cultural and political forces gained strength in the later nineteenth century, it was usually the European-descended fathers of mixed families who were identified in one way or another with these forces. In such settings, given the male-dominated social order that prevailed, Native cultural influences were in a sense "feminized" and weakened. William Berens, however, received his Ojibwe heritage through a line of strong male leaders whose influence seemed little reduced by his

Mary McKay Berens and Jacob Berens, ca. 1906–08? Berens River.
Photographer unknown. Original in possession of Darlene Rose Overby.

father's Methodism, while his main exposure to Euro-Canadian values
came through his mother. As he said in his reminiscences, "I learned
the white ways from my mother and the Indian ways from my grandparents on my father's side so I know what both are like."[22] As an Ojibwe
boy growing up in this setting, William also seemed to achieve a balance
between the two worlds, while "tilting" somewhat toward the Ojibwe
side, at least in his later years and perhaps at least partly because of Hallowell's presence and interest.[23]

Childhood, Mission, and Treaty

The first decade of William's life, 1866–76, saw increased cultural min-gling both in his family and on a broader scale, as Berens River became a crossroads not only for Ojibwe people and fur traders but also for missionaries, treaty commissioners, and other outsiders. His father, Jacob Berens, was a force for some of these changes in encouraging the first missionary, Methodist Egerton R. Young, to come to Berens River and in signing Treaty No. 5 as chief. And he fostered an openness to change in his son. The opening sentence of William's reminiscences ex-presses the essence of Jacob's teaching. "Don't think you know every-thing," Jacob advised him. "You will see lots of new things and you will find a place in your mind for them all."

Jacob's attitude must have helped William to grow up without ex-periencing severe religious conflicts. His parents did not allow their Christianity to cut them off from unconverted relatives and while William participated in Methodist observances, he also experienced Ojibwe ceremonies that left lasting impressions. Besides attending the *Midewiwin*, he saw his grandfather Bear cure people with his medicines and conduct shaking tent performances. In the summer of 1874, William helped in building a church and house for E.R. Young, who arrived that fall. "I wanted to understand what this man was talking about," William later told Hallowell.[24]

The Young family resided at Berens River for two years. Their de-parture was precipitated by Mrs Young's ill health and also by the extent to which they believed their eldest boy, born at Norway House in 1869, was growing up more "Indian" than white under the care of his Cree nurse, whom the family had brought from Norway House, and the in-fluence of the Berens River people, notably William's great-uncle Zhaawanaash, who welcomed him into their lodges and ceremonies. In a memoir written late in life the son, E. Ryerson Young, did not men-tion Jacob or William Berens but vividly described his virtual adoption by some of their relatives. His childhood memories add further insight into the quality of William Berens's early experiences in that setting.[25]

In September 1875 came an event even more momentous than the establishment of the mission. People had been talking about "the great Queen who was buying the country," and visitors were arriving from all over for council meetings and in anticipation of receiving treaty money. One September morning, William was awakened by a frightful noise – the whistling of the first steamboat to arrive at Berens River. Lieutenant Governor Alexander Morris and his party had come to negotiate Treaty No. 5. Jacob Berens was at meetings all that day and got home late at night after signing the treaty.[26]

The terms of Treaty 5 specified that the Berens River reserve was to be surveyed and its size determined on the basis of 160 acres for each family of five. The Indians kept, however, "the right to pursue their avocations of hunting and fishing throughout the tract surrendered … subject to such regulations as may from time to time be made" and supported by the provision of an annual grant of $500 to purchase ammunition and twine for fishnets.[27] Since access to customary resources and occupations was not closed down at that time, few people probably realized that the written treaty reserved the government's right to change the status quo at will.

In the short term, the impact of the treaty appeared limited as it was localized and specific. Jacob Berens, already something of an innovator, had a new elected political role that brought him some standing among a network of Native leaders and in the context of a federal governmental department; he used that role to look after the rights and interests of his people.[28] With church and governmental support, Berens River acquired a school, although its results were very mixed in the early decades.[29] From 1875 on, annual treaty payments of five dollars a person brought a flurry of free traders each summer as "treaty time" approached. These men offered a greater diversity of small goods than the HBC post and of course benefited from the new infusions of cash that the annuities provided.

Just as important as the new mission and school and the creation of a new band structure and reserve were the broadening connections that were beginning to link Lake Winnipeg communities to an increasingly complex economic and political universe. Through his already extensive family ties, and presumably through inclination, William Berens was drawn into the new and rapidly evolving regional socioeconomic order in a variety of ways.

Work Experiences

Between 1876 and the mid-1880s, William had the equivalent of about two years of schooling with the missionary teachers who succeeded the Youngs at Berens River.[30] He was not comfortable with writing, as shown by his seeking help when drafting letters to Hallowell. But his reminiscences record that he quickly acquired other skills and knowledge of the wider world. He travelled by dog team with his father when Jacob Berens carried mail from Berens River to Winnipeg and visited the Indian Affairs office there.[31] On a summer visit to Selkirk, an older acquaintance provided a first miserable experience with brandy. He fished, trapped, hunted, and helped harvest the family's potato crop in the fall. Later he held several jobs assisting government agents in their travels. In 1886, he found summer employment with a government survey party on Lake Winnipeg. He also worked around the HBC post at Berens River, haymaking, digging potatoes, and rowing the skiff.

The early 1880s saw the start of a new era on Lake Winnipeg with the opening of the first commercial fisheries. The first Icelandic fishermen settled on the west side of the lake in the mid-1870s and soon began shipping fish to Winnipeg on the new steam schooners that were also used in the lumber trade. The spread of steam and rail transport and the use of ice for keeping fish frozen brought growing access to American markets. The years 1883–86 saw a quantum leap in the fishing industry. In 1883, two sailboats harvested 72,867 pounds of whitefish for one firm. In 1886, seven tugs and sixty-five sailboats produced 1,400,000 pounds for several companies.[32]

Berens's reminiscences describe the many new kinds of summer jobs that the fishery brought, such as setting nets and hauling and buying fish. In the winter, he continued to go trapping in the bush with his father. Then, in about 1887, the local Hudson's Bay Company post, evidently facing some competition for labour in the changing conditions, offered him more permanent employment for the first time and he contracted to serve as an interpreter and do other jobs at the Berens River post.[33]

In the summer of 1888, Berens took advantage of a different work opportunity. A survey party arrived at Berens River to start an upriver journey to lay out the new reserves for the inland Ojibwe communities covered by Treaty 5.[34] In his reminiscences and in a story he told Hallowell (94–6, this volume), Berens vividly recalled his two-month trip with them to Little Grand Rapids and Pikangikum. His memories of that adventure encouraged him to seize the opportunity to return to those upriver communities with Hallowell over four decades later.

Aside from this trip, another event at some time during these years kept William vividly in touch with his Ojibwe universe. As a member of the Methodist church, he had never gone on a dream fast. But the *bawaganag* sometimes visit without being sought and on one occasion William had a dream experience with the same personages, the *memengwesiwag*, who had favoured Yellow Legs, his great-grandfather. They invited him into their rocky cliff abode on a branch of the Berens River. As a Christian, he did not accept their offer of blessings and, since no bond was established, he felt no restriction on recounting the dream (see 92–3, this volume). He felt, however, that at any future time he could revisit the spot and accept their gifts. Faced with a traditional choice he did not take, William confidently expected the option to remain open to him in later years.[35]

Berens spent the next years partly in HBC work but more often in a variety of jobs with commercial fishermen. His reminiscences mention dozens of places he visited along the 300-mile length of the lake (see map) and dozens of people he met, both Aboriginal and non-Aboriginal. As a young man caught up in working for a boom industry, he was not in a position to grasp the extent of a problem that quickly became apparent to older people along Lake Winnipeg – the serious depletions of the near-shore fish populations on which Native communities relied. He was probably working in the fisheries in July 1890 when his father, Chief Jacob Berens, held a council about this issue at Berens River, attended by representatives from Poplar River, Black River, and other communities and presided over by Dr John Christian Schultz, then the lieutenant-governor of Manitoba and the Keewatin District.

At the meeting of 12 July, an account of which is preserved in Schultz's papers, Jacob Berens was a strong, articulate speaker for his people. He began by discreetly reminding Schultz of an episode twenty years before, alluding "to having met His Honour in 1870." William Berens's reminiscences (38–9, this volume) explicate that allusion: the Berens family had given shelter to Schultz, a strong opponent of Louis Riel, after Schultz fled from Red River into the Winnipeg River area that winter. Jacob Berens went on to describe how the commercial fishermen with their big boats were placing huge nets near the mouths of rivers, capturing the sturgeon and other fish on which the Indians relied, and how the whitefish had almost disappeared from Berens River down to the Red River at the south end of Lake Winnipeg. As he pointed out, "if we cannot catch fish we must starve." The communities had complained, the missionaries had spoken out on their behalf, and the young men had considered cutting the big nets loose but had refrained, but the people's distress had received no response. Schultz's response was patronizing and unhelpful, and the depletions continued.[36]

In 1899, William Berens married Nancy Everett, daughter of William Everett and Nancy Boucher of Berens River. Both Nancy's parents were of mixed descent. Her paternal grandfather, Joseph Everett, was an Ojibwe who had been adopted by the Metis leader Cuthbert Grant. Joseph had married the daughter of a Scots trader and an Indian (both unidentified), who had been raised by the wife of William McKay at Trout Lake. On her mother's side, Nancy Everett's grandfather was Joseph Boucher, said to be a French Canadian from Montreal, who had married a Norway House Cree woman and settled at Berens River.[37] Hallowell said little about Nancy, and her husband's reminiscences covered few of their forty-eight years together. (She was still living when Berens died in 1947). But her background had similarities to her husband's: while strongly Ojibwe in her community ties, she also had a diverse ancestry.

During these years, Berens sometimes worked for and travelled with agents of the federal Department of Indian Affairs. His recollections of them and their conduct furnish a rare record of work experiences narrated from the Aboriginal side. In 1897, while working for a fishing company at $35 a month, Berens was approached by Inspector Ebenezer McColl, who offered $45 a month if William would help him on his rounds. Berens was impressed with McColl's care and attention to his work and his treatment of his employees – "the best inspector the Indians ever had since treaty was signed."[38] Another experience working with an Indian agent was far less pleasant. For instance, when he and the agent were preparing to leave Selkirk for a tour of duty around Lake Winnipeg, the agent over-indulged in drink, leaving Berens to finish their preparations for the trip, by dog team in winter.[39]

William Berens's reminiscences largely tell of secular events without much overt cultural or religious content. Two incidents, however, one before his marriage and one after, demonstrate that he lived very much in an Ojibwe world in which sickness and other mishaps were often attributed to animate agents, human or nonhuman, whom their victim had offended.

The first occurred when Berens was working in the town of Selkirk. He bought a bottle of gin to share with a few of the other men working on the lake boats there. One man in the party was unintentionally overlooked. The next day, Berens was suddenly hit by a terrible pain in his leg. The reminiscences vividly describe the sequel – his three-week hospitalization and his return to Berens River for an Ojibwe cure at the hands of his father. Jacob Berens's diagnosis was that the injury occurred "through an Indian's magic powers [those of the man who had been slighted]." After ten days of home treatment, William was able to walk, though the leg was stiff for another two months.

A second incident occurred soon after he was married. Berens and his wife were camped on an island in Lake Winnipeg near Poplar River while he was buying fish for the Dominion Fish Company. One evening, after some alarming premonitions, they were hit by a dreadful thunderstorm. Finally the storm passed. "I jumped up and walked out then," Berens recalled. "I said, 'This old fellow did not kill us yet.'" The "old fellow" was a man whom he had seriously offended some time before, when he was working in the HBC store. The man was camped nearby when the storm hit and was trying "to do something to me by his magic power." Both this and the Selkirk incident illustrated Berens's strong sensitivity to Ojibwe norms of social interaction – sharing, respecting the requests (and potential powers) of one's elders, being careful not to offend them, and being highly sensitive to the danger of the possible consequences.

Although Ojibwe values about sharing and obligation guided Berens's thought patterns and personal relationships, they did not keep him from functioning in an economic universe that was increasingly dominated by entrepreneurship, wage labour, money transactions, and new and more specialized occupations. Early in his history of intermittent contract work for the Hudson's Bay Company, he negotiated a raise when his duties were increased. His reminiscences also record a number of successful deals in the fish-buying business. In 1899, he was put in charge of the HBC Poplar River post north of Berens River. The post at the time "was in bad shape before I took hold. I pulled the post out of the hole and I asked for a raise." When the Berens River manager refused, Berens went back to fish-buying.

During the winters of 1901–04, Berens had mail-carrying contracts to points around Lake Winnipeg. He also began buying fish and furs for a free trader, making the rounds of the Indian camps before the Hudson's Bay Company men got there and causing grief to the Berens River post manager, Frederick Disbrowe. He clearly enjoyed the tactical challenges of outwitting the Hudson's Bay Company, though he periodically returned to its employ in later years.

Berens's reminiscences break off in 1904. Other sources, however, including the recollections of family members, help to continue the story. In the following decade, he again worked at least intermittently for the Hudson's Bay Company at $150 a year. His son John recalled that William was allowed to set out traps when carrying supplies to the Indian camps and thus supplemented his income with his own furs while picking up those of others for the company. Berens also worked for a while at Norway House and then had charge of the HBC outpost at the Bloodvein River, south of Berens River.[40]

Serving as Chief

William's father, Chief Jacob Berens, died on 7 July 1916. In an election held on 6 January 1917 William succeeded him as chief of the Poplar River, Bloodvein, and Little Grand Rapids reserves as well as of his own band. The resident Methodist missionary, Percy E. Jones, was happy to find "the people were all practically of one mind" in choosing him and added, "I am sure he will do all he can to help his people to better living ... I believe all the people respect him."[41] In 1921–22, the other bands began to elect their own chiefs, relieving Berens of the pressure of trying to visit these reserves several times a year while continuing to work for the Hudson's Bay Company.

As chief, Berens was assisted by three councillors, later two. The federal government paid him $25 annually for his services and his councillors received $15 plus a new outfit of clothes every two years. The chief's jacket had "brass buttons and a one inch wide gold braid around the collar and cuffs; the pants had a two inch wide red stripe on each leg." Twice yearly, Chief Berens traveled to Selkirk and Winnipeg to check on rations and other matters; he also had charge of distributing monthly food supplies (flour, tea, lard, rolled oats, bulk beans, salt pork, and molasses) to the old people on the reserve.[42]

Berens's descendants remember that he placed much emphasis on agriculture. He had two large gardens that each yielded up to one hundred bushels of potatoes. He also kept livestock and at one point had two steers and thirteen cows. While his family used some of the potatoes and milk, a large portion was given to families on the reserve. Each summer, the Berenses and other families would cut and stack hay for the cattle for two or three weeks on hay land six or eight miles from Berens River; in winter, it would be hauled in with wagons and horses that were kept for hauling hay and firewood. William Berens's influence and example led Berens River to be "the only reserve on Lake Winnipeg to practice agriculture to such an extent," according to family recollection. After his death, "the practice went into decline" and the horses died.[43]

In the 1930s, Chief Berens was instrumental in opening commercial fishing on Lake Winnipeg to Indians. Previously, Indian fishermen had not been licensed to operate and their fish-selling activities had been clandestine (although Berens in his reminiscences mentioned no encounters with police). Berens worked with Roxy [Daniel Roy] Hamilton, Liberal member for Rupertsland of the legislative assembly in Manitoba, and with representatives of the Catholic church to remove the restriction. He also negotiated contracts for the Berens River band to cut and haul wood for the HBC post and for the lake ships that visited Berens River. The HBC woodcutting employed thirty men, and the company also paid $.50 a cord as stumpage fee to the band's account.[44]

Working with Hallowell in the 1930s

During these busy years, William Berens also found time and "a place in his mind" for A. Irving Hallowell, the visiting anthropologist. Encouraged by a good listener, the man of history, deeply enmeshed in the secular activities of chief and entrepreneur, became, at intervals, a man of myths, reaching back to his Ojibwe religious traditions and family stories. Berens was in his mid-sixties in 1930 when he first met Hallowell, who was then in his late thirties. It would have been natural enough for him, at that age, to start thinking more about his heritage and his ancestors. But other factors may also have made him responsive to Hallowell's questions and interests. Berens had seen more than six decades of change and diversification in the Lake Winnipeg area. While he had benefited from some of those developments, he was certainly aware of losses, of customs and ceremonies that no longer flourished.

Additionally, one particular incident, although not mentioned explicitly either by him or by Hallowell, may have helped trigger a sympathetic response to the anthropologist. In the summer of 1926, one of Berens's sons, aged seventeen, who had been attending the local Methodist-run day school, became one of its first two students eligible to take the high school entrance examination. He apparently overslept and missed the examination and was not allowed another chance because of "a serious misdemeanor," its nature unspecified. Chief Berens, angered at his son's treatment, withdrew his other children from the school and there was bad feeling between him and the teacher for at least two years.[45] This falling out may have caused Berens at least to reassess (though not reject) his church connection.

As noted earlier, Chief Berens made a practice of meeting the summer lake ships that stopped at Berens River on their way between Selkirk and Norway House. His meeting with Hallowell on 1 July 1930, during the brief stopover of the S.S. *Keenora,* that evening, was seminal for both men. Hallowell was, as he realized, extremely fortunate to make the immediate acquaintance of Chief Berens, the knowledgeable and experienced guide and collaborator who would make his work possible.[46]

A look at the relationship between Hallowell and Berens and its aftermath as reflected in Hallowell's later writings suggests ways in which Berens's memories and outlook guided and shaped Hallowell's perspectives and syntheses of data, just as Hallowell influenced the framing of Berens's reminiscences. Writing in the 1960s, Hallowell was explicit about how Berens had influenced his own intellectual framework and orientation: "from the beginning of my association with him, I became historically oriented as a matter of course because we made constant reference to the persons of past generations in the genealogical material we had collected together." Hallowell's richest genealogical materials came, naturally enough, from Berens himself. As a consequence, Berens's own four-generation family history came to serve as

William Berens and Nancy Everett Berens, surrounded by family members.
Clockwise from lower left: Ida May Berens, Alice (Dolly) Berens (Everett) with infant,
Rosie Berens, Percy Berens, William Berens, Jr., Mary Rose (his wife), John Berens, and Bertha
and Matilda Everett (Alice's daughters). Identifications courtesy of John and Maurice Berens,
1991. Berens River, ca. 1932. Photo by A. Irving Hallowell. Hallowell papers, American
Philosophical Society, Philadelphia.

Opposite:
Chief William Berens's house at Berens River, Manitoba, ca. 1930–32. The house was originally
built for a local fish hatchery manager, and burned down sometime around 1990. Photo by
A. Irving Hallowell. Hallowell papers, American Philosophical Society, Philadelphia.

an implicit prototype for Hallowell's explicit model for the Berens River Ojibwe.

Berens and Hallowell agreed on one matter: the upper Berens River communities were still a traditional world where the old ways survived almost untouched. To visit Pikangikum or Poplar Hill was to visit "the living past in the Canadian wilderness," as Hallowell entitled chapter 1 of his ethnography, for here one could still observe the ceremonies and lifestyle that William Berens's father and grandfather had experienced. Hallowell's abstract spatial "cultural gradient" from pagan and Aboriginal Pikangikum down the river to Little Grand Rapids and Lake Winnipeg, had its temporal analogue in the four generations from Yellow Legs down to his grandson Jacob and great-grandson William Berens.[47]

The correspondence between the two gradients, temporal and cultural-geographic, was powerful and convincing to both men. It did not, however, take into account information that was beyond their reach in the 1930s. For instance, neither Hallowell nor Berens had an accurate idea of how much Ojibwe-European interaction had occurred along the Berens River in the previous two centuries. Not until the 1980s did Victor Lytwyn's detailed archival research reveal the extent of early fur-trade activity, both HBC-and Montreal-based, in the upland regions known as the Little North, east of Lake Winnipeg.[48] In the 1930s, Pikangikum and Poplar Hill appeared relatively "unacculturated" compared to the downriver communities, but their people, like those down the river, had long experience with outsiders and their goods. Their ancestors had lived through the region-wide fur shortages that occurred during the intensive trade competition before the Hudson's Bay and North West companies merged in 1821, although in later periods they were certainly more isolated than the lakeside people.

Although Berens and Hallowell may have agreed on cultural gradients and got along well enough to collaborate during several summers of intensive fieldwork in the 1930s, Hallowell at times asked much of their relationship. In 1935, a year in which he did not visit Berens River, the anthropologist sent Berens nine pages of detailed queries on Ojibwe names and genealogies, leaving spaces for answers to be written in. Berens, with help from others, managed to fill in quite a few blanks.

But after one attempt to sort out some confusion, he added, "I am not want to say things to spoil your work. You Better stay with your own notes. I know we are trying to do our best to get everything correct about those people."[49]

An incident that occurred in the summer of 1937 led Hallowell to conclude that Berens sometimes found their work together burdensome. On a deeper level, it suggested that in some areas, such as dream interpretation, the two did not always reach an accord. One morning, while they were traveling upriver to Little Grand Rapids, Hallowell asked Berens if he had had any dreams the night before. Berens related that he had dreamed he was out traveling with a boy, on snowshoes: "I sighted a camp but there was no one in sight … As we came closer a man [a stranger] appeared. This man handed me some money, over one hundred dollars in bills. I could see an X on some of them. But the bills were the color of that [pointing to Hallowell's yellow-brown sleeping bag]. This man also gave me some silver and I gave some of it to the boy." (See 102–3, this volume).

Hallowell then asked what Berens thought the dream meant. Berens took it as auspicious, believing "it might indicate that he would catch a fox the next winter," and inferring this from the color of the bills, which he thought very curious; he linked the fox to the money it might bring him. This interpretation, as Hallowell knew, reflected the customary Ojibwa outlook on dreams as prefiguring what might or could happen. But Hallowell, at the time, had great interest in psychological tools of analysis. He proposed his own interpretation, which he published in 1938: "The Freudian symbolism in this dream [feces = money] is so transparent that it needs no further comment. On account of the color of my sleeping bag it could hardly have been more forcibly emphasized." To him, the dreamer's seizing on the colour of the bills demonstrated the centrality of that element. Hallowell added that when he attempted to explain the Freudian symbolism of the dream to Berens, the chief "seemed in no way resistant to the idea."[50]

Of course, this did not mean that Berens accepted this interpretation. Although he himself evidently considered the dream as positive, he was undoubtedly skilled at the Ojibwe custom of showing respect and not contradicting an outsider, no matter what curious things he might say.[51] But Hallowell's own flat acceptance of Freudian interpretation in this instance is striking. To use more recent terminology, two different frames of reference for dream interpretation confronted each other on this occasion: while Hallowell accepted Berens's interpretation as emic, representing an Ojibwe insider's understandings, and his own as etic, applying an objective frame of analysis, readers may be struck by how emic both interpretations were, with Hallowell's being strongly influenced by the neo-Freudian anthropology of the 1930s.[52]

In the next paragraph of his discussion of the dream, Hallowell, still speaking in psychological terms, revealed his own uncertainty about their relationship and Berens's attitude towards him. As he noted, Berens, then aged about seventy, had been "his interpreter and mentor" for several summers:

> He has become rather tired of the work, however, and rationalizes this by telling me that I have already written down all I need to know. Here he was then starting off on another trip ... This dream is probably the expression of repressed aggression towards me. I was the man he failed to recognize ... I gave him the money, which approximated the amount he would earn, but the money was also faeces, metaphorically speaking ... At the same time, since we have been close friends, he could not turn me down, and he needed the money as well. But ... internally he very much resisted going. Besides, the journey up the river is not an easy one. There are 50 portages ... and W.B. has been accustomed to do his share of the carrying, besides the cooking. Then when we are encamped there are (to him) the endless inquiries and hours of translating what other people have to say.[53]

The episode is revealing. Berens, while puzzled by some aspects of the dream, took it as predicting some successful trapping and the receipt of cash. Hallowell read into it his own doubts and insecurity about the nature of their relationship.

Creating the Reminiscences

Hallowell and Berens worked together for two more summers after this event, in 1938 and 1940. In light of Hallowell's reflections on their relationship, the attention that he finally gave to Berens himself is of interest. He probably had a mixture of motives in taking down Berens's reminiscences in 1940, even though he evidently had no plan in mind for how he might use them. Certainly he would have realized that Berens might not be around much longer to record his life story and that their time together was limited; indeed, this was Hallowell's last sojourn on the Berens River. As his Freudian dream analysis hinted, he also felt some guilt that, in using Berens as his bridge to the upriver people, he had rather overlooked and sometimes overworked the aging chief, the man who made it all possible.

No doubt the many hours that Berens spent talking while Hallowell wrote became tedious at times for both of them. Indeed the task never got finished: the manuscript ends abruptly with events that occurred in the winter of 1903–04. But, at least for Berens, this time the "endless hours" were, for a change, not spent on "what other people have to say." The document they created, even if cut short, offers a close, personal view of the man who made Hallowell's work possible.

The reminiscences also mention, aside from family members, the names of about sixty people, Aboriginal and non-Aboriginal, whom Berens met and knew around Lake Winnipeg from the 1870s to 1904. Berens travelled widely around the lake, to the growing city of Winnipeg, and briefly to North Dakota. He worked for or with missionaries, fur traders, commercial fishermen, and Indian agents and seemed to remember them all when he talked with Hallowell: the reminiscences are remarkable for their detail and the wide range of names mentioned – of people, places, and steamers and even the fishing boats on the lake. Together, he and Hallowell created a unique personal record of his memories of three decades of enormous change in the Lake Winnipeg region, which they complemented in the 1930s with their collaborative ethnographic studies of William Berens's people.

Last Years

A letter that Berens sent to Hallowell in July 1941 suggests that the chief was beginning to miss his former visitor: "You must not think I'm forgetting about you. But I never forget about you, but I had now body to write a letter for me." After giving various family news, he added, "Even the children are not forgetting you yet. I'm thanking you very much those books you send me. We like to read those. I know you must be very busy every bod[y] trying to do something about this war ... Closing with best regards to you." (Berens likely did not realize that the Americans had not yet entered World War II.)

The war years, which for Canada began in 1939, had brought new challenges to Berens and his community. Warfare was not something Berens personally feared; indeed, in his youth, he had had a dream (91–2, this volume) that gave him confidence that in battle, bullets would never hit him.[54] But he did not want to involve his people in the war and, since band members required his permission to enlist, he had the means to uphold his position. His grandson Maurice Berens explained his controversial stand and its results: "William's attitude was that he would not send men overseas to kill people that he did not know; in this he was supported by the other chiefs around Lake Winnipeg and there were no enlistments from Poplar River, Little Grand Rapids, or Bloodvein."[55]

Berens, however, did aid the war effort through peaceful means. As chief, he recruited both treaty and non-treaty Indians to help harvest crops on farms in Manitoba and Saskatchewan to make up for wartime manpower shortages. The Indian agent would tell the local HBC manager how many men were needed and Berens gathered them, accompanied them to Winnipeg, and brought them back after the harvest; for this, he received $5 a day.[56] Meanwhile, he and Hallowell still corresponded occasionally. Berens's two last surviving letters gave news of various people and activities and expressed hopes that they would meet again. On 31 July 1945, he described his wartime work: "I've been looking after the harvesters. Last summer I was in Winnipeg for two months. This year I am going in again about the fifth of August ... I am taking

Chief William Berens and A. Irving Hallowell at Pauingassi, Manitoba, ca. 1933. Photographer unknown. Hallowell papers, American Philosophical Society, Philadelphia.

men from Arnold [Island] Lake, Oxford, Norway House, Little Grand Rapids, Berens River. I'm taking them in all over Manitoba to Boissevain, Holland, Carmen, Sioux Lake."

He also still looked forward to seeing Hallowell again: "I am very glad to hear from you. Lots of people always been talking about you. They don't forgot you – even my grandchildren always mention your name … We might be seeing you again at Berens River. I think I'll be all right for six years. Your true friend." His final letter is dated 3 January 1947: "I was very glad when I receive the Christmas card from you … You might think we forget you. But we don't forget you yet at all. Even the people from Little Grand Rapids are always asking me about you. Asking me if you are coming for a visit … I am the oldest here now. But will be very glad to meet you again. I will tell you lots of things when I meet you this summer."

The meeting never came about. Chief Berens died at Berens River on 23 August 1947. A *Winnipeg Tribune* obituary praised him as "a fluent and gifted speaker and an energetic leader of his people."[57] Closer to home, one of his old friends, Tom Boulanger, described the funeral and paid a personal tribute in his own reminiscences: "When the body was took to the church the people were walking. They started singing … a beautiful song … I was feeling in my heart that it's very kind. I think that was what they felt too. That was the last of Old Billy Berens. I knew he was a very honest man and he was a nice speaking man when he lived in this world."[58]

The story of William Berens could be told in different ways, from different perspectives. One theme, however, remains central: while interacting with many facets of a changing world, Berens remained strongly Ojibwe, even though his mother, according to family tradition, was categorized as "white" (patrilineal descent was the norm in both her ancestral lines). Just as William "identified with his father, Jacob," so his sons in turn "considered themselves Indians,"[59] despite having a mother and three grandparents of mixed descent.

The extent to which William Berens remained Ojibwe in identity, culture, and personal ties while functioning in a diversity of occupations and social settings presents a challenge to Hallowell's tendency to draw a sharp contrast between the "acculturated" lakeside Ojibwa (such as Berens) and the upriver "pagan aboriginals." A closer look at Berens through the magnifying glass of the texts that Hallowell himself gathered from him and through familial and other sources reveals more complexity than emerged in Hallowell's published studies (which were also largely written for social scientists interested in other matters).

The close collaboration of these two men and Hallowell's record-keeping over several years made this book possible. Each of them, through his recorded interactions and responses, also brings the other into clearer focus. Hallowell's writings and published works, referring

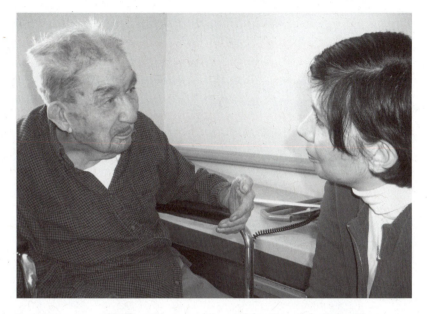

Percy Berens, son of William Berens, and Susan Elaine Gray at the Fisher River personal care home, Manitoba, March 2008. Photograph by David McCrady.

repeatedly to "Chief Berens," "W.B.," and "my most valuable inform-ant," pointed to a need to bring this man out of the shadows and place him centre-stage, speaking with his own voice to the extent that he and other sources would allow. But it was William Berens who chose to share his reminiscences, the stories and myths he knew and the dreams that he experienced, with a visitor he valued, one who cared about hear-ing and preserving them. We are all richer in knowledge and under-standing thanks to his patience, good will, and generosity.

PART II

Map of Lake Winnipeg and the Berens River area, showing places mentioned in William Beren's Reminiscences. Prepared by Victor P. Lytwyn and Weldon Hiebert.

Reminiscences of Chief William Berens: "A Place in Your Mind for Them All"

Introduction

The "Reminiscences of Chief William Berens" consist of about sixty handwritten pages (a few inserts are unnumbered) that A. Irving Hallowell wrote in the summer of 1940, probably mainly while camping next to the chief's house at Berens River. The first thirteen pages are neatly written out and appear to be recopied; the rest are in telegraphic prose with many abbreviations. On the first several pages, Hallowell added a few brief footnotes, some of which he wrote in about 1963 to judge by the dates of works cited; their contents have been absorbed in the annotations provided here, placed within parentheses. He drew upon the text to an extent in the early 1960s as he prepared his Berens River ethnography (unpublished until 1992), but did not manage to do further work with it.

We have added annotations (within square brackets) that supply the full names and identifications of persons and places referred to wherever possible, along with dates and other contextual information. Since

Hallowell evidently wrote much of the manuscript in some haste, probably as Berens was talking, we have silently completed and spelled out
abbreviated words and initials and inserted numerous dropped pronouns to improve clarity and readability. Where interpretive questions
remain, we provide emendations or queries in square brackets or in the
endnotes. With due caution to avoid changing meaning, we have also
silently and minimally supplied or modified punctuation and para-
graphing and have entered correct spellings of names as they occur in
documentary sources. Subheadings have been added in square brackets to demarcate and highlight the topics covered.

[Childhood Memories]

My father used to say to me: "Don't think you know everything. You
will see lots of new things and you will find a place in your mind for
them all." My father was a very wise man and I have never forgotten
his words. I have seen lots of new things in my life, things I never
dreamed of when I was a boy. I am still seeing new things and I expect
to see more!

I can't tell you the year when I was born but I can remember when
we were down at White Dog, the year that Louis Riel took possession
of Fort Douglas [Upper Fort Garry, 1869–70].[1] My father was hired
by the Hudson's Bay Company to work at White Dog [Eagle Nest]
for the winter.[2] There was a big trader there, a fellow by the name of
William Sinclair.[3] What I remember is a pile of house logs. My sister
Julia was holding me by one hand helping me to climb up those logs
when we saw a bunch of cattle coming running towards the house.
This was the first time I ever saw horned animals like that. I was
scared of them and tried to climb on the logs; my sister helped me.[4]

That winter my father was travelling a lot, visiting the Indian
camps to try and get ahead of that trader Sinclair. The same winter
Dr. [John Christian] Schultz and Dr. Vaughn [Walter Robert Bown]

camped at our place on their way east. They were heading for Ottawa or somewhere else.[5] They had three dogs to carry their baggage. Old Joseph Monkman was doing the dog driving.[6] Dr Schultz was running away from Riel.

In the spring after the trading was over, we left White Dog to go to the Stone Fort [Lower Fort Garry] on the Red River. My father was asked to stay on but he did not accept the offer because my [younger] sister Eliza was staying at Berens River and he wanted to get back there. We got into a York boat and came to Berens River.

That summer [1870] my father worked as a guide on the York boat. After he got through that season he built a little house at Pigeon Bay. This was the first log house built there. It was a good place for catching sturgeon. This great fish was caught the whole summer. It was smoked and pounded and made into something like pemmican. That's what we lived on then. Berries were our jam – raspberries, saskatoons, strawberries, gooseberries, blueberries. No one had gardens in those days. When the sturgeon moved out in the fall, the whitefish moved in. Then we caught whitefish and prepared for the winter. We hung them up to freeze, 10 on a stick. This was feed for our dogs and ourselves. In the month of September we put up wild rice, too, if it was a good season. Wild rice does not grow good every year. There must be a certain amount of water. If the water is too high it will not grow. If it is too low you can't even paddle a canoe in the rice fields. If there is only six inches of water it is pretty hard to get at the rice.[7]

When winter began the trapping and hunting started. There were no moose then; we hunted caribou.[8] Even in January, the coldest month of the year, we had plenty to eat. Rabbits had to be caught in the winter to make new blankets. My grandmother [Amo, *aamoo*, bee (Victoria), d. 1890] used to make a rabbit skin coat and mitts for me. They were fine for playing. I used to play a lot with snowsnakes (*sósïman*). All the boys used to play with them in winter.[9] We played a lot at tobogganing. Every boy would make his own toboggan out of poplar wood. Then we would look for a high place from which to slide. We sometimes iced the toboggans. Then they would go fine.

The beginning of March we left our house and lived in a birch bark wigwam. We did not stay in one place but moved our camp almost every week. It must have been about in April that my father and uncles picked up the canoes they had left in the fall. My uncle used to make these birch bark canoes. Then we went out hunting for beaver and muskrats.

After the spring hunt was over we used to move close to the Company's post [at Berens River]. This must have been in June. I remember that the leaves were a pretty good size by this time. The sturgeon would begin to arrive by this time too. I can remember as many as 20 canoes going up the river to Sturgeon Falls. When they came back each canoe would be carrying as many as eight or 10 sturgeon. The women would cut these fish in slices and smoke them. Then the dry sturgeon was pounded. It was finer than rolled oats. Then the Indian women would make those birch bark rogans [baskets] and fill them up. In the morning a woman would take a cup full of the pounded sturgeon, dump it on a plate, and mix the sturgeon oil with it. That was a good breakfast for a man. There was no bread for the Indian then.[10]

We boys used to make our own bows and arrows. And we would hunt squirrels and partridges with them. Sometimes we would put up sticks in a row. They would be of different sizes and not too close together. We called them soldiers. Then we would start the fight. The boy who was the best shot would knock all of them down.

We would also cut boats about two feet long out of poplar. We would rig them with mast and sails. Then we made little clay squares. These were the freight we put on the boats. We would pretend that across a little bay was a company post. Then we would set the boats loose and see which one would arrive first with its cargo.

The boys played the moccasin game but not the girls. Both boys and girls played *näpäwan* [the ring and pin game, *naabawaan* refers to the ring] and checkers.[11] The girls used to make dolls for themselves and dress them. They also put up little wigwams and would press petals of flowers on leaves in imitation of patterns of silk work.

I can remember both English and Saulteaux spoken in my home since I was a baby because my mother [Mary McKay] was a Scotch

woman (and part French). My grandfather (mother's father)[12] lived
with us and he and my mother spoke English all the time. But my
mother and father talked in Saulteaux. My mother talked mostly
English to me. As soon as I started to go round and play with the
Indian boys, I forgot all my English entirely. When I was older and
went working among white men I picked it up again because they
spoke no Saulteaux. My father spoke English as well as Saulteaux.
He learned it in the Hudson's Bay Co. service. But none of my uncles
(father's brothers) could speak English.

At the time I was telling you about, my mother's brother, William
McKay [Jr.], was the post manager up the river at Little Grand
Rapids.[13] He was married to Betsey, the daughter of Cuthbert Grant.[14]
He left the Company about this time [1871] and my father gave him
the house at Pigeon River. This was the second house my father had
built there and it was not quite finished. We only used the first one a
year. My uncle opened a store and started to trade on his own. He
went to Red River and bought quite a lot of goods. He also brought
back a cow and an ox. Outside those that the Company had, these
were the first cattle in this part of the country. It was in my uncle's
store that I first saw braces. I thought they were very pretty things.
I used to run into his store to see those pretty things all hanging
bunched together. I used to hear my mother talking about Queen
Victoria – a great Queen. I found it very strange that a woman was
the head of men and everything else and that she was going to buy
this country.

[Mission and Treaty at Berens River]

Well, we left our house at Pigeon Bay and moved to Berens River.
There were only a couple of families of Indians that had built log
houses up to this time. They were at the point. Old [Jim] MacDonald
had a house and so did old Cauwɑnäs [Zhaawanaash] my father's
uncle. All the other Indians lived in old fashioned wigwams.[15]

It was when we got to Berens River that I heard a missionary was coming. Two men from Norway House were sent out to hew the logs for the foundations and framework of a church and dwelling house.[16] They cut the logs on Swampy Island (Berens Island). They had a dog team to draw the logs to the place where the church was to be built. They worked all summer building the house and church. The house had a flat roof.[17] My father was working on the York boat that summer [1874]. I used to go along with my uncle to the church and keep the dogs away from the grub of the workers. I was very glad to do that for my three meals of bannock a day.

I have not mentioned my grandfather, my father's father [Bear] yet.[18] He practiced the old Indian religion. He may have died about the time the first missionary came. But if he lived longer he never changed his beliefs. This grandfather had lost all the fingers of his left hand except the thumb. Yet he was a conjurer. How could he have shaken the tent himself? I used to see him go into the conjuring tent but the voices I heard coming out from it did not seem like his voice. I saw him cure sick people with his medicine and by *nibakīwin* [*nibikiiwin*, use of sucking tubes to draw illness from the body]. I had reason to believe that my grandfather knew what he was doing and that his beliefs were true. I used to hear my mother talk about God but I did not see anything that my mother did that proved to me that what happened was through the help of God. I saw no power comparable to what I had seen my grandfather use. For I saw my grandfather in the *Midéwiwin* once. It must have been the last one ever held at the mouth of the river. My grandfather was the headman. That is another thing I can't forget. I had a small piece of dog meat passed to me that time and I ate it.

When the missionary Egerton Young came and preached to us about the love of God and His Son I wanted to understand what this man was talking about. Finally, I got enough sense to believe in Christianity. A lot of others had the same experience. But even today [1940] some of the people up the river don't know what to believe. The wife of my grandfather – Victoria [Amo]– lived a long time and was baptized. I learned the white ways from my mother and the Indian ways from my grandparents on my father's side so I know what both are like.

I think it was the summer after the church was built and the missionary came that people began coming to Berens River from every direction. They came from across the lake at Jack Head, from Hole River and Bloodvein on the south, Poplar River on the north and down the [Berens] river from the east. The people were talking about the great Queen who was buying the country. I began to wake up a little now. I was curious to know what was going to be. A council meeting was held pretty near every second day. People were taking out "Treaty" debt. It looked as if they expected to get something.[19] I was pretty sure that something was going to happen but I did not understand just what it all meant.

On the 19th day of September, 1875 – I know that date well now – I was asleep in the wigwam. Suddenly a sound woke me up – a sound I had never heard before. I used to hear my grandmother talking about a *wíndīgo* and the terrible shouts he made. So I wondered if it could be a *wíndīgo* and I was a little scared. I heard the sound four times. And I heard my mother get up. Then I heard a man speaking from outside the wigwam. He said, "Jacob," – that was my father – "are you up?" "Yes," said my father. "There is the boat," the man said. "It's out at Barrel Rock whistling for a pilot." So my father got four men and went in a skiff to bring in the boat.[20]

By the time I got up I heard everyone shouting, "*Ktciogima* [*gichi-ogimaa*, the big boss] is coming! The Queen is going to buy the country from us!" A couple of hours after, John Wiskis and I were watching the mouth of the river. We saw something coming around the point. Everybody was out by that time to see this monster boat that was coming in the river blowing her whistle. There was great excitement. The boat dropped her anchor right in the center of the Berens River harbor. A York boat was sent out to get the men who were sent by the great Queen. There was Lieutenant-Governor [Alexander] Morris and the Honourable James McKay, the interpreter. The Indian Agent was aboard too, but at that time he was just a common clerk. Two of the daughters of the Lieutenant Governor were in the party, too.[21]

The York boat did not head for the Company's post but the Indian camp. My father was standing on the bank waiting to meet the party and I was standing beside him. As soon as the boat pulled in those five persons walked up to my father – the two ladies and the three men. I was fooled though. When I saw a man with a big stomach, well dressed and a gold watch chain, I thought he was the big boss. But this man [McKay] was the interpreter. I did not expect to hear a white man speak my language but this interpreter said to my father, "Our great mother Queen Victoria has sent us to make a bargain with you about your country." Then the Lieutenant Governor walked up and stretched out his hand to my father. The first thing he said was, "My grandfather had an Indian name – his name was Sakīgīzik" [Zaagi-giizhig?] (Standing Up and Reaching the Sky). Then he told my father to go to the mission house. I went along with my father. When we got there he opened the mission warehouse. I saw them pitch out little round yellow looking sacks – a big bunch of them. They were hams! Once my father was asked whether there were enough. "No!" he said. "I have a big crowd to feed." So they pitched out some more. There were about 30 sacks of flour taken out, too. After the grub was distributed there was a council meeting in the mission house. The Treaty was signed about midnight.[22]

I don't know what time my father got back home that night. When I got awake the next morning and got up, I saw some new clothes lying there by my father – a red fancy coat and dark blue pants, socks, and boots. There was also a flag and a medal! I heard people say then that my father had been elected chief. (Before this time the only chiefs were the fur chiefs – the best hunters, appointed by the Hudson's Bay Company.)[23]

Next day there was a lot of trading. There were at least ten traders besides the Company. I saw some new things then. Some of the traders had different kinds of candy. The Company only carried peppermints and this was the first time I saw marbles and hats for boys. The traders were only there for one day. Then they left.

The next summer [1876], when the second treaty payment was made, the Inland Indians from Little Grand Rapids and Pikangikum came down to the mouth of the river to be paid. The Poplar River people came here, too.[24] This continued for quite a few years. My father was the chief of the whole bunch of them. There were no separate bands as there are now [1940].

The first missionary, Egerton R. Young, did not stay long. John Semmens took his place [in fall 1876].[25] He was not married when he first came to Berens River. Mr. Semmens stayed on two or three years, and then came Andrew Ross. When Mr. Semmens was here I went to school one winter and part of a summer. And after he left I went to school with Mr. Ross for about six months, and a little while with the missionary that followed him, Mr. Langford.[26] By this time I was working and quit school. I don't believe I went to school more than two years altogether. I finished the third book and then taught myself on top of that. I learned more myself than in school. I'm sorry that I never had the same chance as the boys have today.[27]

[Hunting and Travelling with My Father]

The following winter [1876–77], I went along with my father – tending his rabbit snares. I was too young yet to go to hunt *atik* [*adik*, caribou] – no moose in those days – never saw one yet. In spring when he was hunting beaver, I was too young to carry one end of the canoe. I helped my mother feed the dogs and in getting wood. [There were] quite a few beaver yet in those days – we never bothered with [musk]rats – ten were worth one "skinway" [?] (75 cents). I did not see much flour. A lot of pemmican – buffalo pemmican – (not made here) was sold by the Company. Father bought five pounds of flour now and then – for a week or two; at the New Year, 25 pounds.

I remember the first long trip I made, to Winnipeg. My father carried the mail twice in a winter for the Company – the Christmas packet and the March packet. We took the Christmas packet to Winnipeg. I went into the Indian Office with my father. The head clerk was Laveque [?] and E[benezer] McColl was the inspector of all the reserves. Mr. Clark was head clerk of the H[udson's] Bay [Company].[28] We drove the dogs right to Winnipeg. It was not very big then.

The next summer [probably 1878] I went in with my father and another young man in a birch canoe. It must have been August as the young ducks were beginning to fly. We followed the shore – crossing from Deer Island to Little Grindstone Point, then down the western shore – paddling all the way. When we got to Selkirk, there was a busy time. Building houses – all kinds of work. I met a Poplar River young man who was working there that summer. He said, "Come and take a walk, boys" – my father was away on business. We took a walk with this fellow. He dished out a bottle. He calls it brandy. I never saw it before. "Take a drink, boys," he says – I did not know anything of its strength. We took big drinks – one after the other – all of a sudden I felt funny. So did my partner. We walked down to the canoe. I just knew enough to throw myself in it – flat on my belly – I did not know my own name then. I did not know where I was. My father came down and found both boys drunk and puking inside the canoe. He was mad and was going to jail us. But we did not tell him who gave us the booze.

[Heading home] we got the chance to get into a York boat at that time – from Red River to Dog Head. Young James Settee was opening a school at Jack Head – so put us off east of Dog Head. We paddled from there to Berens River.[29]

The first day from Dog Head we went to Rabbit Point; the next day was calm. We reached Berens River by night – three of us paddling. My father was getting busy then preparing for the fall fishing and getting our potatoes. We used to dig a cellar in the open ground and keep our potatoes there.[30] We were not living at Pigeon Bay then but at Berens River.

After we got enough fish to keep us going for the winter, my father started trapping. I used to go along with him. He did fairly good the first part of the winter. He caught quite a few marten. I had one little trap – and one mink. A wolverine found my father's trapping line. He broke the deadfalls – took the bait away. My father said, "The only thing I can do is throw the traps away. He will not let them alone so long as I bait those deadfalls."

There was only [one] thing I shall never forget as long as I live. I set a steel trap in an open muskeg in a bluff. About two or three weeks after, my father [and I] went back to the same place again. We were carrying our bedding. I carried one blanket and he another and a tea kettle – not much grub – perhaps a couple of bannocks. We could not see anything to shoot – not even a partridge or a rabbit. Lots of *atik* tracks. We followed the tracks every day but we could not see the animals. I do not know how they knew we were coming. My father was breaking trail in deep snow. Two days and a half we did not eat a mouthful. The first night I was without grub I thought I could not last the whole day. I was that hungry. When two and a half days had passed we came to the place where I had set this trap. Father said to me, "You better look at it – I'll have a smoke here." He took off his load and sat on it. I went towards this bluff. Before I reached there and could see my trap, I heard the chain rattling. I knew then I had caught something. When I came close to see my trap, I saw a marten – trying to get away. Nothing else for me to do [but] to try and get the marten before he got away. I knocked it in the head. I shoved him under my capot next to my bosom. I just carried the trap in my hand. My father never asked me whether I had caught anything when he saw the bare trap. He put his pack on his back and I followed behind. I don't think we had walked 300 yards when I asked him whether a marten is good to eat. He said, "Yes – just as good as rabbit – why, you got one?" I said yes. "Where is it?" he says. I pulled this marten out of my bosom. "Now we'll make a fire and have something to eat." It was easy to skin because it was not frozen – caught the night before we came there. After we ate it, father says, "I guess we better go home." Quite a distance to walk – it was between Leaf River and Berens River. We walked all that afternoon and night, arrived home at midnight. Mother gave us whitefish and potatoes – no bannock or butter or any other kind of food.

After we got home that time, my mother was telling my father that my [great] uncle, Cauwαnäs, had died but had not been buried. I went along with my father the next day to see this man buried.[31] I

heard my father say, "I guess [that's] why I could catch nothing on
this trip – this bad luck." We did not stay home long. My father said,
"We will go again." On the second day after we left home we tracked
a caribou. We followed the trail and shot three "deer." We took three
dogs this time; then we came back with a load of meat. My father
fixed up his traps too; it was getting late in the season already. Then
we left Berens River – moved to the north branch – to stay until open
water. Father was doing well in the big fur – beaver and otter, this trip
(nothing to interfere). After hunting was over we came back to the
Reserve – fishing for sturgeon, drying them, preparing for summer.
Father worked on the boats again. In the fall the same thing – catching whitefish again.

It was about this time that the smallpox broke out among the Icelanders.[32] It must have been about the month of March [1877] when
two white men came here and put up a tent in back of the Company.
They were the quarantine officers. The mail man, Johnny Lambert,
struck right out from Lake Manitoba across Lake Winnipeg to Berens
River and then to Norway House. Made a detour to avoid Icelanders.[33]
Mail used to come only twice a winter.

I was beginning at this time to work around the Company post.
My wages was one shilling sixpence (37 cents?) a day. I used to row
the skiff and help in hay making. Sometimes I'd go out for the man
who was fishing for the Company ([to feed the] dogs), and digging
potatoes in the fall.

[Helping to Survey Lake Winnipeg, 1886]

I could not say exactly how many years after that I went into Red
River. But it was the first year that Lake Winnipeg fishing was open at
Bullhead. A new road was cut from Humbug Bay to Riverton – [we
were] meeting teams every day coming to Bullhead – buyers coming
to purchase whitefish.[34]

That same summer [1886] I went out with Wilkins, the man who
surveyed Lake Winnipeg. I carried the "target."[35] In the bow of the

canoe with the cook – Adam Cochran. Jimmie Johnston steered the
boss's canoe. I carried the target in the lead. Before we got to Norway
House, at Shoal Point there is a little lake there – [it was] full of young
ducks. The boss gave me his gun to shoot those ducks – some almost
ready to fly. I was barefooted so I could jump in and out of the water
at any time. Lots of places very shallow along the shore. I happened
to step on a sharp stick. When we got to Norway House, I could not
walk. I knew I could not carry on any farther. I asked the boss to let
me go. "If you can get another man in your place I'll do it," he said,
"but I'm very sorry to lose you. You have just gotten on to the job
now. You know exactly how for ahead to go and land – not too long
a distance."

I found a man there to take my place – a man from Red River,
Willie Cochran. I was left at Norway House and there was an old man
there who looked after my feet. I stayed there about two weeks and I
was then able to walk around a little. And I met a lot of fellows there.
A new company was opening up to trade in the north country – the
Kaskaten [Carscaden] and Peck Company.[36] That's where I first met
some of the post managers. I knew one man – Frank Dixon, who
used to work for the HBC. Another, Simpson, was post manager of
the new Company posts at Oxford House and Cross Lake. I also met
some fellows from Red River I knew before – Stevenson, Foster.[37]

I was going to come back [home] with the traders' boats. When
we came to the [Warren's] Landing there was a south wind. We were
bound storm [stormbound]. A boat happened to pull in there, the
Colvile, the captain [was] Bell; and I saw the Berens River post manager [James Flett] on board. I had wrote a letter back to my father
telling him I was sick. He had sent word by Mr. Flett to bring me
home if he saw me. Mr. Flett said, "You must come on the boat." So
I told the trader I was going to go on the steamboat. Then the captain
says we have to go to Norway House. The crew lowered down the
yawl. Mr. Flett said, "You'll have to come to Norway House." One of
the deck hands, a boy about my age, had a little stone pipe – he was
smoking, I had not begun yet.

We sailed by south wind to Norway House. The Hudson's Bay

manager [was] hiring – two crews to carry stuff to the Company
warehouse at the Landing; the *Colvile* left stuff there – but we took
one empty barge to Big Grand Rapids. First time that I saw it [that
place]. We took two more empty barges from Big Grand Rapids.

There was a bush fire that time on the west shore. The smoke was
so thick we had to lay over at Georges [Island] a whole day. And we
got off our course; we just went pretty near nine miles out. But it's a
good thing that I knew Black Island. I told Mr. Flett about it; [so] the
captain knows – told by Mr. Flett. The captain came to me, [asked] if
I was really sure where I was. I said, "Yes, that is Black Island." "And
how far?" "About six miles." Then he did this and came into Lobstick
Bay. No lighthouse then. He put us off.

That was the summer James Flett left to take charge of Fort
Alexander.[38] This summer there was a big bush fire on the west side of
the lake. Smoke [so] thick [that the] boat anchored. We went aboard
again. The captain made up [his] mind to stay that day on account of
the smoke. Mr. Flett, he got the captain to blow his whistle for a skiff
to come from Berens River. Four whistles twice – eight altogether.
About an hour or more later we heard someone shooting a couple of
shots from a shotgun – towards Barrel Rock. I knew what that meant.
We got our answer. I told Mr. Flett to tell the captain to answer that
signal – four more whistles. In another hour we heard the shots again,
not far away this time. The captain answered again. To make things a
little lively we started to ring the bell. Three men came and pulled up
alongside the boat. One of them was Jamsie Cret, a Company man;
another man from Fisher River, Daniel Williams; another, John
Everett, a Berens River man. They stayed on the boat that night. Early
in the morning the wind changed and it cleared up. [We] got breakfast on the boat. The crew started to pull up the anchor. We got into
the big skiff – Mr. Flett and myself and his daughter, Jane. (This one
married to Alec MacDonald [see below].) Then we went across to
Berens River.

James Flett arrived at his own post then. He got ready to leave
Berens River to take charge of Fort Alexander post. When he was
ready to pull out that morning he took all his best friends to be the

crew of the York boat – my father, Joe Boucher, old W[illiam] Everett, seven altogether.[39] Everybody went down to see them off. I can see all the women crying, even some of the young girls – as if somebody was dead. They all felt as if a father was leaving them. Mr. Flett had stayed so long at Berens River. Jamsie Cret [was] left here to look after the place till the new manager arrived to take possession. Late in the fall young Alec MacDonald was appointed to be the post manager.

[Fishing and Hauling on the Lake]

That winter I was fishing; I was hauling fish to Bullhead the second year the fishing was open on Lake Winnipeg. That same fall a schooner came in here; the man who owned it was named William Bannfeld [Banfield][40] and I was working for him at the mouth of Pigeon River when he was smoking fish. We had two men and his wife. One of his men was called Tom; the other was an Icelander, Chris. This is the same man that later ran the fish hatchery at Gull Harbor. This was the first time I started to earn big money – $2.50 a day, grub on top of that, and a drink of whiskey before supper. Before breakfast a drink all round again. So Bannfeld, he had some stuff [left] over. "You may as well take this," he said to me – five sacks of flour, five gallons of molasses and 50 pounds of sugar, and two pr windows [?]. "I'm going to be at Bullhead buying fish this winter – you can pay me then – send the boy to Bullhead to haul fish."

In the first part of the winter father and I set nets at Coxes Reef, caught a lot of fish. Father says, "You better make a trip to Bullhead." There were four trains of us – good going. I put 130 whitefish in my train of dogs (five). We camped halfway; next day [it was] getting late when we got there. There were lots of traders – everyone after whitefish (purchasing). An old fellow was there – old John Thomas (Doggie).[41] I asked him, "Where is Bannfeld's store?" He said, "That big house over there." It looked like a big stable – just built that fall – nothing fancy.

As soon as I got in Mrs. Bannfeld recognized me. Bannfeld was

in town – not there – getting teams ready to come out. She told the
clerk to get the fish. He was quick as lightning, this clerk – this was
Disbrow[e].⁴² He counted out the fish and gave us the price; my part-
ners took the stuff. I waited until the last. This clerk, Disbrow (the
first time I met him), he asked me what I wanted. This was at night
and we planned to leave the next morning. I told him my father had
an account and we had come to pay. Mrs. Bannfeld said, "How are
you fixed at home for stuff?" "I have enough until the next load," I
said. "You better take a sack of flour," she said. So I took a half sack of
flour and a tin of jam. This was the first time I saw this and I wanted
my mother to see it. She gave me enough rations – the whole four
of us – to take us back to Berens River: tea, flour, sugar, butter and
bacon. I waited till I got home to open the jam. My mother had only
seen homemade jam.

[Working for the HBC, Berens River]

I don't remember how many trips I made up to March [1887] – but
several hauling fish to Bullhead. After this was over, one day I went to
the [Berens River] Post. I had not talked with the new post manager,
Alec McDonald. He talked with me very friendly – said, "You better
work for me. I'll hire you for a month." So I said I could not hire for a
month now. "I have to go with my father on the spring hunt. He had
no one else. I can work by the day if you have anything to do," I said.
"Yes, I have lots of that," he said. "Now, you and I day after tomorrow
will go to Jack Head where I have an outpost. Have to see what is
going on and take stock."⁴³

[It was] thawing heavy so we could not leave – hung around the
post. Ten o'clock at night we pulled out. We went right across to
Commissioners [Island]. He was in the cariole. I was driving. It was
time to boil a kettle; we pulled in, made a fire – tea. "Bring the grub
box here," he says. When I opened it, he said, "Did you see these
tongues? – *atik* tongues – already boiled – very good."

After eating we started off again – got there just at sunrise. He checked the fur and I baled it up when he was taking stock of goods. Stayed there a whole day and part of the night when we slept; then we left. After we got back he gave me a day to rest. Then I helped the men to peel some rails for fencing.

[Then he said,] "We'll have to make another trip. I have to go to Poplar River. This Willie Atkins has been buying fur from my trapper. He has to give me all that fur back – new regulations." I took him up to Poplar River. Willie Atkins had to give [him] all the fur he had bought from a Berens River Indian. He did not like it.

[It was] getting late in April [1887] now. Another dog train came from the south from the Stone Fort [Lower Fort Garry]. Another post manager sent. Alec [McDonald was] sent to Norway House where his father was chief factor. The new fellow was named Maud [Moar].[44] I went with my father trapping now. When this season was over this Mod asked me whether I would work for him by the month – $15.00. I thought that would be all right. I only had one man to cook for and myself and had to milk a couple of cows and fish for the dogs. But it was not long before I had lots to do. I had to set sturgeon nets, bring them in alive and throw them in the pen. I brought in over 100 that month. They were used for summer rations – kept alive there the whole summer. When the boats arrived from Grand Rapids we took a gaff and killed two for each boat. Same for ourselves.[45]

I worked a whole summer, that summer. W[illiam] J. McLean came out; he was a district manager. He hired me for $125 per year – and servant rates in the store. My job was to work in the store as in-terpreter, but [also] to collect debt on the road in Indian camps (twine, tea, tobacco taken along – very little flour), and to do fall fish-ing. I was doing the same thing for about three years. Jamsie Cret was here but left one year before my contract was filled. I did not even know when I signed the contract that I had to give a year's notice before I quit.[46]

[Surveying up the Berens River: Little Grand Rapids and Pikangikum, 1888]

In July [1888] a surveying party arrived. I went to visit their camp.[47] I met a half-breed that spoke my language. So this young man [was] Johnny McKay, from Manitoba Post. When we began to talk about my uncle [William McKay, Jr.], we found out we were some kind of relation. [He] urged me to go along as interpreter – said he did not think he could understand the Pikangikum Indians. I was hired for cook, not interpreter anyway. I used to go see him because I liked him. There was a white man named Angus Steward [Stewart?] from Westbourne. The next time I went over the boss called me in. He asked me to go along at $45 a month to Pikangikum. My uncle Jim hired for one of the canoes as far as [Little] Grand Rapids. Four of us went in the big birch bark canoe. I did not say anything to my [HBC] boss about this; I knew [thought?] my time was up in June.

That night I took my little trunk, took it to my mother and told her I was going to Pikangikum. Early in the morning I started. I don't believe my [HBC] boss was up. When we got to Grand Rapids, treaty was paid. Big dance in Johnny Moar's house – in the kitchen.[48] My uncle Jim turned back from there. The boss hired another canoe at Grand Rapids to guide us to Pikangikum – one of Sagaski's sons, Nitawasīs; and Cacagaīs, young pelican.[49] They took us to Pikangikum. We surveyed the Pikangikum Reserve.[50] When we left Pikangikum – at *Ktcabaga* [portage] – we had the same guides bring us down as far as Eagle Lake. We saw three *atik* swimming across the lake. One of them [guides] said, "You better chase the buck – there are four of you, and I will chase the cow." Three of us paddled as hard as we could to catch up with the *atik*. I knew he was going to get away then – not far from shore. I shot it when it turned its head to one side – hit it in the eye with a couple of grains of shot. Instead of swimming to shore, he swam out again and I had a chance to kill him. Before we came to Eagle Lake we camped at *Ktcibauga bautik* [rapids]. The guide said, "I guess you will find your way now." I was not sure of my way. I was depending on the surveyor. We got lost in a little creek – went around Eagle Lake twice. Finally we found the way. Came to

[Little] Grand Rapids and surveyed that reserve. We stayed there ten days, delayed by rainy weather. Into September already. Then we came to Berens River [20 September]. My boss opened the men's house for the party so they could be comfortable. He lent them a York boat and three of us took his party to Dog Head – my uncle Jim, Thomas Bates and myself. Ponton got the steamboat from there and we came back to Berens River – [got] paid off. I had about 100 dollars. Hung onto it.

[Back to HBC Service]

The first week of October, W.J. McLean came up again to inspect the post. Someone said, "Mr. McLean wants to see you." Then he gave me a little hell. "What have you been doing," he says. "You never gave us notice when you was going to quit. Now you'll come back this winter and keep on. If you want to quit, now is the time to give notice (a year ahead)." I asked him whether I would have to do the same work. I could see plenty ahead because Jamsie Cret was [had been] helping me [before]. "Yes, you will have to do Jamsie's work too." "Well," I said, "I'll have to have a raise if that's the case." "We'll make it at £36 (x $4.50) if you stay for three years." Then I was first tripper – next to the boss.[51] I finished my contract – doing the same thing for three years [presumably 1888–91].

Maud [Moar] [had] left and a new post manager was sent here, Alec Swain – supposed to stay on.[52] He did not have any use for me. He had a young girl there. Told me to drive his ox and to haul wood. [I] said I would not do it. I was driving the dogs and doing all other work.

[Return to the Fishing Business]

Lake Winnipeg fishing was getting stronger – more buyers. Forty-five miles away at Rabbit Point was J.B. Johnson, an Englishman; and Mr. Dulsman [?] and Disbrow and the Hudson's Bay [post] at Dog Head. I was pretty busy fishing and hauling my fish to Rabbit Point. [The trip took] only two nights – two lifts more than one load.

That spring in June [1891, at the end of his three-year contract],
I knew I could not get a job with the Hudson's Bay man, so I thought
I would go south. I got a job at Dog Head; a man by the name of Dan
Matheson was running a sail boat there. Charley Cornish, a brother-
in-law of William Overton,[53] was boss. Dan drank – Dan jumped the
job. Cornish had to take the boat back to Black Bear Harbor; [he was]
no sailor himself. He said to me, "Would you help me take the boat
back? – I'll pay you." So I set the sails. It was a good thing the wind
was light; [this was the] first time I was in a sailboat. But we managed
to reach the harbor.

An Icelander was there in the icehouse; we asked him whether he
could sail her into Selkirk to get another man who could handle her
well. Cornish said, "You better stay here and make some skiff oars.
I'll try to catch the *Glenn Devon* and get it to tow me out.[54] But it
will pull in here on its way from the north bringing three men from
Dauphin River – you get those men to make the skiff oars too." I did
not know just what he was up to; sure enough the *Glenn* pulled in
and dumped three men there. [They] asked for Cornish; [I] said he
went in. When the *Glenn* came from the south, it brought my boss
and his sailor Jim Hampton. "Now you boys get to Jack Pine Point,"
[he said]. "You boys do sturgeon fishing there and we will haul." Gave
us 20 sturgeon nets apiece and two skiffs. We set all those nets. Sometimes in one day we caught 40, sometimes less. Boats came every day
to pick up fish; dressed them, iced, and the *Glenn* took [them] into
town. I was only getting $30 a month for this as a foreman. I was not
very old to have that job. At the end of two months he raised my
wages to $40 and the other boys hired at $30 were raised to $35.

Fishing slacked off the last week of August. I got word to pull up
all the nets and dry them. Next day the boat came back from Black
Bear. We got to move down to Dauphin River for the fall white fishing. So the *Glenn* took the last sturgeon south. On the return trip it
was towing a big barge – that is what it carried – frozen fish – like
an icehouse. It took us to Dauphin River. When we got there our
monthly wages cut out. The head foreman said, "I'll give you nets to
fish on your own hook and board yourself; I'll give you $3.00 per

100." Lots of people from all over – Fairford, Lake Manitoba, and Water Hen. Started to fish – making $6.00 a day sometimes. A tug by the name of *Miles* was hauling fish from Poplar Point. That was the first time I met Tom Pollock – the captain on this boat.[55] All the sailboats were at Poplar Point fishing, and this tug was hauling the fish. Fishing was getting better. Finally the *Miles* brought all the fishermen from Poplar Point [to Dauphin River], sailboats and all. The boss changed me again; he put me on monthly wages – thought I was making too much – $12.00 a day sometimes. This is where I met Mr. Dowling who was making a survey.[56] My boss took him to Mandagi [Montagao?] River for duck shooting. When he came back, late at night, [there was] a dance. Almost every night a square dance; this is where I began to learn something bad. I had been a fairly straight young man up to now. But even when I was on Dauphin River I used to keep away from dances. There was one time when I was sleeping, on a Sunday, daytime. I felt somebody putting an arm around my neck. When I waked up, it was a girl. I had to get up then. I thought to myself – this is a pretty brave girl.

In fall when everything was over, then we had a chance to have a tow to Channel Island, and we sailed across to Flat Head. We had F[rancis] Felix along. He was married to a Dauphin River [woman] then – had his wife along on the boat. Joe Simpson, he was a foreman on that fishery. That's the same fall that I met other men I have known a long time. Charlie French, later the Fur Trade Commissioner of the Hudson's Bay Company, Billy Purvis – all running boats, and Jack Pollock, brother [of Tom].[57] Then it was winter fishing – the same thing again. The fish buyers followed the fish to the north – lots of fish buyers – white fishermen at Commissioners [Island]. These were the biggest days for fish on the lake.[58]

I did about the same work for a number of years. The following summer [1892?] I was sick – did not feel well. I had started building a house for myself; had hewed tamarack for the foundation. I strained my back and could hardly lift anything. My mother said, "You better go see a doctor in town." "I have no money," I said. "I'll give you an order on the Commercial Bank" ([this was] before it busted).[59] "How

much?" "Thirty or 40 dollars. I'll get a job maybe." So she did [give
me the money] – I remember I had only $7.50 of my own. I spoke to
a couple of fellows, Jacob Nanakowup[60] and my cousin Bill – "Take
me to Berens Island." They said they would. So we started out and got
there that evening. I did not know Simpson – (Kept away from big ??)
although he had seen me. I went to him and asked him for a pass
to go in [to town?]. "I'll pay as soon as I get in." "What's wrong?" he
asked. I told him. They were very busy – short-handed. "Can you cork
and lead nets? Well, if you do that I'll give you a free pass. But you'll
have to stay here three days." Three or four boxes every day were prepared for the fishermen to go and set. I felt better – 15 days – I could
lift easy. "How do you feel?" "Better," I said. "Could you work on the
tug as a fisherman?" "I'll try." "You go to Reindeer Island – 45 miles
from Swampy." Worked all the rest of the summer.

In August we got orders – all this crew to double up at Horse
Island. So we all moved – sailboats and nets, etc. Double crew – a big
outfit of men – perhaps 2–3000 people [sic – AIH]. I stayed on the
tug, being shy. A short, nice-looking young man, white shirt, vest and
hat came up to me. He said ([in] Saulteaux) – unexpected, "Where
do you come from?" I told him, Berens River. "What's your name?"
"What is yours?" – "Sheppard." I had heard of him at Dauphin – a
clerk for an American trader (Archer). We began to talk – about girls,
too. (Do you know this one and that?) – a regular chum. He was head
foreman but I did not know it. He took me to the cook; supper [was]
over, but he made him give me something. After supper I saw him
again. "You fellows got to go to Dauphin River," [he said.] "We're
short of coarse salt" – used in freezing fish. We got there late at night
and could not load. Started the next morning. Left at night; the captain ran the whole night. The next day, Horse Island again with a big
load of salt. I did not see my chum. "The boss is very sick," someone
said. He was playing baseball – missed – was hit in the stomach – in-
flammation of bowels. Two days after, that young man died; lasted
only four days. We had to send a telegram east to Quebec where his
father was.

[Bargaining over Fish]

I stayed there till the fishing was over. I got off at Reindeer Island. Captain Vance hired me then. Four of us – his brother Irwin, Jim Black and myself.[61] Two teams of horses; [we were] supposed to cut two cords of wood for the boats and to fill two ice houses. So one night when Sandy V. was talking, [I] decided to buy fish at Berens River (Flathead). He told me to build a stable at Catfish Creek. "I'll take you across to Berens River" [he said]. I took five sacks of flour and some sugar and bacon and six nets. I asked him how to pay the men if I started to buy fish. "I rather glad not to give anything just now – until I get there. They will be well paid for fish. But all the work you [are] going to do. Give them an order on the Company."

So Sandy brought me to Pigeon Bay. I met my father there and Francis Nanakowup took my place; [he] went back to Reindeer Island. First part of the winter I started to fish. I caught 1000 fish myself, my brother 700 of his own. I got about 2000 fish from Indians left in my care till Sandy would come.

Before Sandy arrived at Berens River, Steve Sigerson [Sigurdson] from Naza [Hnausa] came out with eight teams.[62] There was a council held at W[illiam] Everett's place. [Sigurdson] tried to make every Indian promise to sell him fish that winter. I did not know that the price of fish was coming up, and he got after me about my fish. I told him I could not sell. I had gotten nets and supplies from Sandy V. last fall and had to pay. I was getting a little worried about Sandy after I found the price of fish was up. Early on a Sunday morning I hitched up three dogs, I started. When I was at Little Sturgeon Island the sun was just going down and I was bound to get through that night. I thought I would hit for the south end of Reindeer Island; Sandy had stables there.

As soon as it got dark – I had no bells on those dogs but when I was lying on the sleigh I could hear a sound on the ice. I stopped the dogs. [It was] like someone walking on ice. Could see nothing – started again. Heard it. Stopped again – Horses' hooves. I saw something like a star – the lantern carried by a man ahead of the team but so far it was only tiny. It was Sandy. Francis N. was told to take the dogs ahead; Sandy and I walked ahead of the horses. I told him the whole thing – Sigurdson selling flour at $3.00. Sandy said he would sell at $3.00. We left Sturgeon Island at one a.m. and came to Plunketts. We fed the horses there, then came across to Flathead. Had house fixed up and a stable, so all we had to do was walk in. Had a store too. The fishermen came in the next day and were paid off. Had 4000 fish already. Flour, tea, sugar, clothing, etc., he [Sandy] had. [He] made a return trip to Winnipeg in 18 days. Hired two more teams to make four; then he used three in February, his last trip.

About ten days after that I left for Selkirk to make a settlement of my own. I drew some money and put my dogs up in a box stall. Said I would be back in a couple of days. But I had a girl at Pembina and went there for a week. [They were] looking for me everywhere. I did not want anyone to know. [It was] good I only drew half of my money. Finally told Sandy but he kept it to himself. "You better stay here awhile," Sandy says. So I stayed. We had a lot of booze. When we came to Gimli there was a fisherman's dance there. Everyone was drinking and feeling good – I tried to keep straight – my partner Irwin did. A tug built in the east was there – the *Osprey*. It belonged to Sigurdson – supposed to haul fish from Pigeon Point in.

[Getting Engaged and Travelling Again to Selkirk]

I came back to Berens River that spring, but had made arrangements to go back to Selkirk at open water. Before I turned back, I asked Nancy [Everett] to think about marrying me; then I left – engaged. I passed through Horse Island again – put in another summer there. When I came back I found a fellow who told me, "Did you hear that Nancy Everett was engaged to Charlie Long, Fort Alex[ander]?" I asked her. She said, "No – I never even talked to him. Only saw him once and never spoke." The thing hung about three years before we got married. She was 19 at the time.[63]

In the next spring, about April first, there was nobody to take in the mail to Selkirk. Mr. [James] McLachlan was the missionary here.

I said to Mr. McLachlan, "If you are stuck I will take the mail. I have to go in anyway. I'm going to get a job to go out on the fishery at Horse Island" (Reid and Tate [Tait] Fish Company).[64]

I left here in April – I know because there were a lot of geese already at Commissioners Island. My father came with me as far as that, and my uncle Jim. My father said to me, "You better go before the lake gets too bad. Fisher Bay always gets weak soon – shallow." We took the dog train (mine), and my uncle took me as far as Jack Head Reserve, 35 miles from Berens River. I had to walk from there and carry my blanket and grub [and the] mail. I did not even camp at Jack Head – lonesome after my uncle left me. I went about six miles south of Jack Head – alone. Early in the morning I boiled my tea kettle, had my breakfast, and I started off. At noon I had to boil my kettle again – just a little bannock and a bit of bacon – a slim dinner. I got to Fisher River Reserve. I camped at Jamsie Cret's house. He had a son named Willie. Willie asked me where I was going. I told him, into Selkirk. "I wonder whether I can get a job if I go in," he said. I said to Willie, "I'll help you to get a job."

I stayed two days at Fisher River. I went down to the store to buy some grub – the storekeeper was Jakie Brown, an Englishman. I got some butter and he had some moose pemmican. I thought to myself, "This is the best thing to carry." Me and this young fellow, we started – we were striking across to Humbug Bay; there was an old team road to follow. But we did not reach the bay that day. Next day about at noon we just struck where Drake's mill used to be. We followed the shore – we did not manage to get to Darsis.[65] We started again in the morning; we got to Darsis about nine in the morning. Had something to eat there. We had another lunch before we got to Riverton. When we got there it was getting pretty late, about time to camp, but none [neither?] of us had enough money to go to a boarding house to pay for our meals and bed. There were boarding houses in the Icelandic road. We bought two dozen eggs and a pound of butter, about a pound of soda biscuit. We started off to make a couple of miles out of the settlement. Just [as it was] getting dark we left the main road. I said to Willie, "Go and look for some water." So he brought some water and put the kettle on the small fire. When the water was getting hot I saw something splashing the water inside the kettle. "What you got there?" I said. He dipped the water from a swamp and got a frog in there! He had to make another trip. Next time it was all right and we boiled the eggs; then he had to get more water to make tea. Then we had a good supper.

In the morning we did not have to boil any eggs – went to the other side of Drunken Point between there and Gimli; then again we went on with just enough grub for the day. We came to an old fellow I knew. He told us to camp in his house. We had nothing. But he said, "Camp, boys, camp." When it was getting late, he said, "You better boil a kettle for yourselves. I have no grub." "We have none either." So we had no supper. We started off the next day without breakfast. But this man said, "The first house you pass is where a German lives – a new settler." I remember the fellow – Gowler was his name. We watched for it – on the right side of the road, we were told. We came to it. This fellow was an early riser. I saw the smoke. We walked up and rapped at the door; I asked if he had bread to sell. He said, "No – I just put a bannock in the oven – done now – I'll let you have that." I gave him twenty-five cents. He did not want to [take it] but I gave it to him. I asked for butter but he had none. We had to walk another four miles, to a fellow by name of MacKaye. Here I managed to get a pound of butter. It was noon already. That was our supper, breakfast and dinner. We started off again. Came to Netley Creek – six miles from Selkirk. Right on the river there was a wigwam covered with canvas. There was an old woman living there and two girls – two fine-looking girls. We asked the old woman if she would let the girls take us across the river. But the old woman was too wise. "I'll take you across myself," she said. My partner was a little mad. He wanted the girls to do it. The old woman took us across then. "How much, granny?" "Two dollars each," she said. But we had no money. I said, "We don't have enough." "Any moccasins?" she asked. Willie had a fine pair – silk work. So he gave her these. I was going to hand her a quarter. But before I could do this Willie grabbed the canoe and pushed it out. "That's all you'll get," he said.

Then we reached the settlement – stayed at David Shotlow's [?] [house], an old Company man. The next day I went up to Selkirk to take the mail. We stayed there till the work was to start. The third of June, the fish company started out on the lake, and I went to Horse Island to work there that summer.

[Working for Inspector McColl, 1897]

I finished my two months; then Indian Inspector McColl came there. He asked me if I would work for him. I said, "If I can get off. I'll ask my boss." I was offered more money; I was only getting $35 working on the tug for Reid and Tate. Mr. Tate did not want to let me go. "If you want to quit before the season is over I'll dock you five dollars off each month," he said. I told Mr. McColl about this. "He will pay you every cent he promised. He can't do that," he says. I went back and said I was going to quit. So my time was made up. I had $70 all right. He [Mr. McColl] told me to look for another man. I found one by the name of John Chief from Big Grand Rapids. I gave him my job to steer the canoe and I took his job as a cook – I was now getting $45 a month.

We hugged the shore along Limestone Bay, and camped halfway before getting to [Warren] Landing. We started from there on the third day and got to Norway House. We stayed there that day. Mr. McColl hired another man – a guide, Willie Anderson. We camped halfway to Cross Lake. We stayed there two nights, came back, camped halfway, then [returned] to Norway House. The inspector generally put up one half day at each Reserve, talking to people, inquiring whether they had first class articles – everything – rations – any crooked work? (The best inspector the Indians ever had since Treaty was signed – a very clever speaker.) When we left Norway House we camped at the Landing. From there we went to Spiders [Island] – windbound. From there we made an early start but only reached the mouth of Poplar River; we got to the schoolhouse early. Held council in the schoolhouse – half a day, and left in the afternoon. We came to [blank – Mossy?] Point late at night. The next day we reached Berens River a little before six. The following day we had council in the schoolhouse – stayed a whole day. We left there with a

passenger (Anderson left at Norway House) – McDougall – a white
man – only went to end of Commissioners Island.

We got in early at Jack Head; council for another half day. Then
we left Jack Head, camped halfway. The second night we got to Fisher
River – another council for a day. The next morning we left and
struck right across to the south end of Moose Island. We camped before we reached Snake Island; a thunderstorm hit that night. We had
to move the tent before daylight – the water was rising so high. We
stayed there two days and started from there; we did not stop at Snake
Island. We went across and took the east side again – came to Loon
Strait. But this reserve had been broken up already.[66] We camped once
before Hollow Water Reserve, then stayed there another half day. We
started in the afternoon and went to Clements Point, a few miles from
the Reserve. The next day blowing hard; we managed to get into the
Sand River for shelter. Before I built a fire a fellow must have seen us.
He came up and brought us some meat – smoked and dried and fat
meat – the rib part of a moose; my boss called it the government cow.
We stayed there a whole day. Early in the morning we left. We came
to Little Black River – a reserve there.

Then we reached Fort Alexander [and stayed] more than half a
day – council meeting. From there we made Broken Head River –
Scanterbury; Nenagi was councillor. We left there early and had our
lunch at Mr. [James?] Flett's or McIvor's place.[67] We passed Selkirk,
boiled a kettle again just above the Locks, below St. John's. It was
pretty late already. When we got to the St. Louis [Louise] bridge (St.
Boniface), there was a rig that came down to meet the boss and his
two boys who had travelled with us.[68] A young man drove down with
a wagon and we loaded the canoe, the tents, and the baggage – went
to the government warehouse. [Mr. McColl] told us to go into the
kitchen – gave us supper right at his own table, told us, "You can stay
right here and take your meals at our table." How many can you find
today to offer you that? Then I asked John [Chief], my partner, what
he had to say about this. John was older and he spoke to the boss very
kindly in a humble way. "My dear sir," he said, "we are too low, too

common to get our meals at your own table – a regular big boss like you. We'll try to find a place to stay but we will come and see you before we leave Winnipeg."

The next day he [Mr. McColl] told us to go there at noon. He says, "I have been to the bank and I want to settle up with you fellows." He gave us dinner at his own table. And he gave me every cent that was coming to me, and a suit of clothes as a present on top of that. John Chief had the same.

[A Mysterious Leg Injury]

I heard then that Mr. Hires [Hyers, an HBC rival] from Norway House, his boats were down the river. I met this Mr. John Hires the next day. "You better come down and have dinner with me on the boat," he said. I went down and had dinner. That evening we went down again; we stayed there till very late. John Chief met his chum, a fellow called Charlie Spall – the head guide on these boats. John Chief, he gave me the money and sent me to town to get a bottle of gin 80 [proof] and I gave John the bottle after I came back. John said to [his] chum, "I'll give you a taste." But there was a fellow, a man from God's Lake, working on the boat, but he was in bed already. And he knew when I brought the bottle. But this Charlie Spall did not give him a taste. Then the next day I went down again to see them. This is when I got that – two grains of shot and two pieces of metal in my leg.

All of a sudden I had a pain as if somebody was stabbing me with a needle in the knee. I grabbed my knee and started to rub it. The pain was so bad I said to my partner, "let us go up to town." I managed to go about 200 yards. Then I could not move my leg. I stood in one place. Then John Chief yelled out to the men asking for help. One of the men came and helped carry me to the boat where Hire[s] was. "What is the trouble?" he asked. "Did you hurt your leg?" I said no. "Is there anything I can do for you?" "Yes, get me a horse and rig to take me somewhere." Not long [after], one came. So I got in. I landed in the Winnipeg General Hospital. They took me to a room. The doctor asked whether I hurt my leg. "No," [I said]. "What caused it?" "I don't know – can't tell you."

[My] knee was the size of my head inside of an hour. Opened my pants. [I was] put in a ward – 21 beds. The nurse put a rubber sack with ice on it over my knee. Worked at it a long time. Pain was not so bad. Next day [s]he was putting hot cloths on it. Two days I lay there.

The third day after dinner, a couple of young fellows came along with a stretcher. I was in the dressing room then. Lot of people – young students standing around the table. They asked whether I ever took ether; I said no. "You better make sure about my heart," I said. The doctor said, "You are all right; no danger." Then I took the chloroform. I heard [other] people who took this say they dropped off to sleep. I was not that way. I remember as a boy when I [we] used to dive to try and beat one another. Who could stay under longest; that's the way I felt – smothered. I could not breathe. All of a sudden I saw lightning all over and I could hear a funny sound in my ears. Then at four o'clock I woke up with an awful headache. A nurse was watching my pulse. "Are you awake?" she said. "Do you want to puke?" "No!"

The next day the doctor came along, asked me all kinds of questions. I wondered why he asked such foolish questions. He asked me how long my grandfather on my mother's side [William McKay Sr.] had lived and what he died of. He lived [to be] almost 100; I said he died of old age. Then he asked about my grandmother [Julia Chalifoux]. I said she died of cancer (breast).[69] On my father's side I could not say anything about my grandfather's [Bear's] age but he was an old man and my grandmother [Amo or Victoria] the same. He asked me whether my mother and father were alive. I said yes. Asked me whether I ever had a dose.[70] Asked if I liked women. I told him I was not made out of logs. He laughed then. I did not have much pain in the leg.

Then he asked me whether my mother ever told me I was shot when I was a little boy. I said no. "But did she ever say there was an accident before you were born – shot?" "No; how's that? My mother would have been killed." "How then did two grains of shot and two pieces of metal get in your knee?" "Doctor," I said, "there is only one thing I can tell you. I have often found a grain of shot when a duck had been shot, in the meat. I may have swallowed it." "No! It would never work through that way," he says. "You puzzle me," I said. "I don't know of having been shot."

Our missionary MacLachlan came in to see me and he saw what had been taken out of me. After he came back to Berens River he told my father about it. Then my father said [to him], "You white people don't believe it. But I've told you about such things lots of times. This is through an Indian's magic power."

[Home for a Cure]

After 21 days I sent for the superintendent of the hospital, so he came. I said, "It's like this; would you let me go?" "You ought to stay three weeks more," he said. "That's too bad," I said. "If I have to stay, how am I going to get back? It is October [1897]; most boats will quit running. The lake will not freeze till November. It will be December before the teams will travel. I want to catch this last boat. That is my chance. If you let me go now, in ten days' time after I get back I will be walking because my father will look after my leg. He will put medicine on it." "Is that right?" "Yes." "If you promise me one thing – to save your leg. If you come back here again, you'll lose it." "I'll take your advice, I don't want to lose my leg."

I left the hospital after 22 days – went on a streetcar to the CPR station. I had lots of time to go onto the Selkirk train, two hours before the train pulled out. When we came to the Selkirk junction, one and a half miles from the town, the man who handled the baggage put me on top of his load. He asked me where I stayed. An old lady, Mrs. Bell, kept a boarding house where I stayed. So went there. I had my money – 70 dollars from Horse Island and the money from Mr. McColl. One of the boys drove me to the store. I bought supplies for the winter. They sent them to the boat. Next day the boat pulled out. It did not go to Berens River – put [me] off at the lighthouse on Pony Island. I met a couple of Berens River men. They had a big skiff. Brought me across but I had to leave 500 lbs of flour (McLachlan brought it later).

So after my father saw my leg he sent for his brother, Albert. He gave him some tobacco. "I know you are pretty good," [he said] "but I'll tell you what medicine to use." So my father told him what to use. And he got busy. He boiled the medicine in a big kettle, then took a basin – put some in it – washed my leg; then he poulticed it, twice a day. In ten days' time I could walk but my leg was stiff – could not bend it right. In November before freezing, I remember I was fixing my house. Jacob Nanakowup[was] helping me. In December the lake was frozen and I started to fish; my brother was with me. Both of us had three dogs – but stiff – my leg was stiff. I used to open the rabbit skin, wrap my knee, and keep it warm. I was very careful when I was out at the lake the whole day. One foolish thing – I sold my fish to the buyers. I could have sent for a team – keep my own fish and sell them in town for higher price where goods were lower. I kept on till about February [1898]; all fish were supposed to be in by this time. Fish [were] shipped to the States.

[To Selkirk, Emerson, and the States]

After this I went in behind after the team to get the rest of my pay. I took a dog train. When I got to Selkirk I asked Sandy Vance to let me have 40 dollars. I told him I was going to Winnipeg. I left about four or five nights' feed with the stable man for my dogs. Sandy asked me when I would be back. I said tomorrow or day after. Instead of going back to Selkirk I went down to Emerson; I knew a missionary who had been at Fisher River – MacCoffey [?], missionary at Emerson. [He was] glad to see me. He told me to stay two days with them. The next morning we drove across the line into the States – Pembina [North Dakota], and St. Vincent [Minnesota]. I went in a Pembina hotel for dinner and for some drinks besides. I was very careful to not overload myself because I was travelling with a minister and was staying with him. Next day we went again. The third morning I took [the] train back to Selkirk. Sandy Vance [was] a little worried. Even tried to find out if I was in Winnipeg jail. I did not tell him I went to Pembina.

Vance paid me the rest of my money and I bought some stuff. About 600 pounds all together that I had to take on my dog train. Vance said, "Ervin [Irwin] will take your load as far as Grindstone Point"; had to go there, cook too. We started next morning with one train of dogs and a team of horses. Came to Gimli Travellers' Home. A big dance there that night. Next day [we] left there, good going. I had to take my load from Grindstone Point across to Bullhead. Camped there. Next day Catfish Creek, and I got home.

I had to get a dog train to carry me back to Bullhead and then to Selkirk again – Icelanders team, etc. Sandy B. [Vance?] ran a fish tug, *The Fisherman* – [I] stayed that summer with him, and the next summer [1898]. Sandy was then made mate on the *City of Selkirk*. I was a deck hand on this passenger boat. The second summer I was fireman – firing for the chief engineer. When I got through that fall, came back to Berens River. That fall I made one trip to Poplar River. Took Indian Agent there – W. J. Short.[71]

[Travelling with Agent Short]

Then I got to get married, in January [1899].[72] Before marriage I travelled with the same Indian Agent that winter – took him to Selkirk. He stayed at the CP hotel; I went to a different hotel, got in along with my chums – started drinking. I don't know what happened. When I came to my senses, Mark Donahue, the hotel man, said, "Billy, do you know how long you [been] staying here now?" "No." "A week!" he said. I thought I was there only two or three days. I went to the CP hotel. I asked if my boss was down from Winnipeg. [The manager] says yes. "I want to see him," I said. "Can't see him," the manager said. "He is not well." "I got to see him," I said. Asked the number of the room; [he] told me. I went upstairs. I was nicely sobered up by that time. I could see he was laying in the bed. He was worse than me. I said, "We got to go tomorrow morning sure." [He] asked how much dog feed I had spent. "Don't know." Went back to the fisherman to find out – four dollars' worth. I went back and told him. He gave me

money to pay the bill and my expenses. I asked for some money. I
went down to the bus driver – told him to take my boss to Riverton
in the morning; "I'll pay you," I said. Told my boss the arrangements.
I was going to have to cariole myself – not in good shape to run.
This bus driver made an early start.

I left about ten o'clock, first call was at Blacks (boarding house),
must have stayed two – three hours. I got to Gimli that night but
went to a different boarding house. Did not see my boss that night
or the next morning – not till dinnertime at Drunken Point. We
came to Naza [Hnausa] where we struck off to Fisher River – 57
miles I had to make that day. About after noon it started to snow
and we had very heavy drawing. It got dark on us at the portage.
Dogs travelling slow. I was getting pretty weak. I asked my boss if
he had anything to drink. Pulls out an empty flask from his overcoat
pocket. He showed me: "That's all I had – nothing at all, Bill," – and
I had two half-gallon jars on my load. I asked him then if *he* would
like to have a drink. "Have you anything?" "A little," I says. Handed
me his flask. "Put it in there." I filled the flask. I took a good stiff
drink and he had one too. "Fill my pipe," he said; "my hands are
cold." Lit a match. He did not lay long in the cariole before he said,
"I'll go ahead of the dogs," and he took off his overcoat. The old
man did good; made better time for three or four miles, then gave
out. "Better have another drink." We made the place we had to
reach that night.

The next day, council meeting at Fisher River; then from Fisher
River we went to Jack Head. Arrived day before Christmas [1898].
Camped at the Mission House. Mr. Henry Cochrane – Church of
England – he gave us roast duck for supper.[73] That night he got his
cook to roast a couple more. Mr. Cochrane asked me what time I was
going to pull out. I said four o'clock. I was going to try and reach
Berens River by Christmas night.

When we got to Mr. Short's place [at Berens River], the girls came
out – Nancy was staying there.[74] I asked him [her] if celebration was
over at Church, so [s]he told me, "I just came from there – just over."[75]
I was disappointed I was not there.

[Marriage and a Winter Trip to Selkirk, 1899]

All this time Nancy's mother was against me. Did not let me talk to
the girl anywhere. But that did not work. Finally the old lady could
see she could not win against me. And I got married in January. Two
nights after, D[onald] Flett drove up down to W[illiam] Everett's
house – my father-in-law where I was staying. "I want you to go to
Selkirk," [he said] (I had just come back). "You must take important
letters. One of the horses is really badly hurt and he can't work. Need
another team or all the sturgeon fishing will be spoiled – no ice or
ice house. And I'll go with you to Rabbit Point" (45 miles).

I had to take my own train this time – bought from David Mallet
at [Warren's] Landing. The best train I ever drove. We started from
Berens River before daylight, stopped at Catfish Creek for grub, and
got to Rabbit Point, must be eleven or eleven-thirty. Had dinner
there. We met the trader Jimmie Campbell between Flour Point and
Rabbit Point. He told Donald he wanted to get back that night. I don't
know how long Donald stayed; he turned back after a couple of hours
to Berens River. He had a team of huskies. It was eight o'clock at night
when he got back – a total of 90 miles. I went as far as Black Bear Island – all alone. Left there in the morning – five o'clock. From Black
Bear to Fisher River is 39 [miles]; between this and Icelandic River –
50, then from there to Naza [Hnausa] is seven miles (96 miles that
day). From Naza to Selkirk is 75 miles.

I got to Selkirk about five o'clock – before Mr. Fryer left the office.[76] I delivered the mail – only two camps [nights out], mind you,
from Berens River. Mr. Fryer said, "You can't go back tomorrow –
man (?) out to Lac du Bonnet." He gave me an extra five dollars to
wait – 30 dollars for the trip, four days in Selkirk. I started for home
then and came to Naza. Easy from there to Fisher River. From Fisher
River to Black Bear, [then] stormbound there – two days – a real blizzard. On the second day it calmed down. I started. Had lunch at Rabbit Point, six miles north of Black Bear. Boiled kettle again at Catfish.
Fed my dogs. Got to Berens River about three in the morning.

[To Cross Lake and Norway House with Agent Short]

I began to celebrate my wedding now – no time before – made a big
feast for the band. After it was over, the next day, the Indian Agent
W. J. Short sent for me. He says, "We will have to go to Cross Lake
tomorrow; we'll go along with these ministers" (who were holding a
meeting at Norway House) – Mr. McLachlan, John McDougall, and
[Frederick] Stevens from Fisher River. The last drove his own train;
so did McDougall. The latter had a driver, J. Williams. Only went to
Mossy Point – 17 miles, the first day; then Poplar Point the second
day; the third day Spiders (Buck) Island; the fourth day Norway
House. Stayed there one day to rest the dogs. Next day [we] started
for Cross Lake – [got] to John Bulls – second day to Cross Lake. We
stayed three days. Indian Agent visited every house to see conditions,
asking them questions – how many traps, how fixed for grub, etc.
Then we came back. Camped halfway. When we got to Norway
House, same thing again. Stayed over a week, going to every Indian
house. A lot of people there – Council meeting besides, and school in-
spection. Then back to Berens River. We were 22 days on that trip.

[To Selkirk Again]

About in March – end – [1900], there was a fellow came along –
Charlie Clifton. Jimmie MacKay [was] hired from here [Berens
River], and myself, and Jamsie Cret from Rabbit Point. He [Clifton]
was an Englishman. We had five trains of dogs all together; one just to
carry a musk ox head; another had four legs, another the [musk ox]
hide. He had an Eskimo with him.

    When we got into Selkirk when I was passing the hotel where I
used to camp, Mark Donahue noticed this Eskimo. "Billy," he says,
"what you got there, your brother?" I said yes. "Bring him in," says he.
The hotel crowd all wanted to see him. We took him into the bar. We
had to make signs – showed him a bottle. The Eskimo said, "good,
good" – made drinking motion, started to jig around. [He was from]
Marble Island [at the mouth of Rankin Inlet]. Everybody was treated

by the hotel keeper (Donahue); then they took him to the dining room – cake – then went to Stone Fort [Lower Fort Garry]. After we got settled the livery team – the gent – came along. Said to the Eskimo, "You're wanted in Winnipeg." He changed clothes – fur, skin. Had five huskies, sleigh and whip (bare ground). He rode; dogs chained up. I did not stay there very long. I left J[immie] MacKay at the Stone Fort and came home with Jamsie Crate [Cret]. When I got to Black Bear, ice was getting weak; then I got to Berens River.

[Then I] took a Hudson's Bay man to Jack Head. I bought a sail-boat – 26-foot keel boat, the *Sunbeam*. Jeremiah Johnston used to own it when he was missionary at Jack Head. In the month of June when sturgeon fishing was open, my brother and I went to Jack Head and put rigging on it – sailed home to Berens River next day. Mr. Steward [James Green Stewart, see n. 80] was buying sturgeon for the Company and he hired me to buy the fish at Pigeon Bay and gather the fish with my sailboat. I was doing fall fishing [1900]. I had a hired man by the name of John Ross. We were fishing in the mouth of the Poplar River. After we got a boatload we would sail in to the post to hang them up.

[Two Frightening Experiences]

One night about six o'clock – I find it kind of funny – I felt as if I were going crazy. I could hardly see the lamp. When it got later I was worse and worse. Finally I had to tell my man to tie me up and to throw me in the cellar – to nail it up and take my wife to the mission house ([she was] pregnant). Both of them were scared. Did not know what to do. Did not wish to do as I said. "But you'll never be able to hold me, John," [I said]. All of a sudden I thought of something – we had the Bible in the house. I took it and I opened it and tried to read it. I could make out nothing. The first word I made out was God; as soon as I did, things got brighter it seemed.

A year before this I met an old Indian man and he was trying to do something to me by his magic power – but I pulled through. [He] asked for tobacco and a pipe in the store. He had sold a bearskin to the missionary, [so] I told him to go there. Everybody was scared of this old man. This happened in the store – everybody quiet when I talked back. One old fellow told me I had made a mistake. "I'm sorry for you," he said. But I did not give a damn. I did not think he could hurt me. [He] did not get after me at once.

In the spring [1901] I was buying fish at the mouth of Poplar River for the Dominion Fish [Company].[77] After dinner one day it was a nice day – I was staying with my wife – just the two of us. [There was] a big camp on another island; the old Bozeman [see n. 85] was camped about two miles away from the rest. About one o'clock I began to feel scared – even my body was quivering. I looked around – could see nothing – walked around. About supper, sun [still] high, my wife called me into the tent. But I could swallow no food. Something is going to happen on me– I knew it, scared. My wife asked whether I was sick. "No," I said. I thought I should not hide anything from my wife. "Something is going to happen tonight," I said. "I'm scared – I've never been that way before. You better leave me alone here," I said to her. "If you [are] alive you can tell what happened. But if we both die then no one will know." I had the day book and told her about that and the cash I had that belonged to the fish company and everything.

About sundown, I could see a cloud rising in the west – calm, sun shining bright, not a cloud all day; this was the first. Then I could hear the thunder – just as something striking my body when I heard. Then I knew what it mean[t]. I thought I was going to get killed by the thunder that night. Then I tried hard to get Nancy to leave me. But she refused. Was not long till the thunder came; you could see the lightning when it struck that rocky island – running all over like snakes. Fearful. We hid our heads under the blankets. On the other island when they saw the lightning they never expected us to live that night. But I never gave up hope. When I was laying under the blanket it was just as if someone was speaking to me. "If you can see daylight coming – big dark clouds and light between – on the north side, have no fear then – you will be safe." I told the wife about it, and I told her to look. She kept looking now and then – then she saw the day sky coming; then I looked and saw the same as I had with my eyes closed.

I jumped up and walked out then. Said, "This old fellow did not kill us yet." After sunrise it quit raining and it was a fine day again. [I] said, "Let us visit the main camp now." There was a man who was *mändáuwīzī* [*mamaandaawizi?*, had magic power] there – Sandy Bruce. We went to his tent first. He looked at me and said, "You're alive yet – you came through a terrible night – lightning right at your tent." "My time was not come yet," I said. That was the fourth time an Indian tried to do something to me and failed.[78] [This man] killed two in a year – one in fall and one in spring. *Pagitcigan* [*bagijigan?* sacrificing] to make his life longer.[79]

[In Charge at Poplar River]

I bought the sturgeon for Steward [Stewart] that summer. Jackie McD[ougall?] was the district manager at Norway House. He must have told Mr. Steward to hire me to be in charge of Poplar River post – 25 dollars a month. That was the year that the Boer War was on.[80]

Two years after this, Mr. Steward left and Mr. Harding was sent out to be in charge of the Berens River post and I was working under him that winter. George Ray was sent out about the end of March [1901] to take charge and Harding was to go west somewhere in Fort Simpson [district].[81]

My son Jacob was born March 3, 1901, was a baby when I went [to Poplar River]. Poplar River post was in bad shape before I took hold. I pulled the post out of the hole and I asked for a raise. Mr. McDougal [?] was district manager at Norway House. George Ray said same wages. As soon as I collected all my debt at Poplar River that spring, I packed up and left the post. When I got back to Berens River, George Ray asked me whether all my trappers were back. "All but a couple," [I said], "but they do not owe me anything." [He] said, "You should have stayed till all those hunters got down." I told George that if I did not have a raise I was leaving June first [1901]. I knew he did not like it but he couldn't do anything.

[Fishing and Free Trading, 1901–1904: Cat and Mouse]

I worked for the fish companies that summer. I was doing well. In about eight days I made 300 [dollars] in Pigeon Bay – sturgeon and caviar. And Tom Monkman was buying for the Dominion Fish Company.[82] He told me, "I'll hand you over Berens River. You to buy all the fish from the fishermen at seven cents a pound, and 60 cents for caviar." I was doing pretty good. And that winter I got a letter from Captain Robinson to carry the mail from Berens River to Riverton. I drove the mail for three winters, fishing between times in the summer.

Then I got a job to trade for a man by the name of Rogers at Fisher River. He gave me a fair-sized stock. This time Fred A. Disbrow[e] was placed in charge of Berens River post.[83] [George] Ray left. And I was buying fur and fish that winter for Rogers. I knew Mr. D[isbrowe] was worrying a lot – was a pretty hard proposition for him. He was watching me just like a cat watches a mouse. He did not want me to get ahead of him into the trapping camps. I find out that the first man going [who] tells him I was away from my place, he gave him two dollars. I decided to steal a march. I went to church – the morning service – I did not tell anybody. After I got back I picked the goods the Company did not handle and I baled it – I was ready. I told my wife to get up about one o'clock [am]. She got up, no light, blankets at windows – houses all around me both sides of the river. She asked me, "Who are you going to take?" My cousin Peter B[erens?] was my next neighbor below down the river. "I'll go and wake Peter," I said. I rapped at his door. So he opened and asked what I wanted. "You come along with me. I'm going to Rice Lake." "Why didn't you tell me?" "I could not do it – I did not want this to leak out somewhere." Peter says, "I got no moccasins." "I have a lot in the store," I said – "anything you want." "What is in it?" he asked. "I'll give you two dollars a day" (big wages – those days). "Don't light a lamp – come to my house." By this time the meal was ready. We ate. After that, hitched dogs and took bales – led dogs carefully to the wood trail around Dick Green's. Nice moonlight – then we found the road. I had a good train. Willie Jibo [Gibeault][84] was the man travelling for Disbrow[e]. I knew what his dogs could do, could not last the whole day. [I] had driven them.

Went a long way before morning, then gave them three-hour rest and feed. Started again. Then camped. About three in the morning we started – got into Stony Lake at sunrise – to Minanaki?ewītɑm and Jim Bear – their camp. "Open up," said Jim. I bought two lynx. "That's all I have now," said Jim. "Will you trust me some more?" I gave him 10 [dollar?] credit. "Willie Jibo will be here anytime but I've got to head him off," [I told him].

Then we went to Rice Lake – 12 miles to next camp. I got to old Swain's camp. I bought some mink and fox, and his son-in-law Donald sold me a lynx, a mink, and an otter. There was one I could not make out anything – old Kagowīs – a Company man. We stayed there that night. Next morning we started early. I was not caught yet. Followed Poplar River through Sebastik. When I got to Drunken Lake I saw a fresh trail. He left a mark, indicated [his] camp was not far. When I got there, he had a new shirt, pants, moccasins. He looked very clean – old bojeman.[85] As soon as we got in [he] spread out a sack before us. This was about two o'clock and dinner was ready. How did he know that we were coming then? [He] had told his wife that strangers were coming and so he went and marked the road. I got about ten out of the old man. Next morning I left and struck across to *Minanaki? ewītɑm*'s camp again. I asked him if Willie had passed yet. "Just left this morning," he said, "for Rice Lake."

After we had something to eat we left and followed Willie's track. I caught him up before he got to Berens River. Mr. Disbrow asked him if he caught me. Willie said, "Yes, I caught him." It happened that old John Thomas [Doggie?] was there. He did not believe it. "Mr. Disbrow[e]," he says, "I'll bet you a plug of T and B that he never caught him." Disbrow[e] took him up on the bet. I was down at my father's when John came. "I'm going to ask you something – Did Jibo catch you?" "No! I caught him coming back." So John laughed and went to collect his bet. But Disbrow[e] said he must see me. I went to the men's house. Mr. Disbrow[e] spoke up. "Not my business," he said.

"But I know it will be true if you tell me. I want to know what kind of men I have working for me. Did Willie catch you up?" "No, I gave him no chance."

Then I told him about this. "I can steal a march on you any time I like – I know how to do it," I said. "We'll make arrangements now," he said. "We'll travel together." He was pretty clever. I knew I would have a poor chance now. "All right," I said. "We'll travel together. Let me know before you send your man to those camps." He was honest – he sent word when Willie was leaving. So I got ready.

Early in the morning Willie came to my house. He asked me if I had chewing tobacco. "Yes," [I said]. He gave me 50 cents worth (credit) and a pair of moccasins. I said to myself, "I wonder how I can fix this fellow – I think I can buy him out." So I said to him, "If you give me a chance, I'll give you 25 cents out of it." "But look here – if Disbrow[e] knows, I'll get fired," [he said]. "Who is going to tell him?" I said. "Do you think I am? I know he will ask you; you need not tell a lie. Don't come into the tent with me; then you'll not know. I'll tell you later how much I bought."

[End of text.]

PART III

Dibaajimowinan, Stories and Dreams for Living

Introduction

During their decade of work together, William Berens shared a great deal of information with Hallowell, much of it through stories that gave concrete expression to aspects of Ojibwe culture and worldview that he was helping Hallowell to understand. The first twenty-six stories presented here are oral narratives of the type that Ojibwe people call *dibaajimowinan* or, in Hallowell's orthography, *tabatcamowinan*. Berens also identified number 27, "The Boy and the Trout," as belonging to this category, but it has some distinctive features and will receive its own commentary at the end of this section. *Dibaajimowinan* may be translated, as Hallowell said, as "'News or tidings'… i.e., anecdotes, or stories, relating to events in the lives of human beings." The noun is of inanimate gender; hence its plural ending is -an, as above. In contrast, the noun for *aadisookaan* [variant of *aadizookaan*] or myth (*atiso'kan* in Hallowell's transcription), the category of narratives in Part IV, is animate (plural ending, -ag), reflecting the spiritual power of those stories and of the personages they tell about.[1]

These twenty-six stories relate to or were told during William Berens's own life. "Murder Followed by a Daughter's Sickness," and "The Boys Who Tormented the Pelicans" (1 and 4) were told to him by his mother and paternal grandmother respectively; "Love Magic Captures a Girl (and Her Husband)" was told him by the man who was the protagonist of that story (12). William most likely heard the story of Yellow Legs and the windigo from his grandfather's younger brother, Zhaawanaash (d. 1882–83), as his grandfather, Bear, died when he was quite young. The other stories (except 27) all tell of events that happened to William himself, mainly when he was a teenager and young man. They were clearly significant to him, as he vividly remembered them in his later years and considered them important for Hallowell to hear.

More than half of the stories involve a dream experience that either constitutes the core of the narrative or marks a key turning point. Hearing these and other such stories, Hallowell could not fail to notice the significance of dreams in Ojibwe personal lives. Hallowell was also fortunate to be working with William Berens when he was in his sixties and seventies and could speak more freely than in his youth about dreams in which he was offered gifts or blessings (for example, "The Boy in the Red Tuque," and "*Memengwécī*," 7 and 8), whereas in his earlier years he might still have considered claiming those blessings at some point. Discussions of dream quests and the personages who offer powers to the dreamer often emphasize that recipients were forbidden to speak of these experiences because to do so would mean sanctions and the loss of the benefits conferred. In fact, however, people could and did speak of these things under certain conditions: if they were elderly or near death and did not plan to use those powers, if they had become Christian, or if they had declined the blessings or had tried and failed to receive them. Berens met most of these conditions.[2]

Berens also evidently decided that he could speak more openly of some things to the outsider anthropologist than he could or should to church-going family members or to the clergy at Berens River.[3] There is no sign that he ever "adopted" Hallowell as happened to some anthropologists in the field but he certainly became a mentor to the visitor whom he welcomed and who, at age thirty-eight in 1930, was of his older sons' generation. In that role and context his stories, while their form was anecdotal, were also teaching moments, and they all have lessons embedded in them.

The first four stories warn of the dire consequences of violent deeds, irresponsible or disrespectful actions, or insults causing offence. The resultant suffering or illness could even carry over into the next generation, as in number 1. The next six all involve powerful dreams. "The Medicine Stone" (number 5) is a kind of founding dream that recounts the strong gifts that William Berens's great-grandfather, Yellow Legs, received and demonstrated in his ceremonial medicine practices. The other five accounts tell of William Berens's own dreams involving powerful visitors who presented strange or frightening challenges or conflicts with uncertain outcomes. Each dream experience was a kind of test: he had to overcome his fears, defeat an antagonist who might then prove helpful, and find a way out of difficulty. A common theme was the need to exercise strong mental powers.[4] Encountering the boy in the red tuque, Berens set his mind strongly against being hit by his arrows and concentrated successfully on hitting him when his turn came to shoot (number 7). Inside the rock cliff home of the *Memengwécī*, when Berens decided he should leave, "I threw all the power of my mind to open the door" (number 8). And in the dream conflict with the Catholic priests, powerful newcomers, Berens escaped the flames but learned "that the priests can do what they want with Indians who do not think for themselves" (number 10).

The four stories of love medicine, courtship, and cross-cousin joking are intriguing and amusing on the surface, but they also warn or instruct. Love medicine was powerful and could be dangerous, leading to loss of autonomy for both the user and the target of his or her affection and weakening the power of the mind (numbers 11, 12). Berens's dream of his future wife points to the significant role of dreams in presaging and even influencing events and relationships (number 13). For those who were sensitive to their guidance, their predictions could even be self-fulfilling. "Of Course You Can Joke with *Kinim*" (number 14) is a brief lesson in acceptable kinship behavior: male and female cross-cousins could freely engage in jokes and suggestive play that their relatives and even their respective spouses tolerated and enjoyed. Implicit in the story, however, and confirmed by Hallowell's comment, was the stricture that men must not treat any other female relative in this way.

The next seven short stories (15–21) have in common their attention to hearing and seeing sounds, signs, and creatures out of the ordinary. Hunters and travelers in the bush were keenly attuned and attentive to auditory and visual cues that informed them of animals, possible hazards, and the approach of strangers both human and other-than-human, and they interpreted what they heard and saw in the context of, as Hallowell would say, their Ojibwe ontology and worldview.[5] In the Ojibwe cultural frame of reference, encounters with *wíndīgowag*, Pagak, and large amphibious or water creatures or with their sounds or traces (tracks) were all possible and plausible and were to be treated with caution and respect. These stories of real experiences in waking life told people to listen, watch, and take care, as one never knew where such encounters might lead.

In stories 22 through 24, William Berens's dreams of travel and hunting were harbingers of favourable outcomes or success. Dreams could give promise of survival, successful trapping, or good returns. And they gave clues about where to go and what to do next, as when two girls appearing in a dream led Berens to find a female fisher in a deadfall he otherwise would not have visited at the time (22). In stories 25 and 26, dreams also presaged future events, but these were darker, foreshadowing the loss of family members. In number 25, after a dream about an angel ("I wondered what was going to happen"), Berens accepted a chance to make a sudden trip from Poplar River to Berens River, where he found his sister dying and had a last visit with her. Then in number 26, Berens told Hallowell the story of how, when his father, Jacob, died in 1916, he remembered a dream he himself once had when he was very ill; its message was that he would survive to outlive and grieve for his father.

As noted earlier, Hallowell described these stories as anecdotes. The *Canadian Oxford Dictionary* defines "anecdote" as "a short account of an entertaining or interesting incident." But these brief narratives are much more than entertaining or interesting. They are rich in meaning and dense in content. They are like fables that convey a moral or a lesson, even if their messages are understated or left implicit.

Looking back on William Berens as storyteller, it may be that he taught A.I. Hallowell, the professor from Pennsylvania, something about teaching. Regna Darnell, one of Hallowell's students in his last years and a devoted reader of his works, recently wrote, "Hallowell was meticulous in letting the Ojibwes speak for themselves. He was a master of the representative anecdote." She went on to speak of how well he used stories to convey what he learned from Ojibwe people about, for example, the potential animacy of rocks and the ability of certain people to understand what thunder was saying.[6] Many of Hallowell's teaching stories came from William Berens.

Berens taught his student well and Hallowell received lessons that he in turn could pass on with great effect. These stories take us back to the source, as close as we can come.

Misdeeds and Consequences

1 [Murder Followed by a Daughter's Sickness]

Mother [Mary McKay Berens] told me about a man – Cuthbert Grant. He was drinking – two of them. A young halfbreed man happened to pass – called in name James Bird. Grant shot him – nothing said about quarrelling. Where the bullet struck, he [Grant?] blocked the hole to stop wound. Instead of bleeding from the hole [Bird] bled from mouth and nose. Grant was a leader of the halfbreeds – White Horse Plain [just west of Red River]. No laws or courts in those days.[7]

My grandfather was in charge of the post at Big Trout Lake (Severn River). Mother was about 14 so remembers the whole thing.[8] This

Grant and old [William] McKay [my grandfather] were friends –
made arrangement between them to have children intermarry. By
this time Grant had grown up girls already and he wrote a letter to
my grandfather at Trout Lake. William (my uncle) a young man
already. My uncle asked for leave for one year. Went to White Horse
Plain, married there [in 1853] Betsey (daughter of Grant), a light
haired, fair, blue-eyed woman, fairly heavy set, healthy woman.
So when she was about 50 or 55 she used to bleed from the nose –
confessed – on account of [her] father's sin – a murderer.

[A.I. Hallowell's note at bottom]: "One of the criteria seems to be that
there was no good reason for the murder – not in self-defense. It is not
murder then, but unprovoked willful murder that is bad (cf. cruelty)."

2. [Teasing and Retaliation: the Rolling Head]

[I was] just about 16 years old. This man must have intended to kill
me. We were playing ball and I got one of the boys [sons] of the conjuror mad – partly my fault. He was a humpy [hunchback], and the
way he ran, I imitated him, it was so funny. The boy said, "Remember
that." This was in the summer. I did not understand what was meant.

     In March we were living three-four miles up the river, and we were
ready to pull out the next morning – everyone perfectly well. I had
a dream.

     I saw someone coming from the north. This young man came
and stood on [at?] my feet as I lay sleeping. Said, "You're wanted over
here" [motioned]. So I got up. I then started off with him, not travelling on ground but through the air. From above I could see a river
ahead of us and just one tent, a *pi'kogan* [*bikogaan*]. I could see
exactly the kind of trees growing there – lots of straight jackpine
growing there. North side of the river, came down, saw another tent,
walked into it. Then I saw the boy's father in the center. This tent was
stretched out as far as I could see.[9] Knew then – this place was just
chuck full as far as I could see of all kinds of people. Knew then I was
in conjuring tent – no good – "I'm going out," I said. Old man said,
"No! You can't go."

I saw my own head rolling, people trying to grab it. [I] thought I would be OK if I could grab it myself. Tried, [and the] minute I grabbed it I could see my way how to get out. I woke up then at once. I knew it was dawn. But I could not move now, only fingers, [I was] well before. I managed to speak. Said to mother to light a lamp, told her I was very sick. When morning came, I told my father my dream, that someone had done something to me because I had been in a conjuring lodge. Lay [sick] all day and the next.

It was my soul that was drawn away; if it had not come back I would have been found dead.[10]

3 ["The Animals Know When They Are Not Used Right"]

[While trading furs in spring] I got to Thunder Lake. This [was] after sundown. I saw a tent, a conjuring tent, inside the house. House [was] full already – I went to have my supper there. Went to see this séance. Tent started to shake. [The man] asked his *pawágan* why he was not catching any food for his family. Moose spoke to him. "What you been doing to me – you been leaving my carcass all over the bush instead of using it for your own family. That's the reason you cannot get anything now. The wolf spoke then, says, "You should not talk to him like that. If I help him, you can be caught any time." [But then] Wolf said to [?], "Look here, you know what this moose says. It is wrong to leave the carcass of moose all over the bush. Don't leave it all over the bush or you'll never get anything.

Wastefulness – *Kadabéndag* [*gaa-dibenag*], one who owns, one who possesses, owner, lord] of animals punishes the hunter by starvation.

Not supposed to kill animals and leave them in the bush. If you kill a moose make use of him, his meat, dry it and you'll have luck – then if you starve you'll know it did not come from there [that reason].

Seems to me the animals know when they are not used right.

Proper care of bones – like hanging up a bear skull. Not let[ting] the dogs gnaw the bones of animals – you make a stage, put bones on it. The head part in particular. If you trap foxes, hang them after you take the pelt. Don't skin a fox and throw him out on the beaten trail.

If you give the dog the bones of a moose, [you] won't kill any more moose.

If you bring in an animal, put it in a clean place, not laid in door where a woman can step over them.

Even if you shoot a moose at short range you'll not kill him if you don't follow rules. Same with *atik*. You'll not trap any of them – mink, etc., every furbearing animal. For a year you'll have bad luck – if you play with them.

4 [The Boys Who Tormented the Pelicans]

Pelicans are connected with *pinèsï* [*binesi,* Thunder Bird] because if you tease the young ones it will thunder and lightning before the day is over and you will be lucky to escape death.

W.B.'s grandmother [Amo] told of four boys who caught some young pelicans and teased them – put firebrands in their mouths and closed them. [They were] discouraged by elders but they kept it up. It was a calm day, but before night came, there was a big thunderstorm and all the four boys were killed.[11]

The Dreamed Ones: Challenges, Danger, Gifts, and the Power of the Mind

5 [The Medicine Stone]

[This was] a large boulder of granite (?) with mouth and eyes (?). [It was] dreamed of by William Berens's father's grandfather, Yellow Legs, who was the very greatest of the *mitéowak* in these parts (like a Bishop). It was revealed to him that this stone was to be found on one of the Jack Head islands (Egg Island, i.e., Birch Island) across the lake. He would follow a bear's tracks out of the water which would lead directly to it but, to make sure, a few branches directly above the stone

Chief William Berens, Jr., ca. 1960s, and the medicine stone of Yellow Legs, Berens River. According to Percy Berens, beside whose house the stone lay for many years, some years ago a group of boys rolled it into the nearby river. Photographer unknown. Copy in possession of Jennifer S.H. Brown.

would be broken. [He] sent two men [to fetch it]. This old *mitéo* used
to tap a new knife on the stone several times, after which the "mouth"
(a roughly worn indentation) would open. He would put in his fingers and withdraw a little deer skin pouch with medicine in it. The
mouth would then close. He would put the medicine in water and
then pass it to everyone for a drink (just like the sacrament).

W.B. explained that the Indians did not *worship* this stone but
revered it, just in the same way the Queen Victoria medal he sometimes wears is saluted and respected as the symbol of a great queen.
The stone and everything else in nature is made by God and for this
reason can be used by man in various ways helpful to him.

Various *mitéowak* in different parts of the country have offered
him as much as $100 or more in goods for the stone but he will not
give it up.[12]

6 [The Steer with Metal-Tipped Horns]

I have dreamed many times of a steer with metal (brass) tipped
horns.[13] This animal always chases me and I am scared. Once the steer
caught up with me right across the bay there, near the Hudson's Bay
Company post. Then I woke up. Once I met the steer in winter right
in the middle of a large expanse of ice that seemed as wide as the
ocean must be. I got away by riding on a knife which shot across
the ice like a bullet. The steer could not catch up with me because
of the slippery ice.

Another time I was taken up by a duck feather into the clouds
(the wind always blows such feathers this way and that). I could see
the steer on the ground below from where I was up in the air. But
I was scared up there. When I got scared I always came down. This
time the steer found me again. I was taken care of by a bug that lives
in the water. As long as I was under the water the steer could not get
me. I beat him. Then he said, "I won't harm you. I want to talk to you.
I admit you have beaten me. If you ever have to name a child name
it after me." I have not done this because I never have been asked
to name a child.[14]

7 [The Boy in the Red Tuque][15]

I was walking along and came to a house (not a wigwam). I went in.
There was no furniture in the room I entered. All that I saw was a
small boy with a red tuque (on his head). He said to me, "Oh, ho, so
you're here." "Yes," I replied, "I'm here." This boy had a bow in his
hand and two arrows. One was red and the other black. "Now that
you've found me, he said, "I'm going to find out how strong you are."
("I'm going to try you. Now is the time to see which of us is the
stronger.") I knew that if he ever hit me that would be the end of me.
But I went to the middle of the room, as he told me, and stood there.
I filled my mind with the thought (I set my mind very strongly) that
he would not be able to kill me. I watched him closely and, as soon as
the arrow left the bow, I dodged. I saw the arrow sticking in the floor.
He had missed me. Then he fitted the other arrow to his bow. "I'll hit
you this time," he said. But I set my mind just as strongly against it.
I watched every move he made and he missed me again.

"It's your turn now (here's your chance)," he said and handed me
the bow. I picked up the two arrows and he went to the middle of the
room. Then I noticed a strange thing. He seemed to be constantly
moving yet staying in the same place. He was not standing on the
floor either, but was about a foot above it. I knew that it was going
to be hard to hit him. I let the black arrow go first and missed him.
I made up my mind that I was going to hit him with the red arrow
and I did (the second arrow went straight through the boy's heart).
But it did not kill him (he pulled it through).

He took the bow from me, tied the arrows to it and laid it aside.
"You have beaten me," he said. I was very anxious to know who it was
but I did not wish to ask. He knew what I was thinking, because he
asked, "Do you know who you have shot?" "No." ("I will tell you who
I really am.") (You remember those little flies like a bee.) I am a fly"
(smaller than bull-dog fly which is to be seen on flowers – but is constantly moving and does not stay still long) (yellow, hangs in air and
trembles, not a bee, does not sting, has red marks on head).[16] ("That's
me, the one you have shot. Any time in your life, if you're in a fight,
think of me. Your body will be just like me.") (The boy went on to say

that W.B. would never be shot and killed by a bullet unless the marks-
man could hit a spot as small as a fly: AIH)

Then he told me to walk along the road to a tent and go in. I
walked and came to the tent. There was a man in there with a gun. I
had no sooner stepped in than he pointed his gun at me and shot at
me. But I felt no bullet. This proved right then and there how I had
been blessed.

Told [my] wife I would not be killed if I went to war. She asked
how I knew. I told her it was none of her business.[17]

8 [*Memengwécī*, The Man in the Rock]

As I was going around hunting, carrying my gun with me, I came
to a lake. On the lakeshore there was a steep rock, kind of round. I
climbed on this rock to see if I could see anything across the lake –
ducks or a moose. As I looked down towards the water's edge, I saw
a man standing on a rock and leaning on [a] paddle. A woman was
sitting on the stern end of the canoe with a *tikinagan* [*dikinaagan*,
cradleboard] in front of her with a baby in it, a green mosquito net-
ting over the baby's face. The man [held his] head down. I walked
right up to him. Knew he was a stranger to me. He spoke to me –
"You are the first man to ever see me. I'm going to ask you to come
to my place." And I got in his canoe. As I looked at it I saw no joints
or ribs or anything – it was all of one piece (not of bark, could not
understand what it was made of).

There was a high, steep rock on the northwest side of the lake, and
[the man] headed for this. Just one stroke of the paddle in the water
made such a speed that we were across. Then he threw the paddle on
a flat shelf of rock below (steep part); [I] saw the rock moving. About
three feet thick but lifted right up – [he] took his canoe in.

[We] entered a room. Before I sat down, the man said, "See, this is
my father and my mother." The old man's head just like a rabbit skin,
all white, same with woman. I could not see a black hair on their
heads. [He] told me to sit down and I began to wonder. The articles I
could see in the room – knives, pans, guns, clothing they were wear-

ing – and I never saw this man in any store to buy those things. It comes in my head to ask him, "Where did you buy this clothing, etc., when you never saw a white man? He answered, "Did you know or ever hear of people [speaking] about *pagitcigewin* [*bagijigan*? sacrifice.] These articles were given to us. That is how we got such things."

Then he took me in the other room; "Now look at all these things laying here." All kinds of meat – moose, deer,[18] ducks. I was thinking, this man must be a good hunter to kill all these things (not sacrifice). [I] came back to the other room. I wondered, strange thing that no Indian had ever seen this man before – even when sitting there, thinking of my father who never told me anything about this. I never even knew this was a dream to me. Just as if I had seen it with my open eyes. He did not ask me whether I was ready to go, and offer to open the door for me. [The only] thing I could do was to try and open up the door myself. I said, "I'm ready to go," and I got up and shook hands with him. [He said] to me, "Any time you want to see me, this is the place you will find me." And I threw all the power of my mind to open the door without a doubt. And the rock lifted up. And I woke up then and knew it was a dream. It was one of the first I ever had.[19]

9 [A Fight with *Mīcīpījìu*, the Water Lion]

There is a lion that lives in the water – *mīcīpījìu* [*mishibizhiw*]. Cubs [were] seen one time playing near the rapids of that name. [It] may have something to do with bossing the fish. [It's] bad to dream of, especially for a female. [She'll] live to be a bad woman, should a girl dream of this creature.

W.B. dreamed of [it] before he was married (several times). Means illness. After marriage, once when [his] boy was sick, [he] dreamed of the lion. Went to see a man who told him just what the dream was without W.B. relating it. [The man] said he would try to help. The next night, W.B. dreamed he had a big fight with this creature, but it left no marks on him, not even a scratch, and he conquered. [He] told the man, who said everything would be OK now. The boy got better.[20]

10 [The Priests and the Furnace]

I had this dream before the Catholics started their mission here. I
had four or five children at the time. I dreamed that I was close to the
place where the woodpile of the Hudson's Bay Company now stands.
Two Catholic priests were holding me, one on each side. Another
Indian was there, too (named). One of the priests took his head off.
There he stood without any head.

 I was fighting them but they dragged me off towards where the
Catholic mission now stands. We came to a big furnace and these
priests tried to push me into it. At the same time there was an old
man who stuck his head out of the flames and tried to pull me in.
But they were not able to get me in.

 I kept on fighting them and they dragged me to another place
where there was another furnace. Here the same thing happened. An
old man stuck his head out and tried to pull me in while the priests
tried to push me in. This old man had a spear. I got pretty close to
the flames that time. Then I woke up.[21]

[Hallowell's note: "The dreamer commented that he now knew the
meaning of the dream. It gave him foreknowledge of the struggle with
the Catholics in which he is engaged. The first incident shows that the
priests can do what they want with Indians who do not think for themselves. They can put any ideas in your head they want to."]

Love Medicine, Courtship, and Cross-Cousin Joking

11 [A Love Charm at Pikangikum, 1888]

I remember when I was a young man (very young and bashful),
before I ever bothered my head with a woman, I made a trip of 200
miles from Berens. We were working on a survey. One of the Indian
boys, my chum, took me on a visit (one evening) to a camp of Indians across the lake [Pikangikum]. We shoved the canoe in the water –

birch bark [the] only kind – four of us got into it. Went two miles across the lake. Went into a big *cabandawan* (long dwelling with several fires).²² As soon as I got in a box was moved into center of tent to sit on, [a] fire on each side of me (was given some blueberries to eat). Five or six families living in it. As I looked around towards the west door I saw a girl there sitting beside her grandmother. This woman was very old. I knew she was a great medicine woman (*wasi*). I was pretty careful and behaving myself well in that tent. This girl was nice looking – fair enough to be a white woman – dark hair, black eyes. Just as we were ready to go back I can see she was watching me all the time, giving me a side glance once in awhile. Soon as I reached for my hat, she took the kettle and along with another girl walked down to water edge. I knew then what that means. When we arose to go, three of the boys walking before me, I was behind, met the girls halfway from tent to water edge – pail of water each. The girl put her hand on my shoulder, not saying a word. I did not say anything to her either. I never thought of this at all.

Went back to camp. We made our bedding. I laid right in the center (six men), the door closed. After I lay in bed, it was not long before I fell asleep. I dreamed that I heard a drum across the lake. I saw the girl coming across the lake towards me. I was looking straight at her. She seemed to be walking on top of [the] water. She stopped at side of tent (not door). Spoke: "You're wanted over there." I could not tell how I got out of the tent. Next thing I knew (was out of the tent and calling for a boat), there were two men holding me, one by each arm, asking, what is wrong (was I crazy?) I woke up then, could not tell how I got out, must have been from side, not door. Next day, went up in the bush again to cut our [survey] lines – my heart and mind on that girl all the time. I could not even eat that day. We stayed there three days. We finished our work. It was the same all the time with me. I was that sick to see her. I asked my boss to let me quit. But he refused – said he could not do without me. Of course they did not understand white man's language. I was doing interpreting (talking for him). The fourth day we left, ten o'clock in the morning.

I had a vest which I wore constantly (noticed it was gone; never knew where it got to). It was a mystery to me how I lost it – I never took it off. But I missed it. (Whole thing was result of a love charm.) (Put into effect when she touched him; must have had medicine in her hand – AIH.) Only time I felt so strange about a girl in my life.[23]

12 [Love Magic Captures a Girl (and Her Husband)]

This man was a thoroughbred Indian. The girl was ¾ white. [Her] father came from White Horse Plains; mother from Trout Lake (a Scot halfbreed from an Indian woman). This halfbreed came to Norway House, then [was] at Berens River, old man [Joseph] Everett, took treaty. Youngest daughter, Mary, [was] fine looking, well built, tall, very handy with needle – fancy work. When she was about 18, all the young men had their eye on her [W.B. himself was one – AIH]. This man had a thin crooked face, no house, just made living by trapping. [W.B. working on contract for the Bay at the time. Used to go see her. Knew she loved him. If he did not see her used to come to the Fort – AIH]

First thing I knew she went with this Indian. Only one thing for me to do, to drop out. Let her have her way, no argument. [But] I thought I would find out [what happened].

The Post manager hired this man to do the fall fishing at the mouth of Berens River. He gave me this man to be my helper when I'm fishing. I asked him one night how he got this girl to love him so much. Says, "I'll tell you but keep it to yourself – only between us. The girl would not even look at me; [would] have nothing to do with me. So I went and bought some love medicine. I went and visited that house. She was living with her brother. I had this medicine in my vest pocket. I never even touched her but I saw her shawl hanging. I touched it, handled it, admiringly. A few minutes after, I left the house. Before I reached home she caught me on the road already. I could not get rid of her. I had to marry her."

So he says, "if you want this medicine, I'll tell you where I got it. Gave suit [of] clothes ($20), shirt ($2.50) and a belt ($3.00) and tobacco (of course)."[24]

13 [Dreaming of "The Girl Who Will Be Your Wife"]

When I was 15 or 16 years of age, I used to notice a little girl playing around near where I lived. One night I dreamed that a young girl lay beside me. I heard a voice saying, "This is the girl who will be your wife." I looked at the girl's face. It was the one I had noticed playing.

When I woke up I forgot all about the dream. I would never have believed that this girl, [Nancy Everett] who was so much younger than I was, would ever be my wife. But the girl grew up to be a woman. Suddenly, it seemed that I could not help watching her whenever I saw her, and I could not get her out of my mind. My dream came true. She is my wife today. Yet I was almost ready to marry three other girls before I even thought of her.[25]

14 ["Of Course You Can Joke with *Kinim*"] [your cross-cousin]

Of course you can "joke" with *kinim*. [W.B.] related an incident. When working at the H.B. post at Poplar River he got into a camp early one winter morning with a dog team. Nobody up yet. Found out the tent where his *kinim* was sleeping (with her husband and other relatives) under a rabbit skin blanket. Went in quickly and threw himself down at her side and put his arms around her. She woke up, and when she found who it was, started laughing. So did her husband and everyone else. They had a good laugh. W. later joked about being under the blanket with her. His *kinim*, of course, denied it and he would insist on it.

A man's *kinim* may joke him sometimes by hiding his pants so he can't get up in the morning. [He] can also joke about going into the bush with her. Can 'rough house" – pinch or tickle her. Be suggestive in conversation in a light way but not really smutty. Can joke before and after she is married. If latter, her husband will often enter in … (Joking of this sort is not possible with any other female relative – AIH.)[26]

Sounds and Sightings in Waking Life

15 [The *Pawáganak* of Yellow Legs Defeat a *Wíndīgo*]

A *windīgo* made out of a dream was once sent against my great-grandfather, Yellow Legs. He knew through the aid of his own *pawáganak* that it was coming. He sent his son [probably Bear or Zhaawanaash], a young man 18 or 19 years of age, out to meet the *wíndīgo*. The young man was instructed to tell the stranger that he was not wanted and to ask him to go away. It was a moonlight night and his father told him that he would find the *wíndīgo* near a large spruce tree growing near a creek. When the boy got there, there sat the *wíndīgo*. He had a very big head and he said to the young man, "What do you want?" The boy said, "I was told to tell you that you are not wanted here." The *wíndīgo* said, "You are only a boy. Go back and say that I don't want to see you. I want to see your father."

The young man went back and delivered the message. Then Yellow Legs took a small ax from his medicine bag and went out. Soon everyone could hear all kinds of noises from the fight that was going on. But it was not Yellow Legs that was doing the fighting; it was his *pawáganak*. They must have hid him somewhere. Next day you could see blood on the leaves of the trees and on the ground. You could see where the poplar trees had been twisted high up, where the windigo had clutched at them. Yellow Legs brought back a piece of the little finger of the *wíndīgo*. He said he was going to use it in the Midewiwin in the Spring.[27]

16 [A *Wíndīgo* Voice in Summer]

[We were] coming from Rice Lake – [musk]rat hunting – four men, two canoes. After we made four portages [we] had to cross a lake – two miles – then two more portages (short). When I was running back for last load, to relieve my boy Jacob's load, I heard a shout – in the direction from which we had come – three times. Joe my nephew asked, "Who is calling?" I told him, "That is a *wíndīgo*" (something like human voice but louder). Then we struck the river – paddled for all we were worth to strike the north track.

The next day, Jacob Nanakawop and Jim Bear and his mother came through. They saw this *wíndīgo*. The old lady said, "He was not very big. But I don't think he was a man – Had a rabbit skin coat on and bare legs."[28]

[Hallowell's note added below]: "This kind of roaming *wíndīgo* dies in summer – can't stand heat and mosquitoes. [Most are] only found in winter and spring, principally spring – used to cold (association with *kiwitin* [north]).

Wíndīgo is a *pawágan* – can be a helper – but [one] must have other stronger helpers to hold him down. It is this *pawágan* that helps a human being to make a 'dream' *wíndīgo*.

17 [A *Wíndīgo* Winter Gale]

One night [at Poplar River] before we went to bed, my wife went out. When she came back she asked me what was going on – whether a dance or conjuring. I said I did not know. [She] said, "There is not a light on the north side of the river (W.B. was on the south side). Blowing a gale (blizzard), terrible.

The next morning a fellow came in (Cingabis). Asked him, "What was going on last night?" "Why – you did not hear what was said yesterday?" "No!" "There was a *wíndīgo* passed here last night." Sandy Bruce, one of the leading conjurers, had conjured to have it pass without hurting anyone. That is why it blew so. He commanded everyone to leave the north side of the river and go on south [side]. If any families remained they would be eaten up. [I] said, "You're a fine bunch of people. You know I have a wife and child here. Next time, let me know – I'll kill him myself (mocking him). You tell me the direction, I'll go meet him." Scared of me after a while, thought I was a real man.

The biggest part of the people, not all, went into a large house where the conjuring was held. Two-inch auger [was] used to bore holes in floor for sticks.[29]

18 [Rescuing a Woman *Wíndīgo*]

[At Poplar River one winter] the Indians were all excited and fearful because of an old woman about four hours by sleigh up the river, who was becoming *wíndīgo*. The minister heard of it, asked one of the Indians (a councillor) to go and get her, but he said he would need 15 men.

W.B. who was there at the time offered to go. Found the old woman in camp with her husband. Had not eaten for days, would not eat, although offered food. [She] said if she became *wíndīgo* she would be as tall as the trees, and nothing could stop her. Kept crying, "Oh hai," and sighing. W.B. asked her to go with him; [she] said she could not look at the snow (may have something to do with heart of ice). [He] bundled her up, she put [her] head in cloth, [he] took her with him to main camp. Finally got her to eat after a couple of days and she recovered. [He] visited her every night and cheered her up.[30]

19 [Hearing Pagak]

[William Berens] was travelling with Isaac Bear. They were up before dawn expecting to start off with the dogs. W.B. heard a shout. "Hey——." Said nothing. Another one – closer. Then another very plain, overhead.

"What's that?" said Isaac. "Don't know," answered W.B. Thought it might be a *wíndīgo*.

[They] decided not to start until dawn when they could see every-thing.

Later [W.B.] spoke to an old man about it. He said it was Pagak they heard. He had seen their fire and wanted to let them know he was there. No harm would have come to them.

"Now you'll have a long life," said the old man. "And I have," com-mented W.B. (In other words, to hear Pagak is a kind of blessing.)[31]

20 [Giant Frog Tracks]

William Berens along with Joe Berens [landed their sailboat] on Birch Island, pulled in to boil a kettle. W.B. had a gun, went to shoot ducks. He came to the lakeshore – saw tracks as big as a man's hand, formed just like frogs' tracks – with jump of about six feet towards the water. "I would have seen him if I kept on, but went back to the others." They came to see track – fresh – scared, would not investigate. W.B. wanted to shoot him. Joe wanted to get out as soon as possible. Must have been as big as a beaver.[32]

21 [A Giant Snake]

[Gordon and William Berens were] down on the Pigeon River below the second rapids – a clear day – not a cloud. Lot of *anickanwakon* in the river – a creek – saw him swimming in water towards the south shore of the river – head as big as a jumper. [He] turned and looked at us, thought it was a jumper. I said, 'Get ready, you'll shoot him before he reaches shore. "Where is the jumper?" said Gordon. [I said], "It's a big snake." [Gordon was] only 15-18 feet away in a canoe. [He] saw the back – stripes; the head had disappeared by that time.[33]

Willie [Gordon?] wanted to shoot. W.B. wanted to see the head again. "If he turns we will make for the shore – better chance to shoot." [It] slid through the water with no agitation, must have been 30 feet long altogether. Yellow and red stripes along the side, five inches broad. The rest of it [was] black.

Auspicious Dreams of Travel and Hunting

22 [Otters and River Rescue]

When I was a young man I dreamed that I fell through the ice of the river at a spot … where the current is very swift. I found two otters in the water there. I turned into an otter, and swam along with them to a hole in the ice. There was my father waiting to help me out.

Ten years later I fell through the ice at the same place I had dreamed about. At first I lost my senses. The swift water swept me along to a place lower down where the river was open. My father called out, "Hold up your hand." I heard him, did so, and he saw me coming. He pulled me out by my parkey [parka], just in time.[34]

23 [The Girls and the Fisher]

Once when I was out hunting, I was discouraged. I had no luck at all. And I kept worrying about my "debt." One night after I had finished making the rounds of my traps, I lay down for a bit while my son was chopping wood. I fell fast asleep. I dreamed of a long trail running north. I was travelling on it. I saw a girl coming towards me. She was very pretty and dressed in white. She moved along as if she were skating, with very graceful motions. Then I saw another girl, closer to me, who was setting a table with lots of good things to eat. I started off towards the girls and first I came to the one who was setting the table. "This is all for you," she said.

Then I woke up. Almost before I realized it, I grabbed my hat and started off to visit a deadfall straight north of our camp. It was about 15 minutes walk and I began to think that it was rather foolish of me to go to this trap, since I had set so many steel traps on my line. (This deadfall was not in his regular trap line. He had made it in a spare moment: AIH.) But I kept on, and when I got there I found a fine fisher in the deadfall. It was a female. Then I knew what my dream meant. If I had been a pagan, I would have made a feast then and there and smoked to the "boss" fisher.[35]

24 [Meeting a Man with Money]

[Hallowell, introductory note]: "One morning [in 1937] when we were travelling together on our way from the mouth of the river to [Little] Grand Rapids, I asked W.B. whether he had dreamed anything the night before. He told me the following:"

I dreamed I was out walking on snowshoes. It must have been in spring because there was not much snow on the ground. I was travelling with a boy. I sighted a camp but there was no one in sight. Then I heard the sound of chopping in the bush. As we came up closer a man appeared. This man handed me some money, over $100 in bills. I could see an X on some of them. But the bills were the color of that (pointing to my [AIH's] sleeping bag which was yellowish brown). This man also gave me some silver and I gave some to the boy. I asked whether this was all right and he said yes.

[Hallowell: "I asked W.B. what he thought the dream meant. He said it might indicate that he would catch a fox the next winter. He inferred this from the color of the bills, a fact that he emphasized because he thought it very curious. I may add that he could not identify either of the persons in the dream. They were complete strangers to him."][36]

Foreshadowings of Loss

25 [An Apparition, Poplar River, 1900]

While I was living at Poplar River, my wife and I went to bed about the same time as usual one night, but I did not fall asleep at once. My head was turned towards the door leading to the kitchen and all of a sudden I saw a woman standing there. She was slender, dressed in white, and had golden hair that fell to her shoulders. I caught a glimpse of wings springing from her back. I trembled all over, I was so scared. But I managed to nudge my wife with my elbow. She had gone to sleep but turned over at this. When I looked again I could not see the angel, for that is what the figure seemed to be. All I could see was something misty and white like a cloud. My wife saw nothing but I told her what I had seen. I wondered what was going to happen.

The next day, which was Sunday, my boss drove up with his dog team. He said that he was on his way to Berens River and asked me to go along with him. I told him that I was not prepared to go and that I had no grub. But he insisted. So I got ready and went with him. When we arrived at Berens River I met my brother-in-law. He told me my sister [Eliza] was very ill. She had been continually asking for me. They were even thinking of sending a dog train for me but they could not get one. I stayed at Berens River for 10 days. My sister grew worse and worse. Then she died. I was getting worried because I was away from my post so long, but my boss, who had returned from a trip up the river by this time, set my mind at rest. He told me that he was glad he had brought me along so that I was able to be with my sister the last days of her life. It was very strange that he asked me because he did not seem to have any good reason, except that he wanted company. Yet I got there in time although I did not even know my sister was sick when I started.[37]

26 ["My Time Has Not Yet Come"]

I dreamed that I would bury my (two) brothers and my sisters and my parents. I lived to do this. When my father died [Jacob Berens, 1916] and I walked beside the coffin as it was taken to the grave, everything in my dream came back to me. It actually happened as I had seen it in my dream long before. When I was very sick one time, and no one expected me to live, my father was in despair. One night I said to him, "my time has not yet come. I will stand beside you when you are dead." I told him this because I had dreamed it, but he did not know why I said it.[38]

A Challenge to Narrative Categories

27 The Boy and the Trout

A boy paddled eight or nine miles out to an island in God's Lake [Manitoba] to get some birds' eggs. While he was getting the eggs the canoe drifted away. He remained two or three days with very little food. Heard someone speaking – "*Nózis* [*noozhis,* my grandson], come down," Went to the shore – saw a trout coming up out of the water. "Get right in under my fin," said the fish. "Any fish you wish to eat, you'll get it." So the young fellow felt as comfortable as in a *wīgīwam*. Had all the fish he wanted to eat. Any time he felt hungry all he had to do was to say he wanted this or that kind. Finally one day the fish said, "I'm going to show you something." They came up on top of water. "Now take a look." The boy climbed out on the fish's back – looked around. "Do you know this place?" (Did not know the place.) "Well, this is Oxford Lake."

Down swam the fish again. Again he said, "I'm going to show you something." They came up again. Looked around. Another place. "No, I don't know it." "This is the narrowest place in the sea – Labrador.[39] I'm going to show you something – all the great fish." He took him to a certain place where he saw the big Pickerel, the big Jack fish, the big Sturgeon and the big Sucker. The fish pointed out the Pickerel. "This is the wickedest. Another wicked one is the Jack Fish. The Sucker is alright," he said. The boy did not realize how much time had passed. "Now I'll take you back where I got you from." So the fish swam back and came to the top of the water. The boy could see the leaves coming on the trees. "Your family will be here tomorrow. You won't have to stay very long alone."

Now this rocky island was quite a way from shore. It was a very calm day. The boy's father was out on the lake. He saw four otters heading for this rocky island where he had lost his son. He never expected to see his son again. He kept after these otters but this animal is one of the fastest in the water. Finally he came pretty close to the island. He did not see any more otter. The boy had seen the canoe coming towards him. He got up and walked around, waiting. The father noticed at once there was someone walking about. He headed for the island and found the son he had lost the summer before. He was glad to see him – put him in the centre of the canoe and went back but never asked any questions.

Commentary: "The Boy and the Trout" and the Problem of Categories

Hallowell evidently heard "The Boy and the Trout" in 1932 or 1933, as he discussed it in his 1934 article "Some Empirical Aspects of Northern

Saulteaux Religion." This narrative exemplifies some of the complexities and challenges he faced in working with Ojibwe oral materials. Hallowell, like other scholars of oral traditions, tried to classify such narratives into categories or genres. This particular story, however, stymied him. In his research notes, Hallowell wrestled with the question of whether to call "The Boy and the Trout" a myth or a "*tabätcamoin*." William Berens classed it among the latter, for Hallowell made reference to "the subjective classification of this story as a *tabätcamoin* by my interpreter."

Yet Hallowell also came to recognize the thinness of the veil that separated myth from what Ojibwe people experienced as reality in wakefulness or dreams. He admitted that if Berens had not described the story as a "*tabätcamoin*," he himself would probably have classified it as a myth. But he also commented, "it might very well be the narration of a dream experience" [similar to those that Berens told about in this section]. His next comment noted a self-conscious recognition that he was applying an "etic" or outsider's set of criteria in his efforts to categorize the stories: "From an objective point of view the difficulties of classification by *content* may be contrasted with the native viewpoint, which, I am sure, does not distinguish between narratives on this basis ... *reality* is continuous – from the standpoint of the Saulteaux – there is no genuine contrast between the super-natural and the natural."[40]

In his article "Some Empirical Aspects of Northern Saulteaux Religion," Hallowell used this story as an illustration of the weight that Ojibwe people gave to oral testimony. Although this tale was judged by the boy's contemporaries to be fantastic, they passed it on as fact. Again trying to write from "an objective point of view," Hallowell analyzed this story as "indistinguishable in spirit and content from dream experiences or mythology ... Nevertheless the Indians classify it as *tabätcamoin* ... It is a 'true' story, then, and not myth."[41] It is different, however, from the other twenty-five stories in this section in that it happened at a distance, to a person who was not identified and was not related to the storyteller (and indeed we ourselves puzzled over whether to include it in this section). We might perhaps conclude that it falls into a category that Hallowell called "tales," comparable to the European fairy tales that he found were being told and enjoyed along the Berens River.[42] But the Berens River people provided him with no distinct term for "tales" as a different genre. And as Hallowell observed, the two categories they did recognize demonstrated "the extremely close relationship which exists between reputed personal experience and the *mythos* … the unitary character of the empirical universe as it must appear to the natives themselves."[43]

Accordingly, stories from long ago or far away could resemble or eventually shade into myths. Hallowell drew a parallel between "The Boy and the Trout" and a similar dream story that he heard on the upper Berens River from a man who had heard it directly from the old man to whom it had happened. The dreamer as a young boy was fasting on an island when a powerful visitor appeared as a golden eagle, endowed him with feathers, and led him southward on a remarkable journey to the land of the summer birds (which was also the land to which people traveled when they died). In springtime, the eagle brought the boy safely home.[44] Both these stories compare closely, in turn, to a story in William Jones's collection: "The Youth Who Was Led about by the Chief of the Sturgeons" tells of a boy who, while swimming, was carried away by a sturgeon. He himself became a sturgeon and magically traveled the rivers and even a great sea; finally led homeward, he returned to his father after six winters.[45]

In all these stories, a powerful visitor appears to a boy, whether in a waking or sleeping state, and transforms him so that he can embark on a long journey of mythic proportions; then after one or several winters, his guide returns him safely to his father. None of the stories relates the boy's name or indicates a kinship relation to the storyteller or a link to the teller's own life story. Each story may have begun, like William Berens's own dream stories, as a specific personal experience told by the individual to whom it happened. But over time, across generations, and with retellings, the teller's personal identity fades away. Such stories may shade into more generic dream stories that exemplify the powers of the powerful beings they tell about. Maybe they too were told, like the myths, around the fire on long winter nights, when the dream visitors were listening and children were learning about experiences that they too might have, sleeping or waking. And in their retelling, the focus could shift to the *bawaaganag* or the *aadisookaanag* themselves, "living 'persons' of an other-than-human class."[46]

William Berens's story of the boy and the trout serves well as a transition to Part IV, which presents the myths that Berens shared with Hallowell in the 1930s. It suggests that the divisions between genres are not so sharp after all, and category boundaries may be crossed. As Berens taught Hallowell, "reality is continuous."

PART IV

Aadizookaanag, Myths

Introduction

What people enjoy talking about and what they enjoy listening to, what commands their attention, what moves them to laughter or tears, what they accept as true or false, what they deem good conduct or bad conduct, is invariably related to the realities of the behavioral world in which they live. This behavioral world is not the neutral objective world of the physicist, the geologist, the geographer, or even the biologist. It is a world of objects and events fraught with emotional significance as well as intellectual meaning and with complex associations and values for the individual that he has acquired in the course of his socialization from the traditional cultural heritage of his group.

These elegant lines were the opening paragraph of the introduction for a book that A. Irving Hallowell began to write but never completed in the 1940s.[1] Its focus was to be the myths and tales of the Ojibwe people whom he got to know during his Berens River field work in the 1930s. William Berens was the teller of eighteen of the myths. All of them are presented here except for "The Boy and the Trout," which appears in Part III (104–5) for reasons noted earlier. Hallowell first recorded some of Berens's stories in the summer of 1933; eight of them are dated to that year. Possibly the stories that he began to hear that season first led him to consider writing such a book.

Hallowell went on to gather at least another forty texts (not published here) from other storytellers, mostly men, who lived in Berens River and elsewhere.[2] At Berens River four men besides Berens contributed stories: William Everett, Arthur Felix, James Bear, and Alec Swain. At Little Grand Rapids, Hallowell recorded stories from Adam Bigmouth, Potci, Dunsford, Levique, John Keeper, and Alec Keeper. In Pikangikum he was told stories by Wigwɑswɑtik or Birchstick (the chief of the band) and Kágikèasik. In the summer of 1934 he brought a graduate student, Dorothy Spencer, with him, hoping that she would be able to work with the women more closely and freely than he could. However, because the woman who was to interpret for her had moved away, she was only able to collect a handful of women's stories: two from Jane Miller, an Oxford House Cree woman who was living at Berens River; one from Mary Boucher, also at Berens River; and three from a Mrs Pudvin [Potvin] who was married to a white man and living at Little Grand Rapids.[3]

When Hallowell heard variations on a previously told story, he also recorded those versions. Some, he explained, were told in English, some in Saulteaux and translated by an interpreter (usually William Berens). Hallowell transcribed them, making, he said, only those editorial changes necessary to establish "passable English that makes the native meaning clear." Since, he explained, his translators were not masters of English he did not "[render] their grammatical mistakes nor all their colloquialisms" in the texts he prepared for the book.[4] Hallowell, the storytellers, and the interpreters must all therefore be seen as active participants in the stories he collected.

Since Hallowell never managed to visit Berens River during a winter, he also had to rely on the willingness of his informants to tell *aadi-*

zookaanag out of season – an offence punishable by other-than-human beings. William Berens, who was a Methodist, dared to break the taboo – although, as Hallowell saw, he was plagued by toads as a penalty. His Christian faith may have countered to an extent his fears of repercussions. But his courage in the face of those fears also shows the closeness of his relationship with Hallowell, who had become a trusted friend. He must also have enjoyed retelling to a good listener the stories that he remembered hearing night after night from his grandmother (Amo) and his father, Jacob. More broadly, he evidently valued the opportunity that Hallowell provided to communicate important aspects of Ojibwe culture to the world.[5]

Numerous upriver people, however, had misgivings about telling the stories in summer. Alec Keeper of Little Grand Rapids, for example, agreed only with the greatest reluctance to tell Hallowell some bare outlines of the Tcakabec stories during one of his summer visits.[6] As Hallowell put it in his draft introduction:

> The recital of myths outside the proper season, moreover, is believed to provoke an unpleasant penalty. It is said by the Saulteaux that toads or frogs (both called one and the other) will crawl up the clothes of a person who tells the sacred stories in summer. Of course, it is difficult to measure the actual force of such a sanction but Schoolcraft says he was unable to secure the myths out of season. Evasion was "by some easy or indifferent remark," and he goes on to remark that the Indians claim "that if they violate the custom the snakes, toads, or other reptiles, which are believed to be under the influence of the spirits, will punish them."[7] So far as the Saulteaux are concerned toads and frogs, like snakes, are abhorred. In fact the former are associated with the manufacture of "bad medicine," so no one wishes to be visited by these amphibious creatures.

While Hallowell did not presume to call his collection exhaustive, he was confident that the range and content of the oral narratives that he had gathered represented a "fair sample of the myths and tales of the Saulteaux groups in the region east of Lake Winnipeg."[8] At the time he drafted the introduction for his book, the scholarly interpretation of myths and tales as integral to a people's culture was not a strong emphasis of anthropology, although scholars had been gathering collections of narratives for over a century. Yet Hallowell, with his characteristic gift of ethnographic understanding and his innovative thinking, saw that the role of oral narratives in Ojibwe culture was pivotal. It was his intention to provide a clear context for the narratives and also an account of the role of oral narratives in the lives of the Ojibwe along the Berens River.

Hallowell built in part on the work of Henry Schoolcraft, who in 1839 published *Algic Researches*, the first "extensive body of [Ojibwe] myths and tales collected at first hand."[9] Schoolcraft served as Indian agent at Sault Ste Marie, Michigan, from 1822 to 1841. In 1825, he married Jane Johnston, whose mother was Ojibwe. Her knowledge of language and legends, which she shared freely with Schoolcraft, figured prominently in his published work. Interestingly, although Schoolcraft was adamant that the beauty and worth of the narratives depended on their being presented in their original form, he edited the stories rather oppressively, sometimes going as far as to reshape plots.[10]

Hallowell also drew upon the work of ethnologist William Jones, whose two massive volumes of Ojibwe narratives were published in 1917 and 1919 by the American Ethnological Society. Between 1903 and 1905, Jones worked as a research assistant at the Carnegie Institution for Science in Washington, DC. He was assigned the Herculean task of collecting texts from speakers of Ojibwe from the Lake Nipigon area north of Lake Superior, from the Fort William reserve adjacent to Thunder Bay, Ontario, and from communities in northern Minnesota. In 1906, he accepted a position in the Anthropology Department at the Field Museum of Natural History in Chicago. He was preparing to publish his collection when he met a sudden and untimely death in 1917 on an assignment in the Philippines. Franz Boas edited and ensured the publication of Jones's work, including both his Ojibwe and English texts. Jones, an excellent ethnographer, was himself a Menominee Indian who had a magnificent grasp of Algonquian languages.[11]

At the heart of Jones's work was his effort to "get at the religious ideas of a people from their own point of view." Struck by what he saw as the simplicity of the narratives, he stated, "they run along with such an even, quiet pace, that they leave an impression of dull monotony. They are told in a matter-of-fact way, and conscious effort at rhetorical effect is feeble ... Repetition is frequent, not only of an idea but of an expression."[12] Both Hallowell and Jones were struck by the lack of variation and spontaneity in the stories they recorded. In contrast, Theresa Smith, in 1995, cautioned against even referring to Ojibwe myths and tales as "a body" of work because, "this body, like all forms of the Anishnaabe cosmos, is a highly mutable one."[13]

Narrative Categories

Hallowell identified three categories of Ojibwe narratives: anecdotes, myths, and tales.[14] The first group encompassed the telling of personal observations and experiences and made up a fair proportion of everyday conversation. A century after Henry Schoolcraft's assessment that the range of topics involved was narrow, Hallowell found himself in agreement. Both of them found that Ojibwe men rarely discussed the most vital parts of their lives – the beings of whom they dreamed during their puberty fasts. The dream visitors, or *bawaaganag*, who appeared to fasting boys during their sleep had great power to protect and help – or hinder and hurt – a man.[15] In dream quests young men sought the blessings of *bawaaganag* who, they hoped, would become guardian spirits. Once a *bawaagan* assumed that role, however, one had to be extremely careful not to offend the other-than-human being in any way and one sure way to incur the wrath of these beings was to talk lightly about them. Those who were blessed also had to be careful to invoke their *bawaaganag* only when they were especially needed.[16]

One could talk, however, about other human beings, living or dead, in an anecdotal way, although the recent dead were not, as a rule, referred to by name. Another kind of narrative, which Hallowell called tales, involved either anonymous people or people who, even if named, were not the kin of individuals living on the Berens River. Because Ojibwe kinship ties were so elastic (extending far beyond the networks recognized by European kinship systems), such individuals were seen as in a class by themselves. The essential difference that set these kinds of stories apart was, for Hallowell,

> [the] undefined kinship status of the persons that appear in the tales as compared with the concrete identification of persons who are the subject of the anecdote. Both kinds of narratives are considered "true" by the Saulteaux but it is obvious that, from our point of view, the tales are the kind of narratives that seem to offer the best springboard for the development of fiction, in our sense. There seems nothing to control their elaboration. Actually, however, many of the tales are comparable to the anecdotes, and originally may have been told about historic individuals.[17]

Ojibwe people referred to personal and anecdotal stories as *dibaaji-mowinan*, which Hallowell translated as "news" or "tidings." Hallowell evidently did not learn a distinct Ojibwe term for his third category, those stories he called "tales."

The distinction between the two main categories of narratives was a sharp one. One could discuss personal activities as a human being but could not talk about the *bawaaganag* with equal freedom. Where the *dibaajimowinan* were stories of ordinary human beings, stories about the *bawaaganag* were *aadizookaanag*. Ojibwe people used the term *aadizookaanag* to refer to both the stories themselves and to the characters in those stories: Wisakedjak and Mikīnäk, the Great Turtle, were *aadizookaanag*. Another term of respect used for such beings, one that expressed a sense of relationship, was "our grandfathers."[18] The only distinction Hallowell noticed among these terms was that "our grandfathers" and *bawaaganag* included all the other-than-human beings who operated in the cosmos, whereas *aadizookaanag* was normally reserved for the characters who appeared in the myths.

A distinctive narrative device further differentiated the myths from anecdotes and tales. Storytellers closed their tellings of myths with the formulaic saying *pinewītis kágotik* [*binewidis ge-agoodeg?*]: "And so the gizzard of the ruffed grouse now hangs aloft."[19] Tales or anecdotes lacked any set closing phrase – another indication, as Hallowell noted, of the ritualization of myth as a distinct genre.

Since the *aadizookaanag* could only be talked about under the proper circumstances, the myths could be told only after people's migrations from summer fishing settlements to winter hunting grounds, when lakes and rivers were frozen, the trees were bare, and hunting and trapping activities were in full swing. These stories were told at night, with the early arrival of winter darkness helping to ensure that they would be heard just before sleeping.

Hallowell explained that when everyone was "under the blankets," as one informant phrased it, some old man or woman would narrate a myth.[20] The *aadizookaanag* knew when they were being talked about. They listened carefully as humans told the stories without fear of offending the grandfathers, since the conditions were proper and the attitude was respectful. One of Hallowell's informants, prior to narrating a part of the Wisɑkedjak cycle, said that Wisɑkedjak once told the other *aadizookaanag*, "We'll try to make everything to suit the Indians (*änicinábec*) as long as any of them exist, so that the Indians will never forget us and will always talk about us."[21] With the advent of spring the season of myth narration was gone for another year, frogs and toads were no longer dormant, and families left to gather once again by the lakes for summer fishing.

The Roles and Functions of Myths in Ojibwe Society

Thomas W. Overholt and J. Baird Callicott describe myths as having two functions: education and entertainment.[22] The narrations brought the Ojibwes' spiritual grandfathers into the teller's realm, thus serving as a form of invocation. A genuine function of the recitals was to entertain (they were, according to Hallowell, often told in a humorous vein). But they also opened paths of communication with other-than-human beings. Myths were in turn clearly linked with dreams and dreaming was essential to survival and to living a good life.

Hallowell's field notes regarding a Tcakabek story that was told to

him in Little Grand Rapids (no date) provide a good example of the
function of myth for Berens River people. The story ends with Tcakabek
encountering humans and going with them to a Hudson's Bay Company store because he needed some supplies. This, Hallowell believed,

> further documents the nature of Saulteaux conceptions of the *ät-
> sokanak*. Since Tcαkábɛk is believed to be a living entity, not a purely
> fictitious character, and to inhabit the same universe as ordinary
> human beings, snaring the sun, on one hand, and visiting a post of
> the Hudson's Bay Company on the other, are not events occurring
> in distinct or even contradictory levels of discourse, mythological
> and realistic. They are events in a conceptual universe in which "nat-
> ural phenomena," "mythological" characters and human beings are
> all co-existent entities which may interact with each other in strange
> ways.[23]

Hallowell's point was that some stories about Tcakabek and
Wisαkedjak were set in the "genuine historical past" because these characters were not seen to be confined solely to the mythic past. This ensured that myth remained a vital and meaningful force in the lives of the
people. The telling of myths kept alive and reinforced their history and
worldview.

Hallowell was clear about the relationship between myth and truth
for Ojibwe people. To most outside observers, dominated by western
concepts of science and rational thinking, the myths seem utterly fantastic and unrealistic – pure fiction. The Ojibwe, however, could and
did accept events in myths as real happenings because for them reality
was a more expansive and fluid concept.

Myths from Berens River Communities[24]

The stories that Hallowell collected from Berens River, Little Grand
Rapids, and Pikangikum include some narratives that are not often
found among collections of Ojibwe and Cree stories.[25] Many other

stories occur with variations, both within communities along the Berens River and/or in collections from other northerly Ojibwe and Cree communities. For example, Hallowell collected three different versions of the story of Wisαkedjak turning himself into a woman. At times, the versions present very close parallels. At other times, however, only one motif links the stories together. In William Berens's "Four Men Visit Wisαkedjak and Have Their Wishes Granted" (11), Wisαkedjak turns to stone a man who wishes to live forever because stone is the only entity Wisαkedjak can think of that lasts forever. Variations of this story from other communities all contain the idea of Wisαkedjak turning a man to stone so he can live forever, but otherwise the plots are completely different.[26]

Berens River Ojibwe stories – especially about Wisαkedjak and Tcakabek – show some clear parallels with Cree narratives. Even the use of the name Wisαkedjak by Berens River people is worthy of note. Ojibwe people in communities to the south almost always refer to this character as Nanabush, or a variant of that name. The name Wisαkedjak is more common among Cree and subarctic Ojibwe people.[27]

This usage is not surprising given the numerous Cree connections in the community of Berens River and in the ancestry of William Berens. William's paternal great-grandfather, Yellow Legs, was a member of the Moose clan, which Hallowell found to be "pretty uncomplicated" when he traced its ancestry. William's family tree also, however, included ties through his father's mother, Amo, to the Pelican clan– a complicated line with "a multiplicity of unconnected lineages." Hallowell traced this line of Pelicans back to a man named Kepeäs, one of the first men, according to William's grandfather, Bear, to settle at Poplar River, north of Berens River on the east side of Lake Winnipeg. Kepeäs arrived from the western side of the lake and seemingly from the predominantly Cree area of Cumberland House. Kepeäs's daughter, Amo, met Bear one day when she accompanied her father to the Hudson's Bay post at Berens River (there was no post at Poplar River at that time) to take "fall debt" (receiving goods in advance for furs they would bring to trade the next spring). The two married and Bear went to live with his wife's family.[28]

Scholars have not clearly understood the Ojibwe presence in the Cumberland House area. In his 1986 volume about Indian-European trade relations in the lower Saskatchewan River area to 1840, Paul Thistle noted that the HBC Cumberland House journals recorded that between 1784 and 1795 the local Cree, who had already been experiencing many stresses, were additionally strained by an influx of "Bungee" Indians into the lower Saskatchewan area. Bungee usually refers to Ojibwe people, but Thistle, citing archaeological evidence of an influx of Swampy Crees in the 1790s, concluded that these people were likely Swampy Crees.[29] Berens family history as recounted to Hallowell, however, indicated that at least some Ojibwes of the Pelican clan were already residing in that area.

William Berens would have heard Cree stories from his paternal grandmother, Amo, and from another source within his family circle. As noted in Part I, his paternal grandmother, Mary McKay, although identified by Berens River contemporaries as "white," was of mixed Scottish-Cree ancestry. Her mother, Julia Chalifoux, was of mixed French Canadian and Cree descent. Julia died in 1860, but her husband, William McKay, whose mother was also of Cree-Scottish descent, lived on to 1887. As a boy, William Berens may have heard many a Cree tale from his maternal grandfather. Nancy Everett, William's wife, also had Cree ancestry. Her maternal grandfather, Joseph Boucher, married a Norway House Cree woman before settling at Berens River.

Finally, the Berens River area itself was well known to Cree people. By the time Egerton R. Young established the first mission at Berens River in 1874, Ojibwe people had been rubbing shoulders with Crees (as well as British, French Canadian, and Mètis fur traders) for a century and a half. Young himself documented the impact of Ojibwe *and* Cree stories on his two eldest children, Egerton (Eddie) and Lillian. Two Ojibwe men, Zhaawanaash (Souwanas as Young spelled it) and Jakoos, welcomed the missionary's children into their lodges and regaled them with Ojibwe stories. At this time a Cree woman whom the Youngs called Little Mary was looking after their children. Young, in his book *Algonquin Indian Tales*, described his children's tremendous enjoyment of the men's tales – and Little Mary's disdain for them. She told the children that she could easily tell them better stories than anything that old

Souwanas had to offer. Thus Mary, he says, "found herself pitted against Souwanas, the great story-teller of the tribe."[30]

Myths Told by William Berens

The first five stories that follow tell of creations and recreations. In "The Birth of the Winds, Great Hare, and Flint" (1), a man magically impregnates his daughter, who subsequently gives birth to the four winds, the Great Hare, and Flint. Flint tears his mother to pieces with his sharp edges during his birth and the Great Hare, in revenge, breaks Flint into the small pieces that humans use today. The Winds are again featured in "South Wind Enters a Contest with His Brother, North Wind" (2), when the arrogant North Wind challenges his brother to a test of strength (with surprising results). In "The Origin of Summer" (3), the length of winter is determined by a group of animals who, tired of perpetual winter in the north, visit the southern animals, steal Summer from them, and negotiate a compromise to share it.

The recreation of the world occurs in the myths of "Wisɑkedjak and the Water Lions" and "Aásī" (4,5). In the first story Wisɑkedjak goes on a quest to avenge the death of his stepson, a young wolf who was murdered by a Great Lynx. After he succeeds in wounding the lynx, the world becomes flooded by a tremendous deluge. Wisɑkedjak, with the help of animals (notably the earth-diving muskrat) who are floating with him on his life-saving raft, recreates the world. In number 5, Aásī [Aa'aasi, Crow], having survived many dangers, recreates the world after he avenges his abused mother by destroying it in a great conflagration.

The stories in the section "Other-than-Humans and Humans: Blessings and Struggles" all depict relationships between Ojibwe people and other-than-human beings. In "Mätcīkīwis" (6), a young man marries a woman who turns out to be a Thunder Bird and follows her to her home in the sky, living for a time with the other great birds. In "Mikīnäk" (7), a widow with two sons marries the Great Turtle, who turns out to be a wonderful provider. In "Misabe" (8), a man, despite his terror at falling into the hands of this infamous giant, spends an amazing year with him and is guided home safely thanks to Misabe's giant dogs, who help the man back over the sea. This section also features three Wisɑkedjak stories (9, 10, and 11). The first two chronicle the activities of the trickster in which he interacts with women in two very different ways. The final story tells of the visit of four men to Wisɑkedjak who grants their wishes in different ways, allowing one to marry his daughter and turning another to stone.

Many Ojibwe myths involved the use of strong spiritual or mental powers, whether the protagonists were humans or animals. The section "Humans and Animals: Using One's Powers to Save, Kill, or Survive" features four stories on this theme. In "Rolling Head" two boys magically escape their mother's rolling head and one makes further use of his exceptional powers by repeatedly defeating his father-in-law, an evil shaman (12). "Big Mosquito" describes a man who is powerful enough to kill two of the giant mosquitoes that used to prey on humankind, reducing one to tiny pieces – the size of today's mosquitoes (13). The final two stories, "The Bear, the Hare, and the Lynx" and "Wolf and Wolverine," depict struggles for power between animal protagonists (14, 15).

The final section features two narratives about cannibals and the harm they inflict. The two heroes who defeat these strong, dangerous personages, however, are quite different. The cannibal-killer in "The Eleven Brothers" is the youngest and seemingly most vulnerable child in a family of eleven boys. But, as Ojibwe stories often warn, appearances are deceptive. The boy survives to spear the beating hearts of the cannibals. He then revives not only his brothers but also the other victims they have eaten and wins respect as a person of great power (16). The hero in "Wémtigóze" [Wemitigoozhi] is a strong man who manages to stop a reign of cannibal-terror (17).

Myths and Ojibwe Society – Models of Human Behaviour

In the introduction (p. 1) to his planned book on myths and tales, Hallowell wrote:

> Oral narratives of any kind essentially reflect the outlook of a specific behavioral world. This is one reason why the myths and tales of

one people always differ from those of another. For the kind of events which characterize such narratives, the implicit assumptions about the nature of the universe that are expressed, the themes that are dramatized, the quality of the episodes that serve as stimuli to the emotions and any didactic purpose that may be served by the stories, all derive their significance from the belief, attitudes and values intrinsic to the culture of the people who find them of engaging interest. The primary intelligibility of the myths and tales … must be sought, therefore, in the structure of the behavioral world to which the narrated events have reference.

These myths, when studied carefully, reveal a rich treasury of information that sheds light on the underpinnings of their tellers' society, worldview, and values. Themes such as the need for power for survival, the phenomenon of metamorphosis, the crucial importance of blessings, reciprocity, and respect, the perils of disobedience, the power of dreams, the risks of relying too much on appearances, the tensions that may arise between in-laws, between generations, and between men and women, and the continual quest to attain a good life run like currents throughout the myths. Their characters struggle with and for spiritual power, using and misusing it and competing to see who has greater power, since relative power is often difficult to determine except through competition. Shifting balances of power are prominent in the narratives. When North Wind challenges his brother South Wind to a competition, he is confident that his powers are vastly superior and he prepares to crow. He is truly shocked when the humble South Wind bests him. The moral lesson is clear in this and other myths: too much pride in one's own powers is a bad thing; powers can be lost through excessive pride, abuse, and bad behaviour.

Berens River Ojibwe people shared another belief about power that is conspicuous also in the stories told by Omushkego Cree storyteller Louis Bird. Over and over, the Cree narratives show that the smallest creatures, the humble and weak, the orphan, may have the greatest power and that it is unwise to test or mistreat these beings. In the Tcakabek stories told by both Cree and Ojibwe, it is a tiny man who snares the sun and only a tiny mouse turns out to be strong enough to bite through that snare.[31] Aásī's stepfather and the wicked father-in-law in "Rolling Head" (5, 12) never thought that mere boys could usurp their powers and overcome lethal trials. When a widow marries Mikīnäk, Big Turtle, her sons think the idea is a joke, but the joke is on them and they learn to respect their new stepfather when he saves them from starvation. In "The Eleven Brothers" (16), the youngest brother kills the cannibals who ate his older brothers – the same brothers who had protected the little child from exposure to any danger since he was so young and vulnerable. Hallowell noted, "This means that power of an individual can always be challenged ... one must be wary – or alert all the time. Be cautious even in offence – be nice ... cannot even feel trust in one's own relatives."[32]

Manifestations of power allow other-than-humans, humans, animals, and objects to do remarkable things. Tcakabek, a tiny magical man, can break the arms of giants or kill several giants with a magic arrow. The young protagonist in "Rolling Head" defeats his murderous father-in-law every time due to his superior powers. Some characters can predict the future and some can destroy another being or render that being's powers at least temporarily paralyzed, such as in the story of Wolverine bewitching Wolf so that he cannot hunt (and thus compete with Wolverine). The stories illustrate the kinds of help and power that other-than-human beings may confer on boys who approach them through appropriate fasting and dreaming.

As Overholt and Callicot discuss, proper behaviour plays a big role in whether or not a person will receive, and then keep, her or his power.[33] In many Ojibwe stories, disobeying orders or breaking taboos result in terrible consequences. Wisɑkedjak's wolf stepson is killed by a Great Lynx when he fails to heed Wisɑkedjak's warning that he must never leap over water (4). The young man who marries a Thunder Bird loses her and then must pursue her to Thunder Bird Land because he disobeys her instructions (6). Obedience results in reward. Aásī carefully obeys orders to overcome the dangers, such as the two women with sharp elbows who try to attack him on his voyage back to his mother. Arrogant and selfish behaviour is punished. When Wolverine bewitches Wolf he merrily out-hunts him and watches his family starve, but his luck turns and it is Wolverine, his wife, and his children who lose their lives in the end (15).

One of the most striking aspects of the Ojibwe worldview involved transformative metamorphosis – a phenomenon based on varying levels of power. At the top of the ladder were, of course, other-than-human beings. Humans were next in line, although the strongest humans had different levels of powers that were always in flux. Powerful shamans could cause changes or turn themselves into something else to achieve good (attacking enemies, healing, finding out vital information, effecting a prophecy) or to do evil. Metamorphosis was a means to demonstrate the extent of their powers and the uses to which they were putting them. Wisakedjak turns himself into a stump so that he can hide from and then kill the Great Lynx who murdered his stepson (4). Humans can turn themselves into animals. The young man who married a Thunder Bird changes himself into several different animals in order to reach his beloved wife in Thunder Bird Land (6). Other-than-humans can turn into humans, with Mikīnäk intermittently assuming human form (7). Animals and objects can take on human characteristics. William Jones's collection, for example, contains a story about a skunk, a cranberry, an awl, and a miserable old moccasin. Each is portrayed in human terms and at the same time retains the characteristics of a skunk, an awl, a cranberry, and an old moccasin: the cranberry explodes under stress, and to save themselves when they are attacked in their home, the awl flings herself into a tree and the old moccasin flies over to land by the door, where it looks like a miserable old moccasin.[34] Ordinary objects get transformed, as in "Rolling Head" when the objects on the boys' magical flight become obstacles to their mother's rolling head (12). The lines between the categories of things – animate and inanimate – are continually blurred and in flux. This alone makes it difficult for Western audiences to "get their heads around" the contents of the myths and tales, which, as Overholt and Callicott note, may appear to outsiders as "patently weird."[35] For Ojibwe people, however, these stories epitomized their way of seeing the world and the universe.[36]

Dreams, blessings, and power were inextricably linked. Humans could obtain blessings from other-than-humans only in dreams, which "shows the importance and significance of the spiritual over the material experience" for Ojibwe people.[37] Dreams were also vehicles for the discovery of information and clues about the future. William Berens learned in a dream that he would bury (outlive) his father, Jacob (III, 25). He was thus able to comfort Jacob when he was distraught over William's serious illness. It was through a dream experience, too, that William knew he would not be shot if he went to war (III, 7).

Powerful people who have dreamed that they will be able to overcome hardship by becoming something or someone else (human or animal) will be able to do this in real life. In "Rolling Head"(12), the wizard, Wemisos, puts his son-in-law in a terrible predicament, barefoot and without leggings in the middle of winter. The young man suddenly remembers that as a boy he dreamed of a black wolf. Now, in his time of need, realizing that this being can help him, he becomes a wolf. Many people in Western society tend to see a clear, rigid line between things that happen in dreams and things that happen in waking life. For Ojibwe people, that boundary was permeable and in constant flux.

To provide comparisons and context for William Berens's tellings of the following myths, we have added notes to each, citing some of the variants found in other Ojibwe and Cree collections. Of first importance is William Jones's collection of myths of the Ojibwe living west and north of Lake Superior – stories from the northern part of the southwestern Ojibwe territory. The stories of Cecilia Sugarhead also offer useful comparisons. Sugarhead was born in the 1940s and raised in the Lansdowne House area of northwestern Ontario. She grew up at Attawapiskat Lake, an Ojibwe community of 250 people, 450 kilometres northeast of Thunder Bay. The stories recorded by Louis Bird and C. Douglas Ellis provide a useful Cree context. Louis Bird, from Peawanuk, Ontario, spent many years collecting stories from Swampy Cree elders along western Hudson and James bays and has published two volumes of narratives. C. Douglas Ellis gathered texts from 1955 to 1965, mostly while living for three years at Albany Post (now Kashechewan) on the west coast of James Bay. He also gathered many narratives during visits to Moose Factory.[38]

Hallowell annotated the myths with numerous footnotes and marginal jottings on the handwritten and typed texts that he assembled.

Some of his texts survive in two or three forms, ranging from rather telegraphic versions that look like field notes to fuller written and typed versions. Most often, we have taken the fullest version as a base, incorporating his annotations either in the story text (in parentheses, if they are very brief) or as endnotes. ("Big Mosquito," no. 13, however, is handled somewhat differently, as will be noted.) We have set Hallowell's original footnotes in quotation marks and labelled them [AIH] at the end. Within the story texts, Hallowell's emendations and the Ojibwe words that he inserted are included in parentheses. For all the words that we have been able to identify, we have added, in square brackets, their orthography following the guidelines of Nichols and Nyholm, *A Concise Dictionary of Minnesota Ojibwe* (1995), which we have applied to the best of our ability. (From the Berens texts and from Hallowell's published articles, we have also compiled a full glossary of Hallowell's Ojibwe words, greatly aided by the assistance of Rand Valentine, Roger Roulette, and on specific questions, John Nichols; it is included in Hallowell, in press.)

William Berens's stories, all previously unpublished, are a treasured addition to Ojibwe oral literature. They may now be shared with the wider world, as Berens had hoped and Hallowell had planned.

Creations and Recreations

1 The Birth of the Winds, Flint, and the Great Hare (1933)[39]

Long ago the Indians were all gathered together in a camp such as you see here now. One old man had a very beautiful son. He was very proud of him. So he determined to make a great man of his son. He told the boy that he must go into the woods to fast and dream so that he might be blessed. The old man made a fine *wazïsan* [*waziswan*, nest, dream quest nest] for his son in a tree. Here the boy went and stayed alone.

One morning he found his blanket wet. It had not rained during the night and there were no clouds in the sky. The next morning the blanket was wet again. He found this very strange and said to himself, "I won't sleep here tonight." So he took up his bow and shot an arrow from it with all his strength, holding tight to the end of the arrow. Where it dropped he landed on the earth again. (Of course, by this time no one knew where the boy was.) He lay down to sleep that night as before under his blanket. Once again he found it wet in the morning. This time he said to himself, "I will stay awake tonight and see what happens." About midnight he saw a woman come sneaking towards where he lay. She stood alongside of him. Then she put one leg over him and pissed on his blanket.[40] Up he jumped, but the woman ran away and disappeared in the bush. He recognized her at once, however. She was a woman from his camp but one who was not highly thought of. Instead of returning to the camp and telling his father what had happened, which would have brought great shame upon him, the boy resolved to tell no one. "I'll hide so this woman cannot find me," he thought. So he counted the scales on a white spruce.[41] When he had finished he said, "Let one of you hide me." But the woman found him nevertheless and the same thing happened. (She was just as powerful as he.) The next day the boy started out to find some other hiding place. He came to a swamp with lots of cat-tails growing in it. He requested one of the downy (bractless pistil-late?) flowers to carry him far up among the clouds. Here he thought he would at last be free of the woman. He succeeded for although she was powerful enough to follow him aloft on another cattail down she failed to find him. But she had already borne a girl-child (magically sired by the boy). This child grew with unusual rapidity. She was soon running around. Her mother had made their camp on a high piece of ground. She put up a hide-covered tipi. On the outside it was painted in several colors.

While sailing about in the air, the boy saw this dwelling below. "I wonder who lives there," he thought. So he came down to earth again and walked up to the tipi. As soon as he stepped inside he recognized the woman but it was too late to escape then. The little girl was playing about and he watched her. "Give your father a drink," said the woman. The child ran and filled a dish with water and handed it to him. The woman watched him closely. As soon as he started to drink she pushed the dish into his mouth and said, "Let the earth swallow you up." The boy immediately sank into the ground, but he had sufficient power to keep his head from sinking below the surface of the soil. "You'll stay there for good," the woman said. That day she moved the camp to another spot some distance away.

As soon as the woman was out of sight the boy tried to release himself from the earth. He used all the power he had. He called on all his dream helpers, but he failed to escape. "This is the end of me," he said to himself. Then he thought of one thing more. He said, "I wish my head to turn into a blueberry patch." And so it happened.

One day the little girl walked around to see the place where their old camp had been. She saw the blueberry patch and when she went home mentioned this to her mother. The woman said, "Don't you go near those blueberries. They might be your father's head!" But the little girl wanted to eat some of the blueberries. So she sneaked back to the old camping place again and started to pick some blueberries. The boy wished the girl to come closer and little by little she did come closer. Then he wished that her arse be turned towards him. When she was in the right position he blew into her arse and said, "Now you'll have some kids." The girl was so scared that she ran back to their tent crying and told her mother what had happened. "I told you not to go near that blueberry patch," her mother said.

Soon the girl was heavy with child. Then her time came and she gave birth to a boy. As soon as he was born he could speak and walk. But it was an easy birth. "My name shall be Wabanasi (East Wind)" he said, "I shall be fairly kind to human beings." Then another boy was born. He was partly grown, too, and took his place beside the first one born. "Human beings (*änicinábek*, literally "Indians") shall call me Cauwanɑsi [South Wind]," he said, "I'll be very good and treat human beings well, as long as any exist on this earth." The third child born spoke and said, "Human beings shall call me West Wind. I'll be a little rough on them but I'll never be wicked. Be easy on our mother,"

he went on, as another boy popped out. This one said, "Human beings shall call me Kiwetin (North Wind). I'll have no mercy on any
human being. I'll treat them just the same as the animals."

"How do you expect human beings to exist if you are going to
treat them like that?" his brothers asked. Then another child stuck its
head out of the girl's womb. "Be easy on our mother," the other children said. "Easy, nothing," this one replied, and as he jumped out
of his mother's body it was torn to pieces. "My name is Piwánαk
[Biiwaanag] (Flint)," this child announced. His whole body was made
of the hardest kind of stone. The girl's mother cried when she saw
her daughter in pieces, but she picked them all up and carefully put
them in a bark rogan [basket].

One morning the woman heard a noise in the rogan. It sounded
as if something alive was moving around in it. So she picked it up and
looked inside. There she saw a little hare. "Ah, my poor *nózis* [*noozis*,
grandchild]," she said. But when she looked again, there was another
boy. This one said, "Human beings shall call me Misabos [Misaabooz]
(Great Hare)."

Shortly afterwards the brothers decided that they could not all
remain together any longer. The East Wind said, "I'll go to live in the
east." The West Wind said, "I'll sit opposite to you, at the other end
of the earth." The South Wind said, "I'll go to the southern end of the
earth," and the North Wind said, "I'll go to the north end." Then Flint
said, "I'll go down into the swift current (*sóskŭtciwanαnk*) [*zhooshko-
jiwan*] of the water." But Misabos said, "My brothers, I see that all of
you have already made your choices. I'm going to remain here with
my grandmother for awhile. I will not make my choice yet." Then
all of the other brothers went off to the places they had chosen and
Misabos stayed with his grandmother.

Misabos did not know whether or not he had a mother. So one
day he said to his grandmother, "Grandmother, how did I come into
this world?" The old woman did not answer. Misabos asked her again.
Then she told him what happened – "One of your brothers, the
youngest one. He it was who destroyed your mother." Misabos was
mad when he heard this. He knew Flint was strong but he wondered

whether there was anything which was powerful enough to break him in pieces. He made up his mind to find out. He thought the best way was to discover what Flint was afraid of. So Misabos paid a visit to his brother. He said to him, "You have a strong body. Are you afraid of anything at all?" "Nothing!" replied Flint. So Misabos went home disappointed.

Then he paid a second visit to Flint and asked him the same question. And he got the same answer. So he was disappointed again. When he got home, he said to his grandmother, "I wonder how I can make my brother tell me something." But she said nothing. So he thought to himself, "Perhaps if I wait awhile and ask a third time, he will tell me something. He may forget what he said before." So after some time had passed he got ready and started off again to visit Flint. Misabos asked his brother the same question he had asked before. This time Flint replied, "An arrow made of steel. That's the only thing I'm afraid of." But as soon as he had said this, Misabos noticed a change in the expression of his face. He knew that Flint was sorry he had said what he did. It was Flint's turn now and he said to Misabos, "What are you scared of?" "Of an arrow made of a cattail stick with a head of white spruce cut like a spear," said Misabos.

Then Misabos went home. But now Flint knew his brother was after him, and that things would not be easy for him. So he went out and collected cattails and spruce bark and made some arrows. Misabos got busy, too. He made a lot of arrows with steel heads. In a few days he said to his grandmother, "I'm going to see my brother Flint again. I'm going to fight him." So off he went. When Misabos reached Flint's camp he did not go in. He shouted for him to come out. Flint came out and the two brothers started to fight. Every time Misabos hit his brother with one of the steel arrows you could see a spark of fire.

When Flint shot Misabos, the bark heads of the arrows just broke off. That was all. No harm was done. But every time Flint was hit, a piece of his body broke off. He got smaller and smaller as the fight went on, and more and more pieces broke off. Then Misabos said to himself, "He's small enough now. He's had enough." And to Flint he said, "Those pieces broken from your body may be of some use to human beings some day. But you will not be any larger so long as the earth shall last." Then he left and went home.

Not long after, Misabos said to his grandmother, "I'm going to leave you now. I'm not going to stay on the earth any longer. I'm going above. But every human being will know it when I visit this earth. They will call it *kwingwan*, earthquake [*gwiingwan* (comet); cf. Baraga, *tchingwan*, "meteor" (here, properly, "meteorite," as it hits the ground)].

2 South Wind Enters a Contest with His Brother, North Wind (1933)

Once Kiwetin [North Wind] paid a visit to his brother Cauwanɑsi (South Wind). The latter was a very poor looking fellow and very peaceful. There seemed to be nothing much to him. "Do you think you are more powerful than I?" said North Wind to his brother. "I never said so or even thought so," replied South Wind. "Well, how about making a trial of strength?" asked the North Wind. South Wind did not answer. "What do you say?" said North Wind. But South Wind did not reply. "You must be scared of me," said North Wind. "No, I'm not afraid of you," his brother answered. "Oh, yes, you are," said North Wind, "that's why you won't agree to let me try my power. What about it now, will you let me see what I can do?" "All right, then," said South Wind, "I'll agree." This pleased North Wind very much, so he set a day when his brother was to come north. He said he would "try him out" for eight nights.

So South Wind went north to the country where his brother lived. Everything there was covered with snow and ice. Even when he went into the dwelling of the North Wind, he found that it was all made of ice and that he could hear the ice cracking every once in awhile right inside. North Wind said, "You better have something to eat first." But what he offered South Wind was the poorest kind of fare. At one side of the dwelling there was a box. North Wind told his brother to get into this box and lie down. To beat him South Wind had to stay there for eight nights.

At the end of the first night North Wind inquired, "Are you all right, my brother?" "Yes," replied South Wind. The second night he said, "Hello there, brother, are you still there?" And South Wind said he was. The next two nights the same thing happened. But on the fifth night South Wind thought to himself, "I'll fool him this time." So when North Wind spoke to him he only heard a low murmur from South Wind. "Ha! He's getting weak. He can't stand it," said North Wind to himself. The sixth night South Wind's voice could hardly be heard and North Wind thought, "That's good, he's almost done for." On the next night there was no answer at all from South Wind, but North Wind said, "I'll not open up the box yet." Now on the eighth night when North Wind called to his brother, no answer came. He called again. Still there was no answer. "Aha! I've finished him," said North Wind and he opened the box. But there was South Wind, in good shape. He was sweating, just as if he'd been in a sweat lodge. All he said was, "It's hot in here," and then invited his brother to come south. "It's my turn now to try you," he said when he left.

So North Wind had to go to his brother's place. "You'll be comfortable here," said South Wind when North Wind arrived. "All you will have to do is stand there, like this (and he imitated the crane-posture) and look straight at me." Then South Wind began to blow on him. It was a very, very hot wind and soon you could see that North Wind was suffering. Then it started to rain and there was a little hail. But South Wind did not let up. After the first couple of days North Wind could hardly hold his head up. One of his eyes drooped and then the other. Finally, on the sixth night he had to give up. He was beaten. Then South Wind said, "Now you know you're not the boss of everything."

"And we all know he is not the Boss," added the narrator, "for if he were we would never have any summer."

3 The Origin of Summer[42] (1933)

Long ago there was no summer in this part of the country. There was ice and snow all the year round. Finally the fur-bearers and the winter animals got together and paid a visit to the South, where it was sum-

mer all the time. When they reached there they came upon an encampment of all the different kinds of summer birds. But these birds
were away getting a living. To guard their dwelling they left behind
Omɑkɑkï [Omakakii] (toad, frog) whom they called Kïstäsïnän [gis-
tesinaan] (our older brother – Cree) and Wabɑtcïtcak [Waabajijaak]
(white crane). The reason that the crane was left behind was because
this bird's voice can be heard for such a long distance. Now these visitors saw something which looked like a bladder tied to the poles of
the dwelling. This was what made the summer but they could find
out nothing about it.

After they returned north again they told others about what they
had seen on their visit. They were curious to know what was in the
bladder. "We must try and find out for ourselves," they said. "I wonder
whether Kïstäsïnän would tell us," someone asked. So several animals
paid another visit to the country where the summer birds dwelt.
They went to Toad and asked, "What is that hanging over there?"
"Oh, that's nothing," he replied. So they returned home again. But
the animals were not satisfied.

Two more of them went south again. They were told to ask the
toad for information again and if he disclosed the secret they were to
knock him on the head and, at the same time, grab the white crane by
its neck and shove its beak as far into the ground as possible. This was
to prevent the bird from calling and giving the alarm. This time when
the visitors asked the toad what was in the bladder they took him off
his guard and he replied, "nïp-" (the first syllable of nīpín [niibin],
summer). But before he finished the word he put his hand over his
mouth. It was too late. The secret was out. So, one of the visitors
knocked him senseless while the other one stuck the bill of the white
crane far into the ground. They also glued the toad's mouth so he
could not give the alarm when he came to his senses. But he pulled
the glue free with his fingers. This is why the toad has such a big
mouth now.

The visitors ran off as fast as they could with "summer." As soon as
one animal got tired running the bladder was given to another. The
deer ran as far as he could with it, then he passed it to the wolf. The
wolf, in turn, passed it to the moose. Then the bear took it and also

the fox. Every swift animal in the north country did their share. But they heard their pursuers coming. The birds were after them – geese, ducks and many other birds were after them. The fisher was carrying the bladder then and one of the other animals said, "It's no use, we can't beat them. You climb up that tall white spruce and hang it there."[43] So the fisher did this. Then all the birds and fur bearing animals gathered round the tree.

They decided that they would have to have a council. Someone suggested that they get their bows and shoot at the bladder. All the different animals tried to hit it but no one succeeded. One of the last to arrive was *kïstäsïnän*. He had not had a turn so he was told to try. He did and he hit the bladder and summer escaped. None of them could have summer all the time now.

So they decided to divide it. The caribou was asked how many months of winter he wished. "As many as there are hairs on my body," he replied. "How do you expect to live if there is so much winter as that?" the other animals asked. "The Indians will be after you all the year and they'll kill you." Then the moose was asked the same question. He said, "As many as I have hairs on my chin." "That's still too many," the other animals said. "It will make the winter much too long." When the beaver was asked how many winter months he wanted he replied, "As many as there are scales on my tail." But the other animals objected. "How can you manage to live if the rivers are all frozen to the bottom that long? Where will you be?" Finally the Toad was asked the same question. In answer he held up his forepaw (with its five digits). "Five," he said. That's why a toad, when killed, always holds up his hand. But he settled matters forever after. There are just five months of winter.

4 Wisɑkedjak and the Water Lions[44] (1933)

Once when Wisɑkedjak was travelling about during the winter he came to a lake. He saw four wolves sitting on the ice in the center of it. So he started towards them. The old male wolf said to his sons, "Here comes Wisɑkedjak." When Wisɑkedjak reached them he said (to the old wolf), "*nitci,nitci* [*niijii*] ([my] brother), I'd like to be one of you and to go along with you." "Alright," said the wolf. "Now look at *kidozimak* (your stepsons, i.e., brother's sons) there must be a moose near." The young wolves had thrown their heads back and their noses were turned upwards. Wis kedjak did the same thing. The old wolf asked him, "How many can you smell?" "Four," replied Wisɑkedjak. "No! No! You're wrong," the wolf said. "There is only one, a cow. We'll let the young ones run ahead on the trail while we keep behind." So they all started off, but after tracking the cow-moose a long way, they failed to catch up with her.[45]

Then Wisɑkedjak said, "I think we better find a place to camp." So he looked around and found a sheltered place, out of the wind. But the old wolf said, "This is no place to camp – we'll be cold here." "Oh well, you pick a place, then," replied Wisɑkedjak. So the old wolf picked out a high wind-swept rock, right on the shore of a lake. He handed Wisɑkedjak a piece of poplar bark and said, "Lie down on this, but if you find a lump growing under you during the night, don't you look at it until morning.' Wisɑkedjak lay down, curling up just like a wolf. But he was cold and, during the night, he woke up and found that he was lying on a big lump of something. He discovered that the piece of bark had turned into some good fat pemmican. "Well, well," said Wisɑkedjak to himself, "I'll eat some of this." So he did, but saved some for breakfast. Then he lay down again. Now the old wolf knew that Wisɑkedjak must be cold, so he told one of his sons to throw his tail over him. This kept Wisɑkedjak good and warm. He was very comfortable, except for the fact that every now and then the wolf would fart! When this happened, Wisɑkedjak said to himself, "Stinking dog!" It happened again and Wisɑkedjak repeated what he had said. This time the young wolf asked, "What did you say, Wisɑkedjak?" "Oh, nothing," the latter replied, but when the wolf farted again, Wisɑkedjak said the same thing again. The young wolf knew what he was saying alright, so he withdrew his tail.

In the morning each wolf picked up his own share of pemmican and started to make his breakfast of it. But Wisɑkedjak found that the pemmican he had saved had turned into bark again. The old wolf looked at Wisɑkedjak who had nothing to eat. "What's the matter, Wisɑkedjak?" he said. "What were you doing last night? You did not do as I told you, that's the trouble." So Wisαkedjak had to start off without any breakfast. The young wolves went on ahead, the old wolf and Wisαkedjak following. All of a sudden Wisαkedjak saw the young ones sitting in the middle of a lake with their heads up. "There must be a moose near," the old wolf said. Wisαkedjak sniffed and threw his head back but he could not smell anything. However, when the old wolf asked how many he scented, Wisαkedjak replied, "a cow and a calf." "You're wrong," the old wolf said, "There is just a cow." The three young wolves had started off again by this time and soon found the moose tracks. Wisαkedjak and the old wolf followed. Soon they came upon some wolf dung. "Pick up your stepson's blanket," said the wolf. "I don't want to carry dog dung around," Wisαkedjak muttered. "What's that you're saying?" the old wolf asked. "Oh! Nothing," Wisαkedjak answered. So the old wolf picked up the dung, shook it and it turned into a fine blanket. Then Wisαkedjak cried out, "Oh, I'll carry it." But the old wolf said, "No! I heard what you said."

After traveling a bit more, the wolf noticed a wolf's tooth stuck on a tree and he said, "Heh, Wisαkedjak – your stepson has missed his mark. Pull out his arrow." But Wisαkedjak mumbled, "I don't want to carry a dog's tooth." Then the old wolf pulled it out and it turned into a fine arrow. "I'll carry it," said Wisαkedjak. "No! I heard what you said," replied the wolf.

Finally they came to the place where the moose had been killed. There was lots of blood about but no sign of the moose. Wisαkedjak exclaimed, "The greedy dogs, I wonder whether they have finished it up already." "What did you say?" asked the wolf. "Oh, nothing," replied Wisαkedjak "Well, let's make camp," said the wolf. After they had put up a *wīgīwam* and the fire was made, the young wolves brought in the moose meat. "Now we'll all have a good feed," said the old wolf and they started to dry the meat. After a bit the old wolf said, "Now Wisαkedjak, I'm going to give you one of my sons. He may help you kill something so you will have something to eat. We'll part now. You go your way and I'll go mine."

So Wisαkedjak started off, with the young wolf in the lead to scout for food (like a young man and his father). After they had traveled quite a long way they camped. That night Wisαkedjak had a dream.

He dreamed that he followed the trail of his son (as he now called the young wolf) to the end of it, and could not follow him farther. He knew from this that something was about to happen. So in the morning he said to his son, "If you're running a moose don't ever jump across any little creek you come to, no matter how close you are to the moose. Circle around a creek and don't go straight across any lake, either." Now the young wolf tried his best to do as he was told, but it was pretty hard to track a moose and yet to follow the instructions of Wisɑkedjak at the same time.

Not long afterwards when the wolf was chasing a moose and had almost caught up with it, a small creek intervened and in the heat of the chase the wolf leaped expecting to bring the animal low on the other side. But instead of this the young wolf landed in the middle of the water and, in a moment, the current pulled him right down. When Wisɑkedjak came along after a bit all he found was the end of his son's trail. He sat down and cried. Then he noticed a kingfisher, looking down into the stream. "I wonder what he is looking at," Wisɑkedjak thought to himself. He said to the kingfisher, "What are you gazing at?" "I'm looking at Wisɑkedjak's little son," the kingfisher replied; "his skin has been stretched already." "I wish you would tell me about this," said Wisɑkedjak. "I'll pay you well, by making you one of the prettiest of birds. I want you to tell me who did it."[46] So the kingfisher said, "You know those three young lions (*mīcīpījiu*, i.e., really great lynx [*bizhiw*]) who are brothers – well, they are the ones that did it. But it was the white one that really killed your son. Do you see that little sandy hill down there? On a hot day, that is where you'll see them playing with your son's tail. And when they finish playing they go to sleep right there. Make a bow and arrow," said the kingfisher, "and then go where you can watch them. If you want to kill the white one, don't shoot directly at his body, shoot at his shadow (*tcɑgatecing*) [*jaagaateshin*?], then you'll hit him in the right place. And don't forget to make a raft – a big one, and braid a line (out of grey willow bark) too."

So Wisɑkedjak started at once to make a bow and some arrows. Then he made many fathoms[47] of line. He also made a raft and put some big boulders on it. "Be very careful, "the kingfisher said, "that lion will try to kill you." So the next morning Wisɑkedjak said, "I wish I were a stump." And immediately he was transformed into one. All of a sudden he saw the water boiling as in rapids, and up came the lions. The white one noticed the stump at once. "I never saw that stump before," he said to his brothers. "Oh, that has always been there," they replied. "No it hasn't, it is Wisɑkedjak," the white lion said; "he has turned himself into a stump." "If he has, we can soon find out. Throw your tail around it," the lion said; "and you too," he told the other one. "Now pull!" And they pulled. But Wisɑkedjak could not be pulled out although the lions used all their strength. "See, I told you so, that can't be Wisɑkedjak's, he would not be able to hold fast if it were."

So they started to play about on the sand. After they got tired they all stretched out for a nap. It was a fine clear warm day. After they were all asleep Wisɑkedjak sneaked up close now with his bow in hand and an arrow ready to shoot. So as to be sure not to miss, he aimed his arrow directly at the body of the white one. He let fly. But the arrow instead of hitting the lion missed him altogether and landed on the other side. The white lion jumped up. Wisɑkedjak had another arrow ready and this time he aimed at the lion's shadow and hit it in just the right place. The other lions followed by the wounded one jumped into the water and Wisɑkedjak ran to his raft. He fastened his line to a tree. Then the water began to rise. Up and up it came. It rose higher and higher but Wisɑkedjak still clung to his raft. After awhile no trees were to be seen. The water had risen over their tops. As far as one could see, there was nothing but water, a great sea. The lions realized that Wisɑkedjak was safe so they sent a beaver to gnaw a hole in his raft. Wisɑkedjak said to the beaver, "Brother, let me see what you are using to do this work." Now Wisɑkedjak had not forgotten to take some stones on his raft. He now picked up one and when the beaver opened his mouth and showed his teeth Wisɑkedjak knocked his teeth out with a stone. The beaver left him alone after that; he could not injure the craft.

Wisɑkedjak had been on the raft so long by this time that he got tired of sitting in one place. There was a muskrat and an otter who jumped off into the water now and then, swimming about for a

change.[48] Wisɑkedjak said to them, "Poor little brothers. How long
will you be able to stand this? I forgot to bring along a piece of
ground on my raft. If one of you could fetch some earth, I might be
able to do something." So finally the otter offered to try and get some
earth. Wisɑkedjak tied a rope to the otter's leg and away it went down
into the water. But it never even reached the bottom. It was drowned,
the water was so deep. When Wisɑkedjak pulled the otter up, because
he could not feel it pulling any more, there was not a speck of earth in
its mouth or paws. Now Wisɑkedjak said to the beaver, "You try."
"Yes," said the beaver. So Wisɑkedjak tied the line to the beaver's foot.
Away went the beaver. He tried his best but the water was too deep.
He knew that he was beaten. Wisɑkedjak gave him all the slack he
could but the beaver could not reach bottom. Finally Wisɑkedjak had
to pull him up with the line. The beaver was drowned[49] and had not
gotten hold of any dirt. Then Wisɑkedjak said to the muskrat, "My
poor little brother, you are the smallest of all. I've tried the best ones
and I doubt whether you can do any better." The muskrat said he
would try. So he dived straight down using all the strength he could.
He managed to reach the bottom but just had sense enough to clutch
some earth with his paws and to bite into the ground before he
drowned. Wisɑkedjak got the "rat" up again and when he opened the
muskrat's paws and mouth there he saw a little earth, hardly a handful at all.[50] Wisɑkedjak started to blow on this dirt. It grew bigger and
bigger. After awhile it was big enough for an island. But Wisɑkedjak
kept at his job. He kept blowing on it. Finally he said, "I wonder how
big this island is, I'm sitting on?" So he called the caribou and told
him to run around the island. "It's pretty small yet," the caribou said,
when he came back. So Wisɑkedjak kept blowing and blowing. After
awhile he said to another young caribou, "You run around.'" So this
caribou ran around. When he got back he was pretty old. He had lost
some of his teeth. Wisɑkedjak kept on blowing some more and then
he sent a third caribou to run around the island. This one never came
back again. So Wisɑkedjak said, "It's big enough."

But Wisɑkedjak had not forgotten his enemies; he was not
through with them yet. He started off now himself. As he was going

along he heard someone singing. He stood and listened, trying to catch their song. Finally he caught the words and went to see the singer. He came upon a big toad who was singing as he kept hopping along. Wisɑkedjak said, "Brother, where are you going?" "I'm going to see the sick lion that Wisɑkedjak shot." "What are you going to do when you get to his tent?" Wisɑkedjak asked. "Oh, there will be a leather partition between myself and the sick one," the toad replied, "I'll shake my rattle on this side." Then Wisɑkedjak gave the toad a crack on the head and killed him. He skinned the toad, put the toad skin on and off he went. Every time he hopped, the *cīcīgwɑn* [*zhiishi-igwan*, rattle] rattled. The lions heard him coming. "Here comes your grandmother," they said. "Clear up the tent and put up the partition (*pɑskwégɑn*)." The white lion lay there with Wisɑkedjak's arrow in his side. When Wisɑkedjak arrived he took his place behind the partition and rattled. He noticed the arrow in the lion's side at once. The old toad had almost gotten it out. She had been working on it a little each day. As soon as Wisɑkedjak got the chance he jumped out and shoved the arrow into the lion's heart. Then he grabbed the wolf skin (which was the skin of his "son") they were using for a door and off he went. The old lion said to his sons, "See, I told you to leave him alone. Look at what he has done to us now."

The next day Wisɑkedjak sneaked back to the lions' camp again. He found the grave, well made, of the young lion that had died the day before. Then he dug the body up, cut it in pieces and threw them here and there. After this, Wisɑkedjak took the wolf skin and, by singing, brought it back to life again. "Now, my son," he said, "you'll know where to find your parents. That young lion will never bother you any more."

Pinewītis kágotik (there is a partridge stomach [another version of the meaning provided by Hallowell] hanging up)

5 Aásī[51]

Once there was a young man named Aásī (Crow) who was the only son of his mother. His father had taken another wife and the old man thought a lot of this young woman. He treated the boy's mother very badly. One day he sent Aásī and his stepmother out into the bush to hunt partridges. They came upon a bunch of partridges and Aásī started to shoot at them with his bow and arrows. The boy did not try to kill them but just to hit them hard enough to stun them (blunt headed arrows were used) and keep them kicking[52] for awhile.

As he picked up each bird he would shove it up his stepmother's clothes so that the woman's bare legs[53] became covered with scratches left by the expiring birds. It was not long before the old man discovered these scratches. He asked his wife how she got them. She told him that when she had gone partridge hunting with his son that Aásī had shoved each one he had shot between her legs. Her husband replied, "He'll never do that again. I'll stop him for good." So the next morning the old man said to his son, "Let's go out on the lake and get some birds' eggs." Unsuspectingly the boy went. His father suggested that they go to a rocky island far out in the lake, since he planned to abandon Aásī there. It was much too far to swim back. When they reached this island the old man told his son to step ashore and as he did so, said, "You stay there." The boy started to cry because he now understood his father's intentions. But it was no use, the old man would have no mercy.

Aásī stayed on the island. He could find nothing to eat except a few birds' eggs. He did not know what was to become of him. Finally he lay down. He was half sleeping when he heard a voice saying, "*Nózis* [*noozis*] (my grandson),[54] come down to the water." Aásī got up and went down to the shore. At first he could see no one but upon walking along the water edge a short distance, he came upon a monster snake (*k'tcēkinébik*) [*gichi-ginebig*]. The snake said, "Sit right between my horns, I'll take you to the mainland." As soon as Aásī had mounted him the snake started to swim towards the mainland. It was a clear, hot day, and the water was calm. There was not a cloud to be seen anywhere in the sky. Now the snake said to the boy, "*Nózis*, be sure and watch out for any clouds. If you see any rising tell me at once." After a short while, some clouds started to rise and Aásī saw them, but he said nothing. The clouds rose higher and higher in the

west. Still he said nothing. They had travelled quite a distance and
the mainland could be plainly seen now, but they still had quite a
long way to go.⁵⁵ Finally the low rumble of thunder could be heard.
"What's that, *nózis – pinèsï* (thunderbird)?" "No," replied Aásï, "it's
just the sound your body makes swimming through the water." They
were getting close to the land now, but more and more thunder could
be heard. The snake inquired again, "That surely is thunder, this time,
nózis," but the boy only replied, "You are swimming so hard, that's
what makes the sound." Now when they had almost reached the shore
there was a flash of lightning. The snake knew then that he was in
danger. "*Nózis*, jump off," he said. Aásï did so and swam towards the
shore. He had no sooner reached dry land than he saw a flash of lightning flash directly at the place where he had left the snake. He ran
under some trees for shelter from the rain, which was now falling fast.
He could see the lightning striking at the monster snake again and
again. He felt very sad because he knew the snake had no chance to
escape.⁵⁶ The monster had lost his life bringing him to shore. Aásï
walked down to the shore now to see if he could see any sign of the
snake. He only saw his blood here and there. "It's too bad," said the
boy to himself, "that *nimïcomis* [*nimishoomis*, my grandfather] has
disappeared altogether from the earth." He took a little stick and
touched the snake's blood. As soon as he did this the blood turned
into a small snake (*kinebik*) [*ginebig*] which started to wriggle off.
Aásï said, "*Nimïcomis*, you'll be like this one now instead of a monster." (That's where snakes come from.)

The boy started off now through the bush in search of some people (i.e., Indians, *änishanábek*). Soon he came upon a small *wïgïwam*
in which an old woman was living. "Ah! *nokam* [*nookom*] (my grandmother, also used for greeting any old woman)," said Aásï. At this
the old lady turned her head in the direction of the door and said to
him, "Ah, *nózis, nózis*, poor young man, you've got a hard road to go
through." She picked up a tiny kettle and went on, "Now I'll have to
give *nózis* something to eat." She then put one little piece of meat and
a *makïkomin* (moss berry) in the kettle and after these were cooked,
said to Aásï, "You have a hard road ahead of you, but if you eat all I

give you, you'll be able to reach home alright." She handed the young fellow the kettle and he took it, saying to himself, "This is nothing. It's only a mouthful." But when he had finished the contents of the kettle he found that a similar portion remained. He ate and ate and yet the kettle was never empty. Finally he got so full he could hardly eat any more but kept on going until he could not help saying to himself, "I wonder whether this is the last of it?" Finally he saw that the kettle was empty. "Now," said the old lady, "this kettle is yours," and added, "yes, you'll go through alright, but I'm going to tell you about the dangers along the road. You can't go round them."

Aásī stayed with the old woman that night and in the morning when he was ready to start [she] said, "You'll come to another "grand-mother" next and that's the one who will tell you everything you are to do in those dangerous places." Sure enough, Aásī reached the camp of another old woman the evening of the next day. She treated him exactly like the first one did. She boiled a tiny kettle for him and finally he was able to eat everything that was in it. At this camp, how-ever, the old woman kept a red fox for a dog. As Aásī was about to start off in the morning this old woman said, "At the next camp you will reach after this you'll find an old man. This man will give you something to eat, but don't you eat it. Make him believe that you eat, though. I'll give you this 'dog' of mine for company. He may help you."

On the third night after he left the old woman's place Aásī reached the old man's *wīgīwam*. The old man prepared some food which looked very good, but Aásī did not forget what his "grandmother" had told him. He managed to slip the stuff to the "dog" (fox) who ate it instead. Finally the old man said, "You must be tired; lie down and get a good sleep." Aásī lay down but he did not fall asleep. He did not feel safe even though the "dog" (fox) was beside him. At last he got very sleepy and almost fell asleep. The old man knew this and gradually raised his leg. Now this leg was full of disease and once he touched the young man, he would be as good as dead. As soon as the "dog" saw what was happening he grabbed the old man's leg in his teeth and held it fast. The old man called out, "Aásī *kitai ndɑkwamik*"

(Aásī, your dog's biting me). Aásī jumped to his feet now and instead of beating his "dog" he pounded the old man until he was dead.

Next morning he started off again. As he approached the next camp he heard a chickadee calling. He stopped and waited to see if he could discover who was in the tent. He heard a voice inside say, "*ndindawa* [*nindindawaa*],⁵⁷ that is the bird that used to tell us what was going to happen. I wonder if Aásī is going to pass this way." Aásī now went up to the tent and looked inside. He saw two blind old women, one sitting on either side of the door. He went in and one of them said, "Aásī?" "Yes, it's me." "Ah, you're in here now, that's all right," said the other, "be sure and let us know before you go out. Sit down, we'll give you something to eat." The old women finally managed to find some grease which they put in the kettle, but they had no sooner done so than Aásī took it out again with a stick. One of the old women now dipped a stick into the pot and sampled the brew. "This is strange," she said, "it tastes as if there was nothing cooking in the kettle." Now Aásī noticed that each old woman had a stone lying close to where she sat. After awhile he saw one of them rubbing her elbow on this stone as if she was sharpening it. Then he saw the other one sharpening her elbow bone. After this they turned around so that they were back to back, one on either side of the door. Aásī knew they were going to try to bayonet him as he left so he put his coat on a pole and pushed it out the door saying, "I'm going out now." The old witches, in trying to spear Aásī with their sharp elbows, soon killed each other instead.

Off went Aásī again. After travelling some time he found his way barred by a line strung across the trail. From it were hanging the shoulder blades of different kinds of animals and even those of men. They rattled in the wind. Aásī found he could not make his way around either side of this line of rattling shoulder blades because it was strung across the world (in front of a cave). When he attempted to go straight ahead under the line the blades rattled and the dogs began to bark. The old man who lived in the cave said to them, "What are you barking at?" "We are barking at Aásī," the dogs replied.

Now Aásī wore a mink skin breechcloth. He now took it off and running into a cave made a noise like a mink and taking it with his hand like a *kɑskipitagan* [*gashkibidaagan*, pipe or bandolier bag] made believe the mink was poking his head out. When the old man came out and looked around he saw this mink and said, "Ah, it's just a mink they're barking at, not Aásī."

After travelling some more Aásī came upon a band of Indians whom he recognized as belonging to his own people. At one side of the encampment he saw a small dwelling. He thought he would inquire where his mother was living, so he went up to this tent and looked in. He saw an old woman sitting there but did not recognize her. Her face was scabby and her eyes were swollen from crying. After a few moments he realized that this old woman was his mother. He went in and said, "Poor mother." But the old woman said, "You are trying to fool me. You are not really my son." "Yes I am, mother. What has happened to you? You look very different than when I left you. You are all covered with scabs." Then she said, "Your father had two boys by that other woman and if I say anything to them at all he takes me by the arm and pushes me right into the fire. You can see the results of his abuse for yourself." "Mother," Aásī said, "I'll tell you what to do. Go to my father's tent and say, 'my son is back.' I know he'll not believe you. But if he says anything wrong to you, you push one of his kids into the fire and run back here quickly." The mother of Aásī did as he said. Her husband laughed in her face and mocked her. Then she pushed one of her stepchildren into the fire and ran out of her husband's *wīgīwam*. He pursued her but she reached her dwelling where her husband found Aásī sitting. The old man was astonished but cried out, "Let everybody hear. My son is back."

After his father left, Aásī said to his mother, "Now I'm going to set fire to the world." He made two arrows; one he painted red, the other black. Then he marked out a piece of land with sticks and said to his mother, "You pick out all the people who have been good to you and bring them all to this place. Don't mind the others. Tomorrow morning I'll shoot this black arrow into the air. As soon as it strikes the earth there will be fire."

The following morning Aásī shot the black arrow straight up into the zenith. When it dropped to the ground the earth burst into flame. Everything started to burn except in the place of safety he had marked out. Of course the people whom his mother had not selected also tried to reach this place but Aásī would not allow them to come in. His father also came and said, "My son, what can I do to live?" Now Aásī knew that his father had lots of bear oil stored in rogans so he told him to conceal himself in one of these rogans. The old man did as he was told and soon the fire got so hot that the bear oil began to boil. The fire spread and spread. Animals and birds came from every direction to seek safety from the flames in the spot marked off by Aásī. He stood watching everything and knew that the entire earth would soon be destroyed, so he said, "It is enough, let the fire stop." And, fitting the red arrow to his bow, he shot it upwards into the air. As soon as it struck the earth the fire went out. Then, as he stood looking at the earth which had been burned, he said to himself, "It is too bad that I killed my father." So he went to look for the old man's bones. He found them but they were all charred and fleshless. He took the bones and said, "Father, I will make you into a *walɑcip* [sic] (crow-duck [cormorant] – AIH). He threw them into the water where they became a duck as he had said.
Pinewītis kágotik

Other-Than-Humans and Humans: Blessings and Struggles[58]

6 Mätcīkīwis[59]

Long ago there were ten brothers. They left their camp each morning to go hunting. Some of them went in one direction and some in another, but they all returned to their camp every night. The first one back always cut wood enough to last the night. One night the first man to return to camp found wood already cut and a fire made, but he said nothing to the others. The next morning all the brothers started out again as usual. A different brother got back first in the evening and he found the wood cut and a fire burning. He, too, said nothing. The third day the same thing happened, but it was still another brother that returned first and found the fuel and fire. He asked his brothers whether any of them had returned before him. They all said no, but one spoke up and said, "I found the same thing that you did the day before yesterday, when I was the first one to come back at night." Then the other one said, "I found the same thing had happened yesterday, but I said nothing."

Now, Mätcīkīwis was the oldest of these brothers. Next to him in age was a good quiet man who was a *mämändä´wis* [*mamaandaawis?*, wizard]. But his brothers did not know this.[60] His name was "bullet carrier" (Anwĭpémondɑnk) [Anwi-bimoondag?]. All the brothers respected Mätcīkīwis. They listened to what he said and did as he told them. On this occasion he said, "There must be someone around here who wants to see somebody but perhaps they are afraid to come into camp when all of us are here. I'll stay here all day tomorrow myself." They all knew that a woman must be responsible for what had happened.[61] So the next morning Mätcīkīwis did not go off with the others but stayed around the camp all day. But he saw no one and at the end of the day he had to cut his own wood and build a fire. The following day "bullet carrier" took his turn in camp. He saw no one either and at night he cut wood and built the fire. The next day the third oldest brother remained in camp but no one appeared. He, too, cut wood and made a fire at the end of the day like the others. The same thing happened each day as the other brothers took their turns. Finally the eighth brother had his turn. He thought that surely he would find out something. But he didn't, and neither did the ninth. At last it was the youngest brother's turn. All his older brothers thought it was hardly worthwhile for him to stay at all. "You won't see anyone," they said.

As soon as his older brothers left the next morning the young lad sat down inside the lodge. He had not been seated long when he heard some wood dropped on the ground outside the door. He did not look or go out to see who it was. Soon a second load was dropped and then the door of the lodge was lifted. A beautiful young woman stepped in and took her place beside him. The boy was very glad and asked her no questions.

When the first brother returned at night and saw this fine girl sitting beside his younger brother he was very pleased. The young lad said, "Take off your moccasins, your sister-in-law will look after them." Finally all the brothers except Mätcīkīwis had returned. All of them were looked after by their new sister-in-law and all of them were pleased. Finally Mätcīkīwis came back. As soon as he saw the woman, the expression of his face changed. He said nothing but he looked displeased. His younger brother said to him, "Your sister-in-law will dry your moccasins." But Mätcīkīwis replied, "I'm not tired. I can take care of myself."

Next morning all the men went off to hunt, including the youngest brother. But Mätcīkīwis, after travelling a very short distance, hid himself in the bush until he was sure that all of his brothers were far away. He waited until he knew his sister-in-law must be out chopping wood. As soon as he heard the sound of her axe he crept towards her stealthily, from bush to bush. Finally when he got close enough he fitted an arrow to his bow and shot her between the shoulders. His sister-in-law dropped to the ground. Mätcīkīwis did not go near her body. He started off in another direction into the bush.

That night his younger brother was the first one home. He found no wood out and no fire made. Soon he found the tracks of his wife and following them he found her lying bleeding, with the arrow in her back. He thought her dead and cried. Then the girl spoke to him. "Don't cry," she said. "Go back to camp. Bring a birch bark roll (used for lodge covering) here, place some upright sticks all around me and the birch bark roll around them. After that, go back to the lodge. You must not come here again for eight nights. After that you may come. Be sure to do as I tell you. If you don't, anything that happens will be your own fault." The lad did as she instructed but on his way back to the lodge he could not help crying. He felt so bad. When the older brothers returned and found out what had happened they felt sad too. (They all knew who had killed their sister-in-law.) Finally, when Mätcīkīwis returned, the last of all, he found them all sitting in the lodge in a mournful mood. "What's the matter with you all, "he said. "Last night you were all happy. Tonight you are all sad." The "bullet carrier" now spoke up and said, "It's no wonder. Do you think you have done some great thing?" Mätcīkīwis made no reply.

On the sixth night after his wife had been killed the youngest brother thought to himself, "Surely it will be alright for me to go to her tonight." So he decided to go. When he had come within sight of the place where she lay he heard a rattling sound within the bark and then a swan flew out. "I thought I told you not to come here before the eighth night," the swan said to him. "You can blame yourself, you can't have me now," and with this the swan flew away. The lad did not know what to do at first and started to cry. Then he thought of something. He put an arrow to his bow and shot it in the direction towards which the swan had flown. As he did so he said to himself, "I wish to hang on to this arrow so that I can follow my wife." Sure enough, he was able to hang on and when the arrow dropped to the ground he could see the tracks of his wife. He followed her trail and finally reached a tiny *wīgīwam* with smoke coming out of the top. He went in and found an old woman sitting there. "Ah, *nózis, nózis*," she said. "What shall I give *nózis* to eat?" She took a small piece of meat and a berry and put them in a kettle not much bigger than a thimble. "If you can eat everything in this kettle," she said, "you may be able to reach your wife." So he ate what was in the kettle. Although it was only a mouthful at the time the kettle was not emptied, and so he kept on eating until he felt he could not swallow a morsel more. Finally there was nothing left in the kettle and he handed it back to the old lady. She looked in it and was pleased to see that there was nothing left. He stayed overnight in her lodge. In the morning as he was starting off the old woman said, "On the road before you, you will find another one of your grandmothers. She will tell you what to do."

Away the lad went. Towards night he reached another tiny camp. Here he found another old woman who called him *nózis* and fed him from a tiny kettle like the first "grandmother." She also was pleased when he was able to eat all that was in her kettle. In the morning she showed him the trail he must follow and gave him a *kɑskipītagɑn* [*gashkibidaagan*] (a bag with magical properties similar to those used in the *midéwiwin*) made of chipmunk skin. "You'll come to a very high tree," she said, "with no branches on it – this tree reaches right up into the sky. That's where you will find your wife. This bag I am giving you will enable you to turn yourself into anything you wish."

Sure enough, after travelling for some time he came to a tree like the one described by the old woman. With the aid of his bag he turned himself into a chipmunk and began to climb it. But his claws wore out before he had climbed very far so he changed himself into a fisher. He climbed higher and higher but finally his claws were so badly worn that he had to cling to the tree with his arms. So he changed into a lynx and kept climbing higher. When his claws wore out again, he changed into a bear, then a squirrel, whose claws enabled him to travel a long, long way. But finally these wore out, too, so he was forced to change again into a marten and finally reached a hole in the sky.

Here above he found himself in a strange land (*Pinèsiwɑkotɑ-kīwaspīming*, Thunder Bird Land) [*binesiwag odakiiwaa ishpiming*, lit. "thunder birds, their land, above, in the heavens"].[62] He saw a large encampment and heard some of the men in the lodges cry out, "A stranger is coming; a stranger is coming!" Everyone jumped up and looked out to see who it was. He had been told by his grandmother to go into the first tent he came to so he did. There he found an old woman who said to him, "*nózis*, you stay here. Tonight there will be a big feast. Your wife has been the one chosen to go about and invite everyone to attend this feast. But there are people here who will try their best to overcome you (by magic power)."

In the early evening, sure enough, his wife poked her head into the lodge and said, "You are invited to the feast." Although she recognized him she said nothing else and he simply replied, "O! (thanks)." Before he left the tent, the old woman said, "When the soup is ready to eat, there will be a little shell spoon passed around. It is so slippery no one can hold it. If you can manage to hold it no one can overcome you. Wish that you can!" So when the spoon was passed that lad remembered that he had dreamed (at his puberty fasting) that anything he touched stuck to his hands like glue. So when the spoon was passed to him he held it. The feasting and dancing continued the whole night through. The next morning he went back to the old woman's lodge. After a rest and something to eat he was invited to a foot-racing contest. He was told where to stand and the fellow whom he was to race was also placed in his position. While the lad was standing there waiting to start he said to himself, "I'll go as fast as my sight goes." So the orders to start were given. Quick as a flash, he was at the end of the course, although the man who tried to beat him was Kekek [Gekek] (in Indian belief, the fastest flying of all the hawks), who came along as fast as a ball thrown through the air. Next there was a contest with bow and arrow in which the lad was also the winner.[63]

After this his wife came to him and asked him to come and stay where she was living. Although the lad did not know it, his wife, the swan woman, was the daughter of *pinèsï* (i.e., one of the thunder birds), the boss (*kīneganīsī*) of Thunder Bird land where all the great hawks lived. So the lad now lived in a large *càbandawan* [a large multi-family dwelling] along with his wife, father-in-law and several of his brothers-in-law (Duck Hawk [Kekek], American Sparrow Hawk (Pïpïkïwɑsɛs), [Golden Eagle, Kïnïu (Giniw)]. But he became very hungry because there was nothing in the lodge he could eat. Every day his brothers-in-law brought large quantities of frogs (*k'tcimɑkokik*, big frogs, also term for toad), which were dried and eaten. They called them "beavers." He could not eat these, however. Finally his wife said, "Why don't you eat something? You will starve!" "I can't eat those frogs," the lad said.

So one day, taking his bow and arrows, he started out to hunt for himself. He discovered a little creek and some beaver. He shot one, tied the legs together and carried it back to camp. He threw the animal in the lodge. When he did this his father-in-law spoke up and said, "Hai! Hai! Your brother-in-law is bringing in one of the *manîtu* [spirits, ones with extraordinary abilities]. Look out for your wings. You may get them bitten off." The swan-woman whispered to her husband, "Quick, take a stone and break off their teeth." So the lad took a stone and did as she said. His wife then skinned the beavers and smoked the meat so that her husband had a good supply of food for awhile. She did not eat any of it herself but ate frogs like her relatives.

One day when the lad was out hunting he found some *wanáman* (a reddish substance usually found on "dead" water, ocherous in origin) floating on the surface of the water of a little creek. He painted his cheeks with it. When he had returned to the lodge he found his father-in-law giving him a side glance every now and then. Finally the old man said to his sons, "Hai, your brother-in-law has found some beaver." The lad was embarrassed because he had found no beaver. He said to his wife, "I didn't find any." But his father-in-law kept repeating what he had said before, so the lad kept his mouth shut. Finally, his wife explained that what her father meant by "beaver" were monster snakes (*k'tcēkinébikak*) [*gichi-ginebigoog*]. So when his father-in-law inquired where he had gotten the paint, the lad replied, "In a little creek." "Does it come from a muskeg?" the old man asked. "No! From a sandy mountain," his son-in-law replied. "Hai! That must be their house," said the old man. And so he told his sons to get ready to go there early the next morning. "You better go with them and show them the place," the lad's wife told him.

So after they got there the next day and the old man saw the place he said, "Yes, that's where they live, in that mountain, there." He sent one of his sons to one side of this mountain and a second one to the opposite side.[64] "Now, Pīpīgwīses [Biipiigiwizens], you go up (in the air) and chase them out." So this son flew up into the air at once. To his son-in-law the old man said, "You come with me, sit right down here (spreading out one of his wings for protection). Your brother-in-law might hurt you." The next moment there was a terrific crack of thunder and then flashes of lightning directed at the mountain. This continued for some time. Then Pīpīgwīses yelled out to his brother Kekek, "Look out for him, he's coming towards you." There were now even more deafening crashes of thunder and more lightning, until finally the old man said to his son-in-law, "I believe your brother-in-law must have gotten hurt chasing that beaver." The lad replied, "Let me go. I'm not afraid." So he ran to the side of the mountain where the monster snake was thought to be. He saw its head sticking out of a hole in the side of the mountain. So he took his bow and killed it.

Kekek was almost worn out (and he has been smaller than the other hawks ever since) because he had already managed to drag two or three monster snakes from their den. "Hai, that's fine," said the old *pinèsï*, when he saw them. But the young lad could hardly stand the sight of these monsters as [he] saw their heads, half dead, swinging from side to side. They took the snakes back to camp and when they reached the lodge threw them in. The old man stabbed them to death with one of his quills to finish them off. "We'll have lots to eat now," he said.

Sometime after this the old man said to his son-in-law, "You have been staying with me for quite a while. I know you are getting lonely. You must want to see your people. I'll let you go back to the earth, now. You have nine brothers at home and I have nine girls left. You can take them with you as wives for your brothers. I'm related to the people on the earth now and I'll be merciful towards them. I'll not hurt any of them if I can possibly help it." So he told his daughters to get ready. There was a big dance that night and the next morning the whole party started off. When they came to the edge of the cloud-land the lad's wife said to him, "Sit on my back. Hang on tight to my neck and keep your eyes shut." Then you could hear the thunder crashing and the lad knew they were off through the air. This time he obeyed orders and did not open his eyes.

When they had reached the earth his wife said, "Look, do you remember this place?" The lad opened his eyes and looked around but did not at first remember it. Then he recalled that it was the place where his arrow had fallen, the point at which he had started to follow his wife's tracks. Now they set off towards the lodge of his brothers. When they had almost reached there, the young fellow said to his wife, "You stay here with your sisters. I'll go ahead and see my brothers." When he got to the lodge he peeped in. He saw Mätcīkīwis on his knees before the fire, his head bent low towards the ashes and a spoon in his hand. Ashes were scattered all over the inside of the *wīgīwam*. It seems that Mätcīkīwis had felt the loss of his brother keenly. He cried all the time. Even the birds mocked him. They would hop up to the lodge and call out, "Here I am (older) brother." When he looked up they would disappear. Finally Mätcīkīwis got so provoked at being fooled so often that when anyone came to the tent and called him "[my older] brother" he would scoop some ashes out of the fire and throw it at them. But the birds would come back and fool him again. So this time when his youngest brother really came and stuck his head in the door and said, "(O) Brother, I'm here," Mätcīkīwis did not even look up, but took his spoon and scooped some hot ashes in the direction of the door. "I wish these birds would quit teasing me by saying that my (little) brother is here when he is not," he said. "But look at me, look!" his younger brother said to him. Mätcīkīwis looked, but he did not recognize his brother at first because he could hardly see anything. His eyes were so swollen from weeping. When he found out it was really his brother, he was very happy.

"Now, brothers," said the young lad, "straighten up the lodge and put on your best clothes. I've brought women for all of you." When he heard this, Mätcīkīwis cheered up at once. He washed himself, put on his best clothes, painted a stripe of black on his face and told his brothers to make the lodge bigger (so that it could hold them all).

"I'll go and get them now," said his youngest brother. So away he went to where he had left his wife and sisters-in-law. He told them to change into their best clothes and they did. Now the oldest one was called Mätcīkīkwewīs. She took a wooden bowl and tied it in such a way beneath her dress that it looked as if she had a very big *mons veneris*. Mätcīkīwis, whose place was by the door, was the first to see the women coming, walking one after the other with the oldest in front. He was excited and happy to see the kind of woman he was going to get for a wife. As soon as the oldest sister reached the lodge she took her place beside Mätcīkīwis and the others took their places by the other brothers. "Now we'll all have a good time," said Mätcīkīwis, as he got his drum, he began to sing and the women started to dance.

7 Mikīnäk, Big Turtle Marries a Widow[65]

Long ago there was a widow with two sons. She had a hard time
catching enough rabbits to keep those boys and herself alive. When
the boys were older they helped their mother all they could but had a
hard time of it when they tried to catch beaver. One winter they were
camped on the shore of a lake. Often when the woman went out on
the lake she saw a black spot far away on the ice. She could not make
out what it was. Finally she said to herself, "I better go out there and
see what it is." So she started off towards it. When she got closer she
saw something that looked like a big stone lying on the ice, close to
a patch of open water. Upon reaching it she discovered that it was
Mikīnäk. The "big turtle" spoke to her and said, "How would it be
if we got married?" "How can you get married?" replied the widow.
"You are not in the shape of a man. You'd be no good to me." So she
went back home, and Mikīnäk remained lying on the ice. ("W.B.
re M. – 'good natured – never insulted at what you say. That is why
people have so much fun with him'.")

When the widow told her sons who it was she had seen, the boys
asked, "Why didn't you bring him along? We could have him for our
stepfather [*nimīcomis*] (laughing). He would be good company for
us, too, since we have no one else but you." So the widow took the toboggan and went out on the lake and brought Mikīnäk back to their
camp. The boys began calling him *nimīcome* at once.

One day Mikīnäk said to his wife, "You come along with me and
we'll hunt beaver."[66] So the woman put him on the toboggan and off
they went. When they came to a certain place Mikīnäk said, "Now, the
first thing to do is to chop a hole in the ice. Then put me close to the
hole." His wife did as she was told and as soon as the hole was made,
Mikīnäk dived into the water. The woman made a fire and sat waiting
for him. All of a sudden Mikīnäk appeared and crawled out on the
ice. "Everything is ready now," he said. "They are all asleep and I've
dammed up the entrances. All you will have to do is break into the
house and you'll get them all." So the woman took her axe and started
to break the house. "Oh, there's one running away," she cried. "Never

mind that one," said Mikīnäk. "Make the hole bigger so you can kill them." So his wife managed to kill all the rest of them with her axe. She felt very well satisfied now with her new husband. He was a very useful man. It was so easy to kill beaver this way.

When the boys got back to camp that night and saw the beavers piled at the door, they thought it was a wonderful thing to have Mikīnäk for a stepfather. The next day he said, "Take me somewhere else where there are some beaver." The boys said, "There are some houses up the river," and they told him where. So Mikīnäk and his wife went off again to hunt beaver. She cut a hole in the ice quite a distance from the beaver lodge. Mikīnäk dived into the water and, when everything was ready, came back and told his wife to break the house open. She did and they got a lot of them in a very short time.

Some time after this, Mikīnäk said to his wife one day, "It's about time for us to think about having some young ones." The woman laughed at him. "How can you manage that?" she said. "Never mind," he said. "You do what I tell you. You walk over there a little way and stand with your back to me ... that's it. Now bend forwards." All Mikīnäk did then was to blow hard on her. The woman laughed again; she did not believe that she could conceive in such a fashion. But Mikīnäk said, "You'll have twins." Two or three months later the woman knew that she was pregnant.

One day the oldest son of the woman said, "The snow is getting deep now and I don't know how to make snowshoes." "Oh, I'll make them for you," said Mikīnäk. (How he could manage this no one knew, because he certainly could not hold a knife.) "All you need to do is split the birch for me." So Mikīnäk made snowshoes, but no one saw him make them. "I wonder how he managed it," thought his wife. "I'll try and catch him at work one of these days." Mikīnäk knew what she was thinking, however, and forbade her to come near him when he was at work. But one day she saw some shavings he had thrown out and knew he was at work on snowshoes in the tent. So she crept up to it quietly and peeped through a hole. There she saw a fine look- ing young man with a very fair skin, naked from the waist up, with beautiful tattooing on his arms and body. All of a sudden he dropped his knife. "What's the matter with you, spying on me like this?" he cried out and, bending his body forwards, he became a turtle again. For seven or eight days he lay still and would not move. He would not eat and he would not speak to his wife. Finally, one of the boys said to his mother, "What is the matter with *nimīcome*? He neither eats nor speaks." So she had to tell him what had happened. "You should not have done as you did," the boy said. Then the boys talked to Mikīnäk, coaxed him to eat, and after a while he got over being mad.

After the first thaw, the snow froze again and Mikīnäk, after he had fixed his bow and made some arrows, said, "I'm going to run moose tomorrow." He got up early the next morning and was off. It was not long before he had tracked a moose. (He had now assumed a human shape.) He followed it and soon caught up with the animal. Then the moose started off again. Soon Mikīnäk caught up with him again. This time he took his bow and hit the moose a crack with it on his hind quarters. "Run! Run!" he cried. "I've only just started to chase you." So off the moose went again, but soon Mikīnäk caught up with him. "What's the matter with you? I've not run enough yet today. Get along with you." So the moose ran off once more and again Mikīnäk caught up with him. "I can't do any better," the moose said. "I've hurt one of my legs and I can't bear the pain with this crust on the snow." "Hold on then" said Mikīnäk, "I'll fix you up." So he pulled off his otter skin sleeves (*wanakwaian*) [*wanagwayaan?*] and leggings (*okic-kicgtäsin*) [*ogishkidaasin*] and put them on the moose. "Now I want you to run," said Mikīnäk. The moose felt better now, so off he went with Mikīnäk after him. This time the moose was too fast for Mikīnäk and although he followed the animal's tracks on and on and on, he could not catch up with him. "Well," said Mikīnäk to himself, "I'll have to catch him now. He has my sleeves and leggins."

Day after day he kept on the animal's trail until finally the snow started to melt. Then there was scarcely any snow left on the ground at all but Mikīnäk managed to track the moose to open water although he had seen no signs of the animal himself. It was not until midsummer (the season where there a lot of "bull dogs" [deer or horse flies] about and moose seek the water) that Mikīnäk caught up

with the moose. The animal was in the water when Mikīnäk caught
sight of him, and he shouted, "Ho! Ho! I've caught you at last. This
will be the end of you." So Mikīnäk dived into the river and every
once in awhile he would poke his head out to see just where the
moose was. Finally he got close to where the animal was feeding
amongst the grass. Instead of trying to spear him from above (as is
customary), Mikīnäk stabbed the moose from beneath the water
and killed him. He cut up the moose and cracked its bones open
to get the marrow.

"Now I'll have to follow this river and try and find my wife," he
said. "I'll have some fine marrow for my kids, too." So he travelled
along under the water, dragging his load. By the time all the rest of
the Indians had finished hunting and were gathered in their summer
camps he arrived at the place where his wife was staying. He dragged
his load to the edge of the shore and called his wife to come and get
it. She did so and found a lot of fine meat. "Now don't forget the marrow and the liver," he told her. "That is for our kids." After everything
had been brought into the tent, he said to his children, 'Here's some
liver and marrow-fat for you. Eat it and tell me what the other kids
in camp say." Later he asked them what the others said. "Oh, they are
laughing at us," his children told him. "'That's no good to eat,' they
say." "I guess they would like to have some, too," said Mikīnäk.
"That's why they talk like that."
Pinewītis kágotik

8 Misabe[67] (1936)

A long time ago there was an Indian living on the shores of the great
sea. One day when he was out in his canoe he was unable to get back
to the land. He finally drifted off to the shores of another country. He
pulled his canoe up and looked around. He soon noticed some tracks.
They were like human footprints but enormous in size. He knew they
were those of Misabe. This made him very frightened. But there was
nothing that he could do. So he went back to his canoe and, turning it
over, sat down under it. Soon a dog came sniffing around. Then the

man heard Misabe coming along. The man just sat there, hanging his
head like a scared rabbit. When Misabe came up and saw the man, he
picked him up and looked at him. Then he put the Indian in one of
his pockets, the canoe in another and went to his camp. His *wigiwam*
was tremendous in size and at one side of it sat Windigo. When
Windigo saw the man he said to Misabe, "*Nita* [*niitaa*, my brother-
in-law], give him to me to eat."

"No," said Misabe, "I'm going to keep him." So Misabe placed
some food before the Indian. It consisted of huge chunks of marrow.
The man ate what he wanted, but Misabe laughed at his small ap-
petite. "Poor *nózis* [grandson], " he said, "eat more." But the man
couldn't eat any more.

The next day Misabe said, "We'll go hunting, *nózis.*" So he picked
up the man and put him in his pocket again, and calling his dogs, off
they went. Misabe took his bow with him and shot a moose, a big one.

The Indian was given plenty to eat and was well cared for, but
when a year or more had passed he got lonely. He wanted to see his
own people again. So Misabe said, "Poor *nózis*, I suppose I'll have to
let you go back." So the man got ready to go and said, "Grandfather,
make me a paddle." So Misabe made him a paddle and asked, "Is it
too big for you?" "Yes," replied the man, "I can hardly lift it." This
made Misabe laugh. So he made a smaller paddle and placing it
against his thumb, found that it was just the same length. "How's
that?" he asked. "Ah, that's just right," said the Indian. "But it's like
a straw – look how easily it bends," said the giant, laughing.

When he was leaving in the morning, Misabe offered the man a
big pile of meat. But the latter said, "That's too much, it will overload
the canoe." So Misabe told him to take as much as he could carry and
said, "Any time you get hard up or anything scares you, just think of
me. I'll help you. And you will reach home safely and live to be old."

Then Misabe called his two dogs (they were a short-tailed kind)
and told the Indian that they would look after him. He spoke to the
dogs and told them to take the man back where he came from. As
soon as the Indian shoved his canoe out into the sea the dogs began
to shake themselves and with every shake they grew bigger and bigger.

Finally they were so large they could walk through the sea as if it were scarcely more than two hand lengths in depth. It was just like a little creek to them. When the man reached the shores of his own country and had pulled his canoe up on the land, the dogs came ashore and became small again. But as they sat there on the shore they soon pricked up their ears as a voice was heard calling them by name. (One was named Mizizak, Bulldog; the other, Muzwano [Moozwanow], moose tail.) Then they shook themselves again, and off they went, back through the sea to their master.

9 Wisαkedjak Flies with the Geese[68] (1932)

Once Wisαkedjak flew with some geese. An old goose cautioned him not to pay any attention if anyone shot at them and never, under any circumstances, to look down at the earth. Wisαkedjak intended to obey but, as they were flying, a young goose whispered to him, "Wisαkedjak, look at the girls down there." He could not resist looking and as soon as he did so he began to fall towards the earth. The people below saw him falling. They thought that they had killed one of the geese. So they ran to the place where Wisαkedjak fell. They were disappointed when they found out that it was he, for he was now in his human form. These people bound him up with ropes and said, "Now we will give you your punishment." So they left him on the ground outside the camp. When anyone wished to urinate or defecate they went and evacuated on him. Finally an old woman came and Wisαkedjak said to her, "If you unbind me, I'll get you a stick to wipe your arse with." The old woman unloosened [sic] him. But Wisαkedjak grabbed a stick and ran it up her anus and killed her.

10 Wisαkedjak Discovers Women (1933)

A long time ago Wisαkedjak lived with a band of men. They knew nothing of women. Old women and their daughters lived separately. The girls trapped and killed caribou just like men. One day when Wisαkedjak was hunting he struck a trail. He thought he would follow it and pay a visit to the strangers. He came upon a big *càban-dawan* where some women lived. They had heard of Wisαkedjak but had never seen him. So when he entered their dwelling they whispered among themselves, "What shall we give him to eat?"

"Shall we cook you a heart?" one of them said to Wisαkedjak. "Too dry," he answered. "How about a brisket?" said another. "Oh, that's too tough," Wisαkedjak retorted. "What about a head, then?" another girl suggested. But one of her sisters said, "They are all frozen!"

"I'll help you thaw one out," said Wisαkedjak. So one of the women went outside, brought in a caribou head and threw it on the fire. She began scraping the hair off and Wisαkedjak helped her. When they had finished doing this they wanted to get the jaws open to get at the tongue. But the jaws were still frozen together. So Wisαkedjak suggested that they put the head on the ground between them and by bracing their feet against each other's feet they could pull harder. So they did this and pulled and pulled but they could not get the jaws apart. All of a sudden when the woman pulled, Wisαked-jak let go his hold. The woman fell over backwards. He had his penis in her before she knew what had happened and kept working at her. The other women saw what was going on but they did not under-stand it. One of them shouted, "Get an axe, he's killing her." But the woman who had fallen over called out, "Leave him alone. Don't hit him. It's a wonderful thing he's doing." This made the other woman curious and she made her sister get up and let her try it. So Wisαked-jak had to take this woman too. Then the other wanted to have him do the same thing to them. So he had to keep right on. Even the old women wanted to take a turn. But Wisαkedjak objected. "I'm doing this," he said. But they would not listen to him. "It's not for you to say," they told him, and he had intercourse with every one of the women. They all thought him a wonderful man and wanted to know when he was coming to visit them again. Wisαkedjak was completely spent by this time but he said, "I'll come the day after tomorrow."

Wisαkedjak got back to his own camp very late that night. "Where have you been?" the other men inquired. But he did not tell them. He went to the women's camp again as he had promised and again he was late returning to his own camp. He kept doing this so much that the men became curious. "What keeps him?" they said to each other. "He always comes back late." So they kept him awake late one night when they thought he planned to leave early the following morning before the rest of them were up. Wisɑkedjak overslept and this gave them a chance to follow back his trail before he awoke. They came to the *càbandawan* and found the girls. They took a wife apiece. When Wisɑkedjak arrived after mid-day all the younger women had husbands. "We have kept two women for you," the men said. But they were the two old ones. After this everyone knew what women were for.

11 Four Men Visit Wisɑkedjak and Have Their Wishes Granted[69]

Four men went to see Wisɑkedjak. They travelled eight nights. They found Wisɑkedjak living with his daughter. All kinds of animals were to be seen in that part of the country, too. Wisɑkedjak pointed out a place for each man to sit in his *wīgīwam*. "Every time anyone tells a story about me," he said, "it makes me think how foolish I was as a young man."

The men stayed four nights. Then they told Wisɑkedjak that they had to leave. One man asked Wisɑkedjak for his daughter. "You can have her," Wisɑkedjak said, "but do not sleep with her for eight nights." Then he said to the second man, "What is your wish?" This man said, "I want to be a great medicine man." "You will get your wish," said Wisɑkedjak. The third man wished to be a great hunter and Wisɑkedjak said he would get his wish. The fourth man said, "I want to live forever." Wisɑkedjak did not answer him at once. Finally he put his hand on the hair of his head and said, "Yes, you can have your wish. But there is only one thing I know that never dies – a rock."[70] So Wisɑkedjak put him right at the door of his *wīgīwam*. "That's where you will stay," he said.

Then the other men and the daughter of Wisɑkedjak left. Some of the animals followed the girl. As they travelled they could hear the sound of drumming.[71]

The first night passed and the man who had taken the daughter of Wisɑkedjak left her alone. It was the same every other night until the sixth. He wanted her at once. She asked him to wait two nights more, but he refused. The next morning she had disappeared, and along with her all the animals that had followed her. (The Indians used to say that if Wisɑkedjak's daughter had remained here there would be many more animals than there are now.)

Humans and Animals: Using One's Powers to Save, Kill, or Survive[72]

12 Rolling Head[73] (*te`te`pictigwan*) [*ditibishtigwaan?*] (1933)

There was an Indian living in the woods and hunting by himself. He had a wife and two children. He noticed that his wife always combed her hair and fixed herself up nicely before going out to cut wood. And she generally took a long time about it. This made the Indian wonder what kept his wife so long about her work. He decided to find out for himself. So one morning he made an early start. He hid himself near the place where she went to chop wood. Pretty soon he saw her coming along the trail, with a pack-strap in one hand and an axe in the other. She walked directly up to a rotten tree and hit it with the axe. "My husband," she said, "I'm back again." Then she lay down on her back. She had no sooner done this than several snakes came out of the tree and, crawling over to where she was, began tickling her vagina by moving in and out of it.[74]

   The next morning the woman's husband again left his camp early. But this time he was looking for caribou and finally killed one a long distance from their camp. He left the carcass where the animal was killed and upon his return to camp said to his wife, "You go and follow my trail back to the meat. I've made some marks.[75] I'll cut some wood for you." After his wife had gone off, the Indian took an axe and kettle and went to the spot where he had seen her with the snakes. He knocked on the tree and repeated what she had said. The snakes came out. He chopped them in pieces and, collecting their blood in the kettle, took it back to camp and cooked it.

As soon as his wife returned she said, "Have you anything cooked for me? I'm hungry." "Sure," her husband replied, "I've cooked some blood-soup (*miskwabó*) [*miskwaaboo*]." "What kind of blood have you been cooking?" the woman inquired. "Your husband's blood," the Indian replied.

This sent her raving mad. Then the man cut off her head. It started rolling. Now the Indian said to his oldest son, "You take your little brother and run as fast as you can. If your mother's head follows you, throw this awl (*migós*) [*migoos*] in your path and ask that there be plenty of thorn-bushes (*minɛsatɑgok*, genus, Crataegus, hawthorn) [*miinensagaawanzh*] growing right across the world." Then the Indian gave his son a leggin and told him, "If the head gains on you, throw this leggin behind you and ask that the earth open like a crack."

So the rolling head started to follow the children, but the rump of the woman followed her husband, who started off in another direction. But the rump of the woman did not get very far. The Indian grabbed a stick and ran it through his former wife's cunt so that the rump with the stick in it became entangled in the bushes and could not manage to roll any farther.

Meanwhile Rolling Head was following her children. It kept getting closer to them so finally the oldest boy threw down his *migós* and said, "Right across the world let there be thorn-bushes." And thorn bushes arose and Rolling Head could not get through them. Later the bushes disappeared, and on the head rolled once more after the children. It kept gaining on the boys. Closer and closer it came. Then they threw down the leggin and said, "Let the earth open its mouth." Again Rolling Head was stuck. It could not get by the great crack in the earth.

By this time the two brothers had reached a river. On the bank they met a pelican.[76] "Oh, grandfather (here employed as a term of respectful address)," they cried, "take us across the river." And the pelican took them across.

When the bird got back, there was Rolling Head, who said,

"Grandfather, put me across." "All right, I'll do it if you promise to sit quiet," the pelican replied. But Rolling Head kept moving to and fro all the time on the bird's back. The pelican got tired of this before reaching the other side of the river and so bumped Rolling Head off into the water. The head turned into a lot of small fish (*kinozesɑk*) [*ginoozheg*, northern pike?].

The boys kept on travelling and finally reached the shore of a lake with a fine sandy beach. They stayed there and played for awhile. But the little fellow started to cry and his older brother tried to amuse him by tossing a little bell (*cinautcígɑnɛs*) [*zhinaachiganens*?] up into the air and catching it again.[77] All of a sudden the older boy noticed a canoe coming towards the shore. A man was lying in the center of it. After he had beached his canoe the man called to the boys and said, "Come over here and play. I would like to watch you." So they went over to where the stranger was and the older boy started to toss the bell up and down again. As he was doing this the strange man, whose name was Wemisos, struck the bell while it was in the air so that it fell into the canoe instead of on the beach. Now the older boy knew who the man was and knew that he was a wizard. "Throw that bell here," he cried out, "I want it for my little brother." "No, no, come and get it," the stranger said, "just step into the canoe and pick it up." "No," said the boy, "throw it to me." "Oh! Just step in and get it," Wemisos answered. "It's all right."

So the boy stepped into the canoe to get the bell. But as soon as he did so, the wizard struck the canoe and off it went like a shot across the lake. The little fellow left behind on the shore started to cry bitterly for his brother. He yelled out to him, "I'll turn into a black wolf. Any time you see a black wolf you'll remember me."

On went the canoe with Wemisos and the older boy in it. Finally they reached another shore of the lake. Wemisos got out immediately but said to the boy, "You stay right where you are." The wizard went right to his tent where he lived with his two daughters. Upon entering he announced, "I've brought a young man with me. Whoever gets to the shore first may have him for a husband." Both girls dashed out of the tent together but the oldest one reached the canoe first. As soon as she saw the boy she said, "I thought you brought a man. He's no good for anything." But the youngest girl said, "I'll take him." So the boy became the husband of the youngest daughter of Wemisos. He grew up and first had a boy-child by this girl and then another boy-child. But the wizard was tired of seeing him around. He knew that his son-in-law had great powers but he wanted to test him.

One day the young man said to his wife, "I wonder whether there are any birds' eggs on those rocky islands out there?" At this Wemisos spoke up at once, "Ah, my son-in-law, there used to be a lot of eggs over there. We will get some tomorrow." So they paddled out to the islands the next morning and just as they reached the shore Wemisos said, "Jump out, son-in-law." And the young man jumped out. The next moment the wizard struck the canoe and off it went, leaving the young man alone on one of those rocky islands in the center of the lake. And as he went, Wemisos yelled out at the gulls circling overhead, "I'm giving you a feast of my son-in-law." But the young man had his bow and some arrows with him. So he shot a gull, skinned it, put on the skin and, gathering up a few eggs, started to fly back to the camp. As he passed Wemisos, lying on his back in the canoe, watching the gulls flying overhead, the young man defecated on his father-in-law's head. "I never smelt a gull's feces like that," he said to himself, "the gulls must have eaten my son-in-law already." The young man arrived home before Wemisos and told his wife to cook the eggs he had brought. He gave an egg apiece to his two boys and said to them, "Go look for your grandfather. If he asks you where you got those eggs, when he sees you eating them, you tell him, 'Our father brought them.'" Sure enough, when Wemisos saw the children eating the eggs he said to them, "Where did you get those eggs?" And they replied, "Our father brought them."

"Your father!" exclaimed Wemisos, "there is not much left of him by this time." But when he entered their tent he saw his son-in-law sitting there. Wemisos was chagrined, but the young fellow never let on what happened.

Later the young man was making arrows. After he had finished the shafts he had no feathers to put on them. He asked his father-in-law where he could get some feathers. "Oh, my son-in-law, there are some great eagles (*misaziwak*. The ordinary term for bald eagle is *migazi* [*migizi*]) over on an island I know," replied Wemisos. So the next day they set out again in the canoe and after reaching an island in the middle of the lake the same thing happened as before. The young man was deserted there by his father-in-law. But he shot an eagle, put on its skin, and taking some feathers with him arrived in camp before Wemisos. The young man gave his children some of the quills to play with and when Wemisos arrived and saw what his grandchildren had he inquired, "Where did you get those things, grandchildren?"

"Oh! Our father brought them," they replied. Wemisos laughed at this and said, "I guess the great eagles are eating him by this time, my grandchildren." Then he entered the tent and saw his son-in-law calmly sitting there. Wemisos felt worse than ever, but he said nothing and neither did the young man.

One day the young man remarked, "I wonder whether any sturgeons are to be found?" "Oh yes," replied Wemisos, "I know where we can get some fine ones." So they got their spears ready and went out together to spear sturgeons. The young man speared one of these monster fish. Just as he did so, Wemisos called out, "Misinaméok [Misinamewag], Great Sturgeons], I'm giving you a feast of my son-in-law." At the same moment the fish started to swim off. The young fellow refused to loose his hold on the spear shaft, however, and was dragged into the water after the fish. He said to it, "*Namisómis* [*nimishoome*] (paternal uncle, stepfather), take me right home." He had dreamed of the great sturgeon,[78] so the fish did as he requested and the young man killed it after he arrived. He told his wife to hurry up and boil it before her father got back. When the sturgeon was cooked he gave a piece to each of the children, and told them to be sure and tell their grandfather where they got it if he asked them. Soon the old man landed. He saw what the children were eating and asked them who gave them the sturgeon to eat. "Oh! Our father brought it," they answered.

"Hai, there's nothing left of him," said the wizard, "I made a feast of him with the great sturgeon." Then he turned and saw his son-in-law. Wemisos could hardly think of any way to beat him now.

But later he said to his son-in-law, "Suppose we go and play together. We will play at the high jump." "All right," said the young man. So they took a canoe and went across to a point nearby. "We'll do the jumping here," said Wemisos. Now he had chosen this place because, on the far side of the jump, a sharpened stake had been placed in such a position that the jumper was almost sure to impale himself on it. But the young man had noticed this stake. As he ran to make the jump he thought of a white crane (*wabɑtci`tcak*) [*waabajijaak*][79] about which he had dreamed. He not only made the jump successfully, but cleared the pointed stake without a scratch. Wemisos jumped too, but the stake could not harm him as it was of his own doing. Then they went back to camp.

"Oh, my son-in-law," said Wemisos soon after, "I have made a fine swing (*mictigwewébɑzin*, wooden swing) [*mitig-wewebizon*].[80] You get on and I'll swing you." The young man knew it was dangerous, but he could not refuse. As soon as the young man seated himself in the swing, Wemisos started to push him up into the air. "I've dreamed of glue (*nɑmekwen*, lit. sturgeon) [cf. Baraga 1853:263, *namekwan*, glue], he can't throw me off," the young man thought to himself. So the old wizard was beaten again. He did not know how to get rid of his son-in-law. But he almost overcame him. This is how it happened.

One winter Wemisos said, "Let us go hunting together." His son-in-law was willing, so off they went together. When camping time came they made a brush tent (*cingúbigan*) [*zhingobiigan*] in which to spend the night.[81] After they had built a fire in the center Wemisos said, "Now, my son-in-law, you better dry your socks and your moccasins and leggings." So they both hung these articles of clothing up to dry. Then they lay down to sleep. But Wemisos did not go to sleep. As soon as he saw that his son-in-law had dropped off to sleep he got up quietly and threw the young man's foot-gear in the fire. Then he lay down again and as soon as believed them to be all burnt up he roused his son-in-law. "I smell something burning," he said, 'look, your socks and moccasins must have fallen into the fire. They are all burnt up."

In the morning Wemisos got up and was soon ready to leave. "I'm going now," he said to his son-in-law, "you can stay right here where you are." The young fellow felt pretty bad at first. He did not know what to do. He could not travel in bare feet. But then he remembered that when he was a boy (presumably in his puberty fast) he dreamed of a black wolf. "This is the time he should help me," he thought. So he took some charcoal from the hearth, mashed it up, and blackened his legs. As soon as he stepped outside the tent he turned into a wolf. Once more he managed to get home ahead of his father-in-law. When the latter arrived he was again chagrined to see his son-in-law there.

Still, he did not wish to acknowledge his defeat. So, in a day or so, he asked his son-in-law to go hunting with him again. The young fellow made no objection, so again they started out. They made a brush-tent as they did before and soon were ready to settle down for the night. But the young man was wiser this time. When his father-in-law went outside for a few minutes before lying down to sleep, he exchanged their socks, leggings and moccasins. He hung his where the old man's were. But Wemisos did not know this. After he thought his son-in-law was asleep he got up and without knowing it, threw his own socks and leggings and moccasins in the fire. Just as before, he aroused the young man by exclaiming, "I smell something burning. It must be someone's moccasins." This time his son-in-law got up and, picking up those remaining, said, "Well, these are mine, the others must be yours!"

In the morning the young man prepared to leave. His father-in-law did not know what to do. Finally, he spoke and said, "My son-in-law, what is to become of me, now?" But his son-in-law only replied, "You know what is best for you." Then he left. When he had gone Wemisos took some charcoal and blackened his legs. He thought of the caribou of which he had dreamed. He started to run but his *pawáganak*[82] must have been weak because he did not get very far. It was very cold and he said to himself, "This is not going to do." He was standing alongside of a tamarack, so he said, "Hereafter, the people shall call me a tamarack-cone" (*maski kwatikopi`kwakwat*) [*mash-kiigwaatigo-bikwaakwad*].

13 Big Mosquito (*k`tcizɑgimé*) [*gichi-zagime*][83] (1933)

Long time ago – there were some people living – there were also some
man eaters – the mosquito family. So there was a man at one time. He
saw the snare set by the Mosquito people. "I'll lie down here and see
what happens" [he said]. So he lay there. Mosquito came along. "Aha!
My 'moose' (for this is what the mosquitoes called the human beings
they hunted) – I wonder what has killed him? Just to see my snare is
enough to kill him. I have a wonderful snare." Ties him up and throws
him on his back – carries him home. Threw him in his tent. Wife
loosens him up now – just like an animal. This man watches – eyes
half closed. "You better heat your kettle" (said Mosquito). Wife turns
and looks for knife. Man jumps up and runs out of tent. "He!" the
Mosquito says and it starts to laugh. "I'll follow up." Took bow. Man
ran – Mosquito gained – man climbs up *minäik* (a spruce tree).

Soon the Mosquito caught up – fixed his arrow to bow to shoot
the man. "No! No – don't shoot me. My blood will be a waste to you.
You'll love it." "Yes, yes that's right – my 'moose' is teaching me," says
the Mosquito. "How am I going to get you?" "Climb up after me," says
the man. "*Tapwe, tapwe* – yes yes" – Cree. The Mosquito starts to
climb. The man said, "I've been dreaming of *eskin* [*eshkan*, chisel] – I
wish I had it in my hand." He had it then. "Don't look up," he said to
Mosquito. "Alright – my 'moose' is teaching me – I look down."

When he got close, the man stabbed him in head with chisel and
the Mosquito fell down. But the Mosquito managed to get home.
What to do now? Go and get wisest man in camp [who] was the bull
dog fly (*mizisak*) [deer fly]. Said, "We sent for you – what is best thing
to do?" "Well," he says, "this is easy. Take a mallet and drive it thru"
(chisel was still in Mosquito's head). [He] took mallet – struck the
chisel. His head was split – killed – all started to laugh. "What will we
do now?" "Hang up your kettle – cook and eat. I'll follow the 'moose',"
his brother said.

The man knew he was being followed. Came to lakeshore. "I wish
I could find an old canoe or something." He found one. Said to Mosquito, "Don't shoot – you'll lose the blood – follow me." Mosquito

jumps in and tries to catch the canoe. The man kept paddling out –
the Mosquito got weak. "I'll take you ashore," he says. Mosquito [was]
so weak he could do nothing – almost frozen by being in the water so
long. Made a fire – a big one. Laid the Mosquito close [with his] back
to the fire. While he watched him [he] saw that the Mosquito's skin
began to burn – but the Mosquito lay there – did not feel it. Finally
his back cooked and the Mosquito was roasted to death. The man
took his knife and cut the Mosquito in pieces. Threw them around.
"You'll be small now. You were too big before. If the big ones keep
up, no human being will be able to live." So the little mosquitos
began to fly and have found man ever since.

14 The Bear, the Hare, and the Lynx[84] (1938)

Once a Bear and Hare were living together in a *wīgīwam*. Hare said,
"Let one of my grandchildren sleep with me for company." Bear
agreed and sent one of the cubs to sleep with his grandfather Hare. In
the morning something had happened to the cub. It was dead. Hare
cried and said, "Let me go and bury my grandchild." So Hare took
the cub off into the bush. There he cooked and ate it. The next night
the same thing happened. Hare said to Bear, "I can't manage to sleep
alone. Let one of my grandchildren sleep with me." So Bear sent
another cub to sleep with Hare. In the morning this cub was found
dead. Hare had strangled it. Hare cried again and said, "I want to
bury my grandchild." So he went off with the dead cub and instead of
burying it he cooked it and ate it. The third night the same thing happened again. In the morning the third and last cub of Bear was found
dead. So Hare said, "We are having bad luck. We better separate now.
You go your way and I'll go mine."

   But Hare only went a short distance and then came back to the
wīgīwam where they had been living. Hare went in and sat down.
Soon he heard someone speak to him. It was a couple of young lynx
who poked their heads in the *wīgīwam*. "Come right in, my grandchildren," said Hare, who was sitting with his back to the fire. "Scratch
my back for me, my grandchildren." So the young lynx rubbed their

paws on Hare's back but did not put out their nails. "What kind of scratching is that, anyway," said Hare. Then the lynx put out their claws and scratched for all they were worth. Hare was soon torn to pieces. Then they started to roast him. The grease could be smelt for a long distance and the old lynx smelt it. So they crept up to the *wīgīwam*. When they saw what was going on one of them said to the other, "Something smells greasy, our kids must have killed something." They went close to the tent. Sure enough there was Hare on a roasting stick, and grease was dripping. "We'll take the thing away from them and eat it ourselves." So they jumped into the tent and grabbed for the roast hare. The young ones wanted their share so they grabbed the hot hare too. It was so hot they burned their faces. That is why the lynx have the expression on their faces that they have today.

15 The Wolf and the Wolverine (1933)

Long ago Wolverine was married to the daughter of Wolf. They all lived together. But Wolf hunted moose and caribou while Wolverine hunted beaver. Wolverine was very good at this. One day he asked his father-in-law to go along with him to kill beaver. Of course this was something new to Wolf. So he paid close attention to every move which his son-in-law made. He wanted to see exactly how it was done. After Wolverine broke the house the beaver went down into the water. Wolverine ran along the edge of the bank. Every once in a while he hit his tail playfully on the ice, as if he were dancing. Wolverine did not like to have his father-in-law watch him so closely, so he said to him, "Why are you looking at me all the time? Do I appear any different than usual?" Wolf never answered him. He knew Wolverine was getting mad. After they had caught some beaver they went back to their camp. That night the Wolverine bewitched Wolf. He used his magic power to condemn him to starve. He made it impossible for him to catch any of the animals he hunted. When Wolf followed the trail of a moose something always seemed to warn the animal that it was being tracked. While formerly Wolf had no trouble in catching the moose and caribou, they now escaped from him. He never succeeded in overtaking them. Things kept on this way for a long time. Finally, Wolf was getting weak. He was always out on the run every day but he could kill nothing. He knew now what the trouble was. He was sure his son-in-law had bewitched him. But he said to himself, "I'll ask him to go out hunting with me tomorrow."

By this time Wolverine had two young ones that used to run in and out of their grandfather's tent, so he [their grandfather] said to one of them, "Tell your father to come out with me tomorrow morning." Wolverine was willing to go with his father-in-law but, of course, he did not expect any luck. So off they went the next morning. They tracked a cow moose. Wolf said to his son-in-law, "You chase him." So the Wolverine chased him a short distance. But he knew he could not catch him. When Wolf came up to where his son-in-law was, the Wolverine said, "If he had a longer tail he would be worth catching."[85] Wolf knew he could not depend upon his son-in-law for this kind of hunting, so he followed the moose they had tracked. He found that he was gaining on the animal. The tracks began to get fresh. Finally he caught sight of the moose and called out, "Hai, *djíbai* [*jiibay*, ghost].[86] Now I have the sight of you." Then Wolf dashed off at full speed in pursuit of the moose. He caught and killed it. He took home a leg to his wife and children. It was already dark when he arrived. After tearing the meat off he cracked the bone in order to give the children some of the marrow. Wolverine heard the crack and said to one of his kids, "Go into your grandfather's tent and see what that noise is." (Of course Wolverine knew what made the sound.) Wolf's wife heard the child coming so she hid the bone of the moose, and picking up a two-handed scraper (*pakwatcigan*) (*atik* [caribou] lower hind leg), tapped it on the ground. "Oh, I'm going to make some soup for your grandfather out of this scraper." So the child went back and told its father this.

The Wolf then gave his children something to eat and said to his wife, "Let us get up before daybreak. We'll take the covering off this tent and move down to where I killed the moose." So they got an early start the next morning and made their camp near where the moose was killed. Wolf dressed the meat and brought it to the dwelling. The moose's stomach was frozen solid. He hung it up on the side of the tent. Above the fire, on the *kwawanatik* [agwaawaanaatig, meat or fish drying rack], the Wolf put lots of the fat. Soon Wolverine came along. He was drawing a loaded toboggan. He threw the line across his mother-in-law's knees. "Draw my load in," said he, "there are some nice fat beaver tails on it for you." But the old woman thrust the line aside. "I should have received this long ago," she said, "now I don't need it."

When Wolverine looked up and saw the fat dripping now and then into the fire he said, "Ho! Ho! The grease is dropping in the fire." Wolf said, "Get a dish and let him eat of it." So his wife put a dish before her son-in-law and he ate some grease. "It's very good," he said.

"Well, it might taste better if you closed your eyes while you ate," Wolf said. So Wolverine did as suggested. Then his mother-in-law got up and unfastened the frozen stomach of the moose which was hanging above Wolverine's head. She pretended that it dropped accidentally, but it fell on her son-in-law's head and knocked him senseless. "Take the axe and kill him," she said to her husband.

So Wolf killed him with the axe. Then they took Wolverine's body down to the trail they had followed in the morning and laid him there with his tail facing the direction from which they had come.

Soon the two little Wolverines came along. They were running ahead of their mother. They saw their father's tail with white frost already around it. They ran back to their mother. "Our father's tail has white frost around it," they said.

"That can't be," said their mother, "what will become of you if your father's tail has white frost around it?" But sure enough, when they came to the place, she saw that her husband had been killed. She stopped there. She was afraid to go on. Wolf said, "What shall we do with them?"

His wife replied, "Kill them all, since they have tried to starve us to death. Do you want to spare them?" So he took the axe and killed his own daughter and grandchildren.[87]

Humans Against Cannibals

16 The Eleven Brothers[88]

Once there were eleven brothers. One night the two oldest ones did
not return to camp. The next morning the two brothers next to them
in age said, "We must follow the tracks of our older brothers and see
what has happened to them." So they started off. They did not return
that night either, so the second morning two more of the brothers
followed their tracks. They never came back. So the third morning
two more brothers went off to find them but at night they had not
returned. The same thing happened the fourth day so that now there
were only three brothers left in camp. They knew that something had
happened to their brothers, so one of those remaining said, "I'll go
alone and you stay with our younger brother." So he went off but did
not come back. Now there were only two brothers left. The oldest
said, "Younger brother, I'll have to go and look for our brothers." Now
this man had a white fisher *kɑskípītagan* [*gashkibidaagan*, term used
for bags made of animal skin in the *midéwiˑwin*] and he hung up this
skin. "Watch this," he said. "As son as it starts to swing you'll know
that I have commenced to fight."

Later in the day the youngest brother noticed the fisher skin began
to swing (and it had rattlers on it too).[89] The bag kept swinging all the
rest of the day. The youngest brother knew that it must be a long and
hard fight. In the evening the bag gradually began to swing slower
and slower. Finally it stopped swinging altogether. Then the boy knew
that his brother had been killed and that he was the only one left.

Next morning he heard someone speaking. He knew it was not the
voice of any of his brothers, so he was frightened. As there were some
partridge feathers lying inside the *wīgīwam*, he picked up one of these
and wished that he would turn into a partridge feather. It so happened. The next moment some strangers entered the tent. They were
talking and one of them said to the other, "I wonder whether any
people are left in this tent." "It looks like it," said his companion.

"Look at the fire" (which was blazing). "It can't be," said the one who had spoken first. "We killed the last one of them yesterday." Then they began to search the place. They looked everywhere inside the lodge and out in the bush but could find no one. Finally they got tired and said, "I guess we did kill everyone." Then they left. (These men were *wíndīgowαk* who went hunting people to eat.)

In the morning the youngest brother started out to trail the cannibals. The only weapon he carried was an awl (*migos*) [*migoos*]. It was not long before he came to a lake, the whole length of which was lined with snowshoes stuck up in the snow on either side of the trail. "These must be the snowshoes of all the people they have killed," he thought. Then he came upon the place where his brother had been fighting with the cannibals a couple of days before. The snow was closely packed all over and blood was spattered here and there. He crossed the lake and saw a water hole cut in the ice and judged that the cannibals' camp would be on the hill-top nearby. Then he caught sight of their *cábandawan*.[90] The boy was watching everything closely now and he espied a barked tree with what appeared to be a nest in the top of it. "I wonder what is in that nest," he said to himself. So he climbed the tree, which was quite tall, using his awl as a hold and pulling himself up hand over hand. Finally he reached the nest and looked in. It was lined with human hair, and in it lay twelve hearts. The boy could see that they were throbbing. "Ah!" he said, "I know now why my brothers could not kill these men. Their lives are here." So he concealed himself in the tree from where he could plainly see the cannibals' camp.

Towards evening the boy saw one of the cannibals coming along towards the *càbandawa*n. He was carrying the heads of two men. The other ten now soon returned, each one bringing two or three heads apiece. Then the two oldest cannibal men started to dance; they were so glad to have something to eat. As they danced the boy took his awl and touched a heart which he believed to be that of one of these old cannibals. The heart beat harder and one of the old men dancing in the *càbandawan* cried out, "Ah! I believe someone is after our hearts."

As soon as he said this the boy stabbed the heart with his awl and the old man dropped to the ground, dead. The others now jumped to their feet, seized their bows and arrows, and rushed out of the *càbandawan*. One after the other, the boy quickly stabbed the hearts as quickly as he could until every cannibal was dead.

Then he climbed down the tree and went over to the *càbandawan* where he plainly saw the results of his work. He made a bow and two arrows. After these were finished, he gathered together all of the bones which had been thrown out of the *càbandawan* after the cannibals had eaten the flesh. He piled these up. Then he got one of his arrows ready and shot it in the air, shouting at the same time, "Look out men, I might hit you. Jump to your feet." The dead men jumped up at once. He had saved them. And all of his brothers were surprised to see him. The boy said to the others, "Go back to your hunting grounds." He was now considered by everyone to be a very powerful man. *Pinewītis kágotik*

17 Wémtigóze [White Man][91]

Long ago there were two old men, both of whom had the same number of children. One had ten sons and ten daughters; the other had the same. The latter's name was Tcóbatɑm [To Pass Anything from One Side To Another Between the Lips] and he had a daughter called Ningikskwezis [Otter-Girl]. She was married to one of the other man's sons. These two families camped and hunted together but they found that this was not going to do. There was too big a crowd for them to feed. Game was getting scarce and they were not getting enough to eat. So each family decided to go their own way for awhile and to meet again in a month or so.

Now the young man who was the husband of Otter-Girl treated her very badly and after the two families had separated he killed her. After he had done this, he covered her body with brush.

One night the girl's father said, "I'm getting lonely for Otter-Girl. I'd like to see her." When he got up the next morning he said to his wife, "I'm going to visit my daughter." So he started off. He soon struck the trail of the other family and followed it. Finally he came to the place where they had last camped. He noticed a pile of brush nearby and wondered what they had covered up. Under it he found his daughter's dead body. After this he kept on the trail of the other family and in the evening reached their camp. The other old man inquired, "Where did you strike our trail?" "I struck it below where Otter-Girl is buried under the bush," Tcóbatɑm replied. The other old man was not at all pleased to see that Tcóbatɑm had already discovered that his daughter had been killed. Next morning, Tcóbatɑm said to him, "*Ndinawa* (the term used between parents of married couples), I think I'll come over here and camp with you again." Then he started off in the direction of his own camp.

After he had gone the other old man said to his son (the husband of the deceased Otter-Girl), "It was wrong to do what you did. You don't know what may happen to us now." He was very much scared.

When Tcóbatɑm reached his camp he told his wife and children about what had happened and what he had decided to do. "We'll not stay camping with them very long," he said. "When they move camp, I'll tell you what we'll do. Each one of you boys must manage to keep one of your brothers-in-law ahead of you on the trail, and the girls must do the same with their sisters-in-law.[92] I'll keep the old man behind as if we were going to be the last to leave, but I'll kill him right there. Have your axes ready in your hands. Watch your brother who is the farthest ahead. The moment he steps on the heel of the snowshoe of the man in front of him, you do the same to the person in front of you.[93] Then kill him with your axe before he can get up."

The old man's plan worked out very well. After otter-girl's people had joined the other family and camped with them a few nights it was decided to move on the next morning. Tcóbatɑm kept the other old man behind while the others started ahead. "What do you call this moon?" the former said to him. "This is the mid-winter moon (February)." "No! You're wrong; this is eagle-moon (*Migɑzīwīkīzis*, March) [*Migizigiizis*, Bald Eagle Moon].[94] Look! There is an eagle

now passing behind you," Tcóbatɑm said, cutting his throat, as the
old man turned around to see it. "Did you expect to see an eagle
this time of year?" he added.

Then Tcóbatɑm followed the trail of the rest of the party. He saw
bodies lying all along it, one after the other. His eldest son asked him,
"What are you going to do with these people? You can't eat them." But
his father only replied, "Make a big long fire. Roast all the meat we
have, everything – moose, beaver, bear, porcupine and roast a couple
of these children too." After everything was cooked, the old man took
his knife and, cutting a piece from this animal and that, began to taste
everything. "Moose! No! There's too much willow taste to it. It's no
good. Caribou! It has too much of a dry mossy taste. Beaver! It savors
too much of poplar. Otter is too fishy. Wolverine! Pretty near right."
(Because the wolverine will eat human flesh, will dig up human
graves.) Finally he tasted a piece of one of the children that had been
roasted. "Ah," he said, "this is the best of all. It tastes just right! From
now on this will be our meat. We'll hunt nothing else but people."
So they began to hunt for nothing but people. And when the news
spread, everyone was scared of them, because the old man was
likewise a kind of wizard (kīmändauzī).

Now there was a man named Kaiánwe who was also called
Wémtigóze. In the fall of the year he knew (through his dreams) that
he was going to meet the witch-man. So he told his father-in-law
about it and asked him to help him prepare for the occasion. They
built a house with a partition in the middle and a kind of slide of ice
which would precipitate anyone approaching it into the front part.[95]
They lived in the rear end of the house themselves.

One morning Wémtigóze told his father-in-law, "I'll see him
today. I'm going to go and meet him on the river." So he set out with
his dog, dressed in the poorest clothes he had and carrying a very
badly made bow and some arrows. This was to fool the witch-man.
But Wémtigóze did not neglect to take his best knife with him.

Now Tcóbatɑm, the witch-man, had heard of Wémtigóze and
wanted to keep out of his way. As Wémtigóze was working on the

river, pretending that he was damming the river for beaver, the witch-
man came along. The latter was glad to see a man, since he thought to
himself, "Here is a good chance to get some fresh meat to eat." But all
he said to "white man" was, "I'll come over with my sons tomorrow
and they will lend you a hand. The boys will carry down all the sticks
you need to close up the creek." So the witch-man went back to his
camp and "White Man" went home too.

When the former reached camp he said not a word about what
he had seen. "What's the matter?" said one of his sons. "The old man
doesn't have a thing to say. He must have seen an orphan somewhere."
"Yes, he is an orphan by the look of him," said the witch-man. "He's
all rags and his bow is just like a bare rib,[96] but he has a good knife.
And he's terribly white!" Then the old fellow started to sing and shake
his rattle (*cīcīgwan*) [*zhiishiigwan*], but he had scarcely started when
the rattle burst. He threw it aside and said, "He'll never get away from
us, anyway." Then he got up and hung the kettle in the door. "If we are
going to have good luck it will be full of blood," he said. But when he
looked at it again it was full of ashes.

Meanwhile the "white man" had been making his own plans. He
got up very early the next morning. First of all he made a trail up into
the bush. Then he hid his best bow there. After this he cut some timber but scattered the rails (intended for the dam) in all directions so
that the witch-man's sons, in order to gather them up, would have to
separate. Soon the old wizard came along with his sons, the women
being some distance behind. As soon as the men arrived, "white man"
said to them, "Hang up your bows high on that tree. The dogs might
eat your bow strings if you leave them lying about." So the men did as
they were told, and then went off into the bush to get the rails. "You
and I will cut a hole in the ice right across the creek," "white man"
said to the wizard, and they set to work at once. After they had been
working a short time, white man pulled open his shirt and bent down
to drink. The wizard started to so the same thing and immediately
"white man" struck him on the back of the neck with his *èskin*
[*eshkan*, ice-chisel] and shoved his body into the water. As soon as he

had done this, he ran up into the bush, secured his bow and jumped
behind a tree. The first man he saw collecting rails he shot down.
Then he shifted his position and shot another of the brothers. He
kept on until he had killed all of the wizard's sons except one. This
one almost escaped him but he finally killed him. By this time the
women had come along. He found that the wizard was keeping some
women to fatten them for better eating, so he made them step to one
side. He killed all the others.
Pinewītis kágotik

Afterword

In his draft preface (pp. 19–20) to his book manuscript, Hallowell emphasized the importance of seeing the myths not in isolation but in
their full human context, while also recognizing that their prime significance is for the people who tell them and carry them on. His words
make clear why it is important to study and listen to these texts with the
greatest attention:

> While lip service has been given to the idea that myths and tales are
> an integral part of the culture of a people, our folklore archives are
> replete with collections of oral narratives, not only published sepa-
> rately from the ethnographic accounts of the people from whom
> they have been collected, but frequently without even an extended
> introductory statement that indicates to the reader just how they fit
> into the cultural matrix. Yet it must be obvious that the primary
> meaning and significance of myths and tales is for the people who
> tell them. The role which oral narratives play in any society can
> hardly be considered an insignificant detail when the society is
> viewed as a going concern …
>
> The world outlook, the system of values, the attitudes expressed
> in the leading themes of the narratives, also afford us valuable psy-

chological insight into the character structure of the people themselves ... [Franz] Boas has demonstrated that myths and tales may
contain a great deal of ethnographical realism. It can also be shown,
I believe, that they embody a great deal of psychological realism.

Here, Hallowell encourages us to look more profoundly into the dy-
namics of these stories for a better understanding of the people, their
inner thoughts, and their ways of relating to one another and to the
other-than-human beings who were also part of their social and spiritual universe. He never managed, however, to complete his study of
Ojibwe myths and tales; his analyses of them remained partial and unfinished, as he himself would have freely admitted.

We too have not undertaken to analyze the myths systematically but
have decided rather to let them speak for themselves to readers while
pointing out along the way some of the prominent themes and core
values that they express. We hope that readers of these texts will be led
to explore them more deeply from various perspectives and especially
that the many relatives of William Berens, down through the generations, will be glad of the gift that, through Hallowell, he has left for us all.

Appendix:
Thunder Bird
A. Irving Hallowell[1]

Although there are distinct terms for thunder (*animαkï*) [*animikii*] and lightning (*wasamowin*) [*waasamowin*], the causal agent of this meteorological phenomenon is reputed to be the Thunder Bird (*pinèsï*) [*binesi*], whose manifestations can likewise [be] called by this term. It is also the generic term for bird, and in composition the suffix *–esï*, which frequently appears in bird names, has reference to the avian class of creatures and not specifically to the Thunder Bird. On the other hand, in personal names the reverse is usually the case, since a considerable proportion of these have reference to the Thunder Bird, implicitly if not explicitly. As a rule then, the specific and generic usage of *pinèsï* and its derivations can be clearly distinguished either in terms of conventional usage or the context of the moment.

To the lay reader it may seem strange that *pinèsï* is conceived as a bird, while on the other hand the ethnologist will casually point out that the geographical location of the Pigeon River people is such that they are well within the cultural range of a belief in the Thunder Bird, a tremendously widespread conception in native North America and even North Asia.[2] Thus, from the cultural historical standpoint they could hardly be expected to believe otherwise.

On the other hand, from the standpoint of the natives themselves there is a sound empirical basis for the belief. Not only has this creature appeared to men in dreams; there is a lake where its nest has been observed, a few individuals have seen *pinèsï* with their naked eyes and furthermore, the seasonal aspects of thunder and lightning, as well as the direction from which they appear, are analogous to avian behavior.

In May, I was told, when the *pinèsï* first appears it inevitably comes from the south. This is also the month when the summer birds are first appearing[3] and the season of open water begins. Towards the end of the summer – about Aug. 1st – *pinèsï* seems to appear more frequently from the west, but it will then move towards the south, before disappearing. It often happens that if there is a west wind it will turn into a north wind and help *pinèsï* on its way southward. So, like the birds, *pinèsï* goes south in the fall and you never hear *pinèsï* again until the winter is over. The young ones, it was said, are raised during *pinèsï's* sojourn in the west. Thus it is also perfectly clear why it is that *pinèsï's* niche in the cosmos is in the south. And the inference made from the common observation of concomitant phenomena – thunder and birds – is rational. Similar behavior implies a similar nature.

To the north of Pigeon River the next river of any size is Poplar River (*äsatiwïsïbï*) [*azaadiwiziibi*]. This river flows through a large lake, which is on the maps is marked Weaver Lake, but to the Indians it is known as *pinèsïwàbikusagahïgan* (Thunderbird Lake). Formerly, this lake was extremely foggy. Today it is said to be less so and this fact seems to be connected with the local disappearance of the Thunder Birds which frequented the lake. On an island in the lake is a hill, on the top of which was a nest of *pinèsï*.[4] One of my informants once visited the place.[5] Big boulders – some of them four to five feet in diameter – lay in a circular arrangement and formed the outer dimension of the "nest." Concentrically arranged inside of them were a series of smaller rocks graded in size, the smallest in the center. The nest was three or four feet deep, and according to my informant could not have been made by human beings.

The rocks were much too large to have been carried up there and it was not at all obvious just where they had been obtained. I never ran across any Indian, nor did my informant know of any person who had actually seen the *pinèsïwak* which nested in this spot. But Peter Berens (Berens River band) when a boy of 11 or 12, did once see *pinèsï* at close quarters. His uncle's family was camping on the north side off Flathead Point [see map, this volume] (*onapakistakwanisanowin*) about 200–300 yards from the point itself. Lightning was often observed to play about this point and even to strike there. On the occasion referred to, there had been a severe storm. After the rain had stopped but while it was still thundering, Peter ran out of the tent and in the direction of the point. There he saw a large and unfamiliar bird lying on the rocks. It had an enormous wingspread. Its body was bluish gray in color and its feathers were striped. It had a red tail of exceedingly great length. It was very pretty. Peter ran back to the tent to get his uncle. But before he reached there it began to thunder and lightning again, and when his elders returned to the point with him there was no bird to be seen. The boy thought that the bird he had seen was a young *pinèsï* but his story was discredited because while *pinèsï* is frequently dreamed of, it is most unusual to see him with the naked eye. Sometime later, however, Peter related his experience to an old woman who had dreamed of *pinèsï*. She verified his description and told Peter that he would live to be a very old man.[6] This is an excellent example of the mutual support which, in particular cases, dream experiences can lend to what is claimed as ordinary observation and vice versa. And through the dissemination of such experiences a secure empirical foundation is built up to support belief. *Pinèsï* still continues to haunt Flatstone [Flathead] Point because a few years ago a man met his death there by lightning. Today no one will camp on this point in stormy or threatening weather.

Another description of *pinèsï* not, however, based on direct observation but on tradition described the Thunder Bird as being as large as a dog, with body feathers something like the wool of a sheep, a huge wing spread, with long feathers like the hawks, a beaked bill and feet like an eagle. The hawk-like traits are those inevitably stressed, and so it comes about that the Thunder Bird is mentally grouped with this avian division in ornithological classification.⁷ This association is further borne out in a myth (Mätcīkīwis) [see Part IV, 6] in which the hero marries one of the daughters of *pinèsï*, a swan (*wabïzi*) [*waabizii*],⁸ when she visits earth in human guise. Later when he visits Thunder Bird Land (*pinèsïwɑkotɑkīwaspīming*) [*binesiwag odakiiwaang*] he finds that his brothers-in-law include the golden eagle (*kïnïu* [*giniw*] or *apisk*), the Sparrow Hawk (or Pigeon Hawk, *pïpïkïwɑsɛs*) [*biipiigiwizens*] and the Peregrine Falcon (Duck Hawk, *kekek*) [*gekek*]. *Pinèsï* is the headman of the place (*kīnegɑnīsī*) [*gii-niigaanizi*]. All these "Thunder Birds" hunt "beaver"; but the animals they call by this term are the great toads (frogs, *k'tcimɑkokik*) and great snakes (*k'tcēkinébik*) [*gichi-ginebig*], which inhabit the earth and are sometimes seen by human beings also. The hero participates in one of these "beaver" hunts, amid the crash of thunder and the flashes of lightning.

Since the Sparrow Hawk, as well as representatives of the *Buteonidae* (Marsh Hawk, Red-Tailed Hawk, Broad-Winged Hawk (*onótcïkinèbikwesï*, snake-hunting bird), etc.) which are also associated with the Thunder Birds, include among their prey batrachians and reptiles, we sense an empirical clue to the notion that the favorite prey of *pinèsïwak* [*binesiwag*] is analogous in character. Only the Thunder Birds hunt the giants of the species. Furthermore toads and snakes of the ordinary varieties are despised by the Saulteaux, if not actually feared. The activities of the Thunder Birds have helped to rid the earth of the monster relatives of these loathsome creatures.⁹ Now there only a few of them left which are not often seen. Without the help of *pinèsï* the very existence of mankind might have been endangered. Thus runs Saulteaux belief.

If human beings are ever struck by "lightning" it is purely accidental. For in the myth of Mätcīkīwis, the old *pinèsï* sends his daughters to be the wives of men on earth and says, "I'm related to the people on the earth now and I'll be merciful towards them. I'll not hurt any of them if I can possibly help it." What the *pinèsïwak* are really after then, when they are heard in the sky and when lightning appears, are the hateful snakes and toads, of giant size. The slowly rolling "distant" thunder with but few "claps" are the old *pinèsï*, while the sharp and active "closer" claps indicate the presence of the younger "birds." What the Thunder Birds actually do their damage with no one knows. One never finds any sort of missile. Only the place that was struck can sometimes be seen. But in the case of human beings, not even that. In view of this interpretation of the character of thunder and lightning it can be understood why the Saulteaux resist the notion advanced by the whites, and particularly by the men of the Forestry Service, that lightning causes forest fires. The Indians will not argue about it but they simply don't believe it. *Pinèsï* would not do that. It is just not his business in life.

And yet it cannot be said that the Saulteaux are unafraid during a severe display of thunder and lightning. In fact one man with whom I was especially well acquainted was particularly jumpy. As a matter of observation it seemed to me in fact that thunderstorms were of unusually frequent occurrence on Pigeon River, during the two summers I spent there, at least [1932, 1933, a clue to the date of this writing]. I also suspect that there is a genuine functional correlation between their beliefs in regard to the harmlessness of *pinèsï* on the one hand and incipient fear reactions to the frequent thunderstorms on the other.

Evidence of this is based upon the custom of giving *pinèsï* a "smoke" when he appears. Smoking to *pinèsï* is a form of sacrifice. This rite is simply performed. A pipe is lighted, slowly turned in the four directions and then smoked. This is accompanied by an inward petition of mercy and sometimes simply the words: *peka, peka, peka* [*bekaa*] ("wait, wait, wait, or go easily") or *peka, peka kisegïmauwak apinungïak* (wait, wait, you frighten them (the) children [*abinoojiinh-yag*].) It would be an overstatement to assert that this is a magical device for compelling *pinèsï* to depart, but it at least contains the overtones of such a notion, and in psychological terms it is undoubtedly reassuring to the performer. Of course if a man has *pinèsï* for a *pawágan* [*bawaagan*, guardian spirit] the ceremony referred to may be performed simply to honor one's protector: this was the interpretation placed upon the following episode, which was related to me by an eyewitness.

Fair Wind (Nämɑwin)[10] was sitting in his tent one day when a severe thunderstorm came up. After an extremely loud clap of thunder and a flash of lightning occurred, Fair Wind turned to his wife [Koowin] and said, "Did you understand what he said to me?" (referring, of course, to the *pinèsï* but not mentioning the Thunder Bird by name, there being a tabu upon specifically referring to one's *pawágan* (if such was really the case) by name.

"Not very plainly," the old woman replied.

"He's asking me whether I have a pipe and why I don't light it," Fair Wind said.

"Well, then, why don't you get your pipe out?"

"You get my pipe out and hurry up about it." So the old woman hunted around and finally located Fair Wind's pipe and tobacco bag and also got out some *sägatagan* [*zagataagan*].[11] She passed these to a *skabéwis* [*oshkaabewis*, servant or usher] who happened to be present at the time. He filled the pipe, put some *sägatagan* on top of the tobacco, struck a spark with the flint and steel and lighted the tinder, after which he passed it to the old man.

Nämawin took a few puffs, then bowing his head he said, "*mïapane*" (here it goes), and turned the stem of the pipe clockwise through the air. Everyone present was extremely quiet, even solemn. My informant did not remember the exact words spoken as this episode happened a number of years ago, but they had reference to the fact that he had not spontaneously made a smoke offering to *pinèsï*. He asked to be pardoned and for merciful treatment.

Since the ceremonies performed on the Pigeon River are carried on in uncovered pavilions, clear weather is essential. Formerly, when the *midéwi·win* [*midewiwin*, medicine lodge] was regularly held it was traditional that it was always clear when this ritual was in progress. Today when the *wabanówïwin* [*waabanoowiwin*][12] is given weather conditions are consciously considered. The summer of 1933, however, was extremely stormy, and the day that the *wabanówigamik* [waabano pavilion] was opened at Pauingassi the sky became increasingly overcast and it was very chilly. Since this particular ceremony was planned for a three-day period, weather conditions were an important item. The drumming started about noon each day and continued until 9 or 10 o'clock at night. Dancing was intermittent. There was rain during the night following the opening day and showers the next morning and early afternoon. Drumming did not start until 3 o'clock and even then there were no real signs of clearing. After starting, the wife of Angus was overheard to say something to her husband about appealing to *pinèsï*.[13] But Angus only replied, "I'll leave it to him." Soon afterwards it began to rain, but only lightly. The drumming continued but at the same time canvas was placed here and there on the windward side to protect those of us inside the structure. Yet sentiment was strong that the rain would not continue and that it would even clear up. I was much impressed with this optimistic view since there were no obvious signs of a change in weather. But within an hour the rain stopped and the evening turned out to be clear and cool. My interpreter drew my attention to this fact and there is no doubt that the change was attributed to the beneficence of *pinèsï* in the minds of the Indians. But it will be noted that in this case there were no overt acts involved. But the clue to the sentiments involved was expressed in the remark of the wife of Angus and his reply. Angus had "faith."

This inward appeal to *pinèsï* in connection with the *wabanówïwin* cannot be thoroughly understood without reference to the fact that *pinèsï* is intrinsically connected with the ceremony itself and receives plastic representation as well. In the *wabanó* pavilion at Pauingassi a roughly carved and extremely generalized avian figure painted green topped the posts erected opposite each of the four doors. Inside, the two center posts also upheld *pinèsï* figures, the one towards the west being considerably smaller in size than the eastern figure. And on the small drum which hung from the roof pole during the ceremonies a device was painted in blue which contained two *pinèsïwak* facing each other.

In John Duck's *wabanówigamik* at [Little] Grand Rapids I also observed carved bird-like figurines, also painted green, upon the top of each of the four posts opposite the doors.[14] When Asagesi [at Little Duck (Barton) Lake] opens his tent a *pinèsï* figure is placed on the pole on the south side of the tent. Afterwards it is taken down. This pole (symbolically) reaches straight up to the sky.[15]

A further search into the iconography of *pinèsï* leads us to the bark records of the *midéwiwin* on which very simply drawn outlines of bird-like figures appear. I was also told that a wooden figure of a bird[16] was sometimes placed on one of the posts in the *midéwiwigamik* during the progress of the ritual.

The conjuring lodge is sometimes called *pinèsï*'s house although I understand that *pinèsï* as such is not usually, if ever, heard in the tent. A further connection of *pinèsï* with ceremonial organization is to be noted in the case of the *potáte* dance [*boodaade*, literally, "something is blown," a reference to the gift or breath of life]. In this case the Thunder Bird is the spiritual "owner" or "boss" of the dance. This dance was introduced on the Pigeon River about 30–40 years ago and was bought from a Long Plains Saulteaux. It is said to be an adaptation of the give-away dance of the Plains. It may be significant that the name of the man from whom the dance was bought was *Nīskatwewïtang* [Niiskaadwe-widang], "when he calls it rains." The reference here is to *pinèsï*.[17]

This brings us, finally, to the subject of personal names. A large proportion of these have reference to *pinèsï*. Since these names originated in dream experiences of the namer and consequently the specific context from which they sprang is unknown, and also because the references to the Thunder Bird are often extremely vague and veiled, rather than specifically expressed it is only possible to cite those examples which are commonly understood to contain such a reference. Here are a few examples:

Waskeändjɑbis / Bald Head
Pïmänɑkwɛp / The One That Sits on the Long Narrow Cloud
Kepekïzïkweäs / Sailing Through the Sky From End to End Forever
Nawigïzɑkwɛp / Sitting in the Middle of the Sky
Pawanɑgwebïk / Somebody You Can See Behind a Cloud
Mizäkïäsïk / Hits Ground When Flying
Tetcakamäs / The One That Sails Straight From Point to Point
Aïtɑbï'tɑnk / The One That Sits Firmly
Abïtanɑkwɛp / One Sitting on Cloud From End to End of the Sky
Kɑtebweyasïk / Something Sounding in the Sky

Sekanɑkwébinεs / Touching the Clouds Above While Standing
  Straight Up
Eguidänɑkwïäs / Counting the Clouds While Sailing
Nanákaweweyäs / Making Different Sounds While Flying
Pinesïwas / Thunder Bird Woman
Pεmɑgïzïkwewɑtɑnk / The One That Calls in the Sky
Nïbïtceasïk / Passes Everything Between Earth and Sky
Nawekïzïkwεp / Sitting in the Middle of the Sky
Mízakï / The Thing That Comes down from Above (like a bird
  swooping down)
Kapīmoiweäs / You Can Hear the Sound When He Passes

Notes

Preface

1 The works in question are *Black Elk Speaks, Being the Life Story of a Holy Man of the Oglala Sioux, as Told to John G. Neihardt* (1932), and Raymond J. DeMallie, *The Sixth Grandfather: Black Elk's Teachings Given to John G. Neihardt* (1984). Both books have been reprinted several times.

2 See Clifton, ed., 1989, ix; and Brown's chapter therein, 1989, 204–25.

3 See for example, Brown in Hallowell 1992; the introductions by various former colleagues of Hallowell to his articles collected in Hallowell 1976 (five of these are reprinted in Hallowell, in press); and the biographical memoir by Anthony F.C. Wallace (1980).

4 Stocking 2004, 226.

5 Stocking, 222–6. Hallowell told interviewer Anne Roe in 1950 that his strenuous work pace in the 1930s was in good part "compensatory" for marital and family troubles (Stocking, 222). The two murders of policemen that his son, William, committed in April 1947 may also have kept Hallowell from a last

visit to Berens River. In January of that year, Chief Berens sent a letter to Hallowell expressing hopes of seeing him again that summer, but by the early fall Hallowell was attending the first of his son's two trials for murder in Philadelphia (Stocking, 222). William Berens died in August 1947 and Hallowell never returned to Manitoba.

6 Stocking 2004, 246, 243.

7 Stocking 2004, 252, 243–4.

8 Stocking 2004, 240–4, 246–9, 252.

9 Ingold 2000, 90–1, 109.

10 Darnell 2001, 241, 244, 246.

11 Harvey 2006, xxii; see also his citations of the work of Kenneth Morrison and Theresa Smith, who have drawn on Hallowell's work, and his discussion of Hallowell in chapter 1, "From Primitives to Persons."

12 Hallowell 1992, 108–9; fig. 23 (p. 24, this volume) is Hallowell's photograph of the house, which burned down around 1990.

13 Stephen T. and JoAn Boggs, e-mail, 28 January 2008. See Hallowell 1992, 10, fig. 4, for a photograph of Bittern with Hallowell and Berens at Little Grand Rapids.

14 In the summer of 1966, Selwyn Dewdney traveled along the Berens River, researching rock art and *Midewiwin* scrolls. He wrote to Hallowell on 22 May 1967, "You are well remembered throughout the area you covered, and apparently are still expected to return, for I was flattered by one Saultaux woman's insistence that *I* was the "*Mide-oogemah* from the States!" In the early 1990s, Jennifer Brown and Maureen Matthews found that elders at Pauingassi and Little Grand Rapids still remembered Hallowell by that name.

15 Antoine Bittern, 17 November 1992, Margaret Simmons translating, Fisher River, MB, personal care home. Conversation with Jennifer Brown and Maureen Matthews, recorded and transcribed by Matthews. Bittern died on 1 May 1993, aged ninety-six, in Winnipeg.

16 Gordon Berens, 17 November 1992, Fisher River, MB, personal care home. Conversation with Jennifer Brown and Maureen Matthews, recorded and transcribed by Matthews. Berens died on 7 April 1993, aged eighty-two, in Winnipeg.

17 Percy Berens to Jennifer Brown and Maureen Matthews, October 1992, Berens River, notes by Jennifer Brown.

18 Percy Berens to Jennifer Brown and Susan Gray, 27 November 1994, Winnipeg, notes by Jennifer Brown. In August 2007, he told Maureen Matthews that his father never talked to him about the *Memengwesiwag*; he never heard the story William Berens told in III, 7, this volume (Berens 2007).

19 Percy Berens to Susan Gray and David McCrady, 8 March 2008, Fisher River, notes by David McCrady.

Part I

1 Hallowell 1992, 4; field notebook, 1930.

2 Hallowell, field notebook, 16–21 August 1930.

3 Hallowell 1992, 8.

4 Ojibwe or Anishinaabeg ("people" or "real people") are the ethnonyms preferred by many of the people themselves. Some still use the term Saulteaux, a French name derived from Sault Ste Marie, the great rapids between lakes Superior and Huron where the French first met the Ojibwe, "people of the rapids," in the 1640s. Hallowell alternated between using "Ojibwa" and "Saulteaux." Ojibwe spelled with a final "e" rather than with "-a" or "-ay" elicits the most correct pronunciation of the word. The term "Chippewa," which derives from the same root as "Ojibwe," is commonly used in the United States. For a comprehensive synonymy of the terms by which the people have been known, see Pentland 1981, 254–5.

5 For a full listing of the Hallowell papers housed at the American Philosophical Society Library in Philadelphia, see: http://www.amphilsoc.org/library/mole/h/hallowel.xml

6 Hallowell 1967 [1955], 253–4, "Fear and Anxiety," reprinted in Hallowell, in press. The taboo on myths in summer was quite widespread. Thomas Vennum writes that the Menominee of Wisconsin told such stories in winter "because the snakes and toads were dormant" and hence "could not overhear the people talking about them, become offended, and somehow 'get even' by causing some misfortune to the storyteller once the weather improved. In Indian belief, to get even, a toad would jump on you in your sleep and cause welts on your body." Vennum 2007, 110.

7 The first quote comes from Hallowell 1992, 4. The second is from his dedica-

tion to Berens of his monograph *The Role of Conjuring in Saulteaux Society*, 1971 [1942], xii.

8 William's birth at Berens River on 7 June 1866 was noted in the Berens River post journal of that date: "Today Mary Burence [Berens] was delivered of a son." HBCA B.16/a/7, fo. 23d.

9 Hallowell 1992, 11, 22–4; 1967 [1955], 118; Bishop 1981, 160. See also Peers 1994. "Yellow Legs" is the literal translation of Ozaawashkogaad; the meaning behind the name has not been explained. On naming, see note 13.

10 Hallowell 1992, 10; see also Part III, 5, "The Medicine Stone," this volume.

11 See Thistle 1986, 69, on the arrival of "Bungee Indians" in the Cumberland House region in the 1780s and 1790s. HBC traders usually used the term Bungee in reference to Ojibwe people. Thistle speculated that as used around Cumberland House the term may refer to Swampy Cree, but Berens family memories and other clues suggest that some Ojibwe people did reach that area in that period. Amo was said to be aged eighty or ninety when she died.

12 Hallowell 1992, 10–11. Hallowell spelled the name "Cauwanas," following his usual transcription practice, but "Souwanas" was the spelling used in the books of E.R. Young and, with some variations, in the Berens River post journals. Thanks to John Nichols for recommending the orthography Zhaawanaash. The accent falls on the first syllable.

13 In a page of notes on the Berens genealogy, Hallowell recorded that at William's naming feast he was kissed first by Bear, then by his grandmother, and then by everyone in the *zhaaboondawaan* or long lodge where the ceremony was held (Research, kinship terms and relations). In an unpublished manuscript on Ojibwe views of disease, Hallowell said that when William's grandfather named him, he forbad him "to eat the flesh of birds with hawk-like claws," possibly because of their associations with Thunder Birds. William obeyed that rule "for fear that he might get sick and die" if he did not (noted also in Hallowell 1976, 425). The giving of a personal name "refers to something that happened in the dream experience of the namer ... [and] may sometimes solemnly impose an obligation upon the person named" (Hallowell, unpublished typescript on disease causation, n.d., 12–13). Names that invoked Thunder Birds held great power.

14 Hallowell 1992, 23, map 2.

15 Berens, 42, this volume. The last reference to Bear in the Berens River post

journals appears on 16 October 1873: "The old Bear came from the fishery." On 13 February 1874, the journal reported, "Buried an old Indian today that died here" (HBCA B.16/a/7, fos. 24, 27). This entry could refer to Bear. As of 1875, his brother Zhaawanaash was acting as the local chief (Brown, 2008).

16 For discussion of the name Berens as applied to the river and to the family, see Brown's note in Hallowell 1992, 14–15, n. 2.

17 Gray 2006, 79–80.

18 Rogers and Black Rogers 1978.

19 Thanks to Roger Roulette for the transcription and translation of Jacob Berens's Ojibwe name (e-mail, 26 Jan. 2008). John Maclean 1918, 124–5; Hallowell 1992, 28; Brown 1998.

20 Hallowell 1992, chapter 1, and 13n8 on the McKay family; and 25 (on tea). William McKay family dates derive from Pat McCloy (McKay "table") whose papers are now in the Glenbow Archives, Calgary (copies supplied by Mary Black Rogers).

21 Brown 1980.

22 Berens, "Reminiscences," 42, this volume.

23 Hallowell in the late 1930s drew a different conclusion, stating that Berens did exhibit signs of psychological conflict, although his later writings de-emphasized the psychological. For examples, see Hallowell 1938, and 1967 [1955], 260 ("Fear and Anxiety," a reprint of a second 1938 article,) both reprinted in Hallowell, in press.

24 Berens, "Reminiscences," 42, this volume. The comment typifies the intellectual openness and curiosity that Jacob Berens evidently inculcated in his son.

25 Brown 1987a; Brown 2008.

26 Berens, "Reminiscences," 44, this volume.

27 Morris 1880, 346.

28 The best known instance early in his chiefly career was in the winter of 1876–77, when he successfully prevented the sons of a woman who had turned "*windigo*" from being charged with her execution, explaining the power of Native belief and arguing to HBC officer Roderick Ross, who was serving as justice of the peace, that they did not understand Christian ways. Gray 2006, 66.

29 Dueck [Gray] 1986.

30 Berens, "Reminiscences," 45, this volume.

31 The Berens River post journals from HBCA B.16/a/5 onward contain numerous references to Jacob Berens's carrying mail ("the packet") and other activities.

32 Hewson 1960, 625–39.

33 Berens, "Reminiscences," 52–3, this volume. The Berens River post journal of 1887–88 mentions William Berens bringing in furs from other communities, transporting supplies, and mending nets (HBCA B.16/a/10).

34 The Berens River post journal recorded on 30 July 1888, "Berens retired from service." On 18 August the survey party under "Mr. Ponton" started upriver; they arrived back at the post on 20 September (HBCA B.16/a/10, fos. 56, 57d). Later entries in the same journal indicate that William Berens returned to his post duties that fall.

35 Hallowell 1967 [1955], 97–8.

36 Schultz 1987 [1890], "Notes on Indian Council at Treaty Rock, Berens River, Lake Winnipeg, Man. 12th July 1890."

37 Hallowell, Berens, Boucher, and Everett genealogies.

38 Berens, "Reminiscences," 63, this volume. For more on McColl, see McColl 1989.

39 Berens, "Reminiscences," 69, this volume.

40 Maurice Berens 1985, 3–4. Maurice Berens's father, John (William's youngest son), was an important source for his paper.

41 Percy E. Jones 1917, 299–300.

42 Berens 1985, 7–9.

43 Berens 1985, 10–12.

44 Berens 1985, 13–14.

45 Dueck [Gray] 1986, 94–6.

46 Hallowell 1992, 2, 4.

47 Hallowell 1992, 6–9. The links across four generations are evoked by the Ojibwe reciprocal term for great-grandparent and great-grandchild, *aanikoobijigan* (Nichols and Nyholm 1995). *Aanikoo-* in its various compounds refers to joining one thing to another, "knots in a string," as some Ojibwe and Cree-speakers express the relationship in English. (The parallel Cree term is *aaniskotaapaan*.) This distinctive word appears to mark the four-generation connection as special, as indeed it was for William Berens.

48 Lytwyn 1986.

49 William Berens to Hallowell, 11 July 1935, page "N."

50 Hallowell 1938, 47–8, reprinted in Hallowell, in press. In the late 1930s and early 1940s, Hallowell was much interested in psychological interpretations and in the use of such research tools as Rorschach tests in fieldwork; his later writings shifted from that emphasis.

51 Black-Rogers 1985.

52 Manson 1986, 78–9.

53 Hallowell 1938, 48.

54 Hallowell 1976, 467 ("The Role of Dreams in Ojibwa Culture," reprinted in Hallowell, in press).

55 Berens 1985, 15.

56 Berens 1985, 16–17.

57 *Winnipeg Tribune,* Obituary of Chief William Berens, 2 September 1947.

58 Boulanger 1971, 39.

59 Berens 1985, 18.

Part II

1 William was born on 7 June 1866; see Part I, note 8. In 1869, without consultation with the inhabitants, the old Hudson's Bay Company territory known as Rupert's Land was sold to Great Britain for transfer to Canada. Riel and the Metis, with wide support in the Red River Settlement (now Winnipeg), resisted this arbitrary move, established a provisional government, and achieved provincial status for Manitoba in May 1870.

2 The HBC post where Berens was working was almost certainly the lesser-known Eagle Nest on Eagle Lake, 75 miles east of Rat Portage (Kenora), which sometimes served as an outpost for White Dog (which was not in operation in 1869–79). In any case, Jacob Berens and family were undoubtedly not living at the post but in their own dwelling, likely a cabin to judge by the reference to a house and logs. William Berens told Hallowell on another occasion that while Jacob was working for the company, they were living at White Dog Falls, where Jacob was welcomed among his Moose clan relatives: "The Moose people did a lot for him, gave him food, etc." (Hallowell Papers, Series V, research notes, sibs, totems).

3 William Sinclair was evidently a free trader competing with the HBC men

that winter. He was probably the William Sinclair Jr. who had been a HBC clerk at Eagle Nest in 1866–68 (HBCA, post descriptions); he seems unrelated to the better known family of Chief Factor William Sinclair (d. 1818). The Hudson's Bay Company Archives have compiled an alphabetical series of "Biographical Sheets" for many (not all) HBC employees, and these help to identify numerous HBC men mentioned by William Berens; see http://www.gov.mb.ca/chc/archives/hbca/biographical/index.html. In the annotations that follow, biographies in this source are cited as "(name), HBCA biographical sheet, 2008."

4 William's older sister Julia was baptized at St Peter's church (Anglican) on the lower Red River in July (no date given), 1864. Her father, Jacob Berens, was listed as a servant of the Hudson's Bay Company. Archives of the Diocese of Rupert's Land, Reg. #1, OW G728 (Dynevor), MB. William's memory of pursuit by horned cattle parallels a recurring dream that he recounted to Hallowell (see Part III, 6).

5 Schultz and Bown were strong opponents of Riel in the troubles of 1869–70 and fled Red River to avoid capture. Bown left Red River sometime in December 1869 and Schultz on 21 February 1870. This account indicates that they met and briefly lodged with the Berens family. Schultz travelled on to Toronto and Ottawa via Duluth, MN, reaching Toronto on 6 April. On Schultz, see Clark 1990; on Bown, see Mochoruk on Bown 1994; also W.L. Morton, ed., *Alexander Begg's Red River Journal*, 1956, 250, 296, 363. Annie McEwan in her memoir "Four Years at Berens River" recalled that in 1906–07 Chief Jacob Berens lived nearby. Doug McEwan, her husband, who was working at the fish hatchery there, enjoyed his company. One day he told them about "he and his wife having Dr. S[c]hultz and Dr. Bowen [Bown] stay with them at Fort Alexander. Dr. Schultz for a few days, till he could get a driver and dogs to hurry him away from Riel's men. He had escaped from Fort Garry. Dr. Bowen stayed [at Eagle Nest?] all the winter." AM, A.E. McEwan Papers, MG8 B52. (Bown was a dentist and businessman but not a doctor. Jacob Berens may have mentioned Fort Alexander as being well known; Eagle Nest [and White Dog] were small outposts of this important centre.)

6 An associate of Schultz, George Duncan MacVicar, who had been captured by and escaped from Riel, wrote to his fiancée Josephine Larwell (5 February 1870) that he took refuge at the home of Joseph Monkman, "a fine old

English Half-Breed." AM, MacVicar Papers, MG3 B9, item 6, 16–19. Joseph
Monkman (ca. 1810–1899) was the son of HBC trader James Monkman and
his Cree wife Mary Muskegon and had a varied career. His obituary in the
Winnipeg Telegram, 9 June 1899, and family memories tell of his taking
Schultz to Duluth via Fort Alexander and the Winnipeg River. One time
when Schultz was exhausted and begged for shelter, Monkman found "an
Indian's hut" nearby. Schultz was fearful that it might belong to "a French
half-breed" but Monkman reassured him: "I have not seen the house, but
I can smell the Indian smoke of the willow bark. If the house belonged to a
Frenchman I would smell tobacco" (Monkman 2000, 5–7). Was this the
Berens house? The story is certainly suggestive.

7 See Hallowell 1935, 302–4, "Notes on the Northern Range of Zizania [wild
rice] in Manitoba," reprinted in Hallowell, in press. William Berens told Hallowell that wild rice grew in numerous small lakes and creeks in his hunting
grounds; in 1933, there was enough to feed "three or four battalions of men."
Hallowell noted that this information refuted earlier claims that wild rice in
the region grew no farther north than about 50 degrees north latitude (i.e.,
southern Manitoba). Later work has shown that in the 1800s the Ojibwe
actively expanded the range of wild rice to the north and west of its western
Great Lakes "homeland"; their sowing and encouragement of the crop in
new areas belie the term, "wild" (Moodie 1991).

8 Caribou flourish in old-growth forests and landscapes that have not been
burned over in a long time. See L. Wilkinson and J.T. Fisher, 2005; thanks to
Michael Sanders for this reference. Moose seemed prominent in the area in
later years. A great forest fire that raged along the Berens River in the summer of 1889 (report of Angus McKay cited in Gray 2006, 5) may have been
a factor in the transition.

9 This game was widely played. Frances Densmore described it from her work
with Chippewa people in northern Minnesota. Boys would stand in a row
and each throw their sticks, carved with an upturned tip or with the head of
a snake, through soft snow or across crusted snow, and then run to retrieve
their sticks and see whose had been thrown the farthest (Densmore 1979
[1929], 68; plate 25d).

10 The sturgeon fisheries from the Great Lakes to Lake Winnipeg were immensely productive before the commercial overfishing of the 1880s and

1890s almost destroyed them. For an exemplary study of their collapse, see Holzkamm, Lytwyn, and Waisberg 1991, 119–39.

11 The ring and pin game was widely played; see http://www.nativetech.org/ games/ring&pin.html accessed 15 Feb. 2008. A ring, commonly of bone or hide, was attached to a cord, the other end of which was fastened to a bone or metal "pin" or awl. The ring was thrown upward and the object was to spear it with the pin. The moccasin game was a game of chance. In the Minnesota Chippewa version, male players would hide four bullets, one marked and the others unmarked, under moccasins. Their opponents guessed the location of the marked bullet, while others watched, made wagers, and sang and drummed (Densmore 1979 [1929], 114–15).

12 William's maternal grandfather, William McKay (ca. 1795–1887), was the son of Donald McKay (Scottish) and a woman of Cree-Scottish descent, Hannah Sutherland, and was in charge at the Berens River HBC post 1856–59 and 1862–71, then left HBC service (Hallowell, 1992, 11, 13n8; HBC biographical sheet, William McKay 'a'). McKay married Julie (Julia), daughter of Joseph Chalifoux at Norway House on 13 August 1826. Pat McCloy, McKay genealogical table (original in Glenbow Archives, Calgary), copy provided by Mary Black Rogers.

13 Hallowell spelled this surname "MacKaye"; we have standardized it to McKay as spelled in fur trade documents. William McKay 'e' (his HBC designation to distinguish him from others of that name) was an interpreter and postmaster at Trout Lake, 1843–65, and then post master in charge at Little Grand Rapids, 1865–71 (HBCA biographical sheet). Travel from the mouth of the Berens River to Little Grand Rapids involved traversing about forty rapids and portages. The place was early known as Big Fall or Great Falls; "Little" was added later to distinguish it from (Big) Grand Rapids on the west side of Lake Winnipeg.

14 Mary McKay's marriage to Chief Jacob Berens and her brother William's marriage to Betsey (Elisabeth), daughter of Cuthbert Grant, Jr., linked families that reached across the spectrum of Rupert's Land society. Grant was the Metis leader who stirred strong feelings for his role in Metis and North West Company opposition to the Hudson's Bay Company-supported Red River Settlement, 1812–21, and in the Battle of Seven Oaks in June 1816 (see also the

story referring to him in Part III, 85). Of Presbyterian background, he converted to Roman Catholicism through marriage. Later appointed "Warden of the Plains" in Red River, he associated mainly with Metis traders and buffalo hunters of French and Canadian ancestry. In August 1849, James Hargrave at York Factory wrote to Grant noting that his Trout Lake interpreter McKay and Elisabeth had formed an attachment, and proposed to facilitate their marriage, which took place in St. Boniface in 1853 (MacLeod and Morton 1974 [1963], 89, 101, 139–41). Hallowell's manuscript here footnoted Berens on the children of William and Betsey McKay: "His eldest boy was Donald, the second Cuthbert, who used to be a minister at St. John's [Cathedral, Winnipeg?]. He had a girl named Sara who married a man by the name of Stout. There was another girl Mary and a boy Alexander who was my playmate. The youngest boy was John Charles."

15　The "first log house erected by an Indian" stood on a point on the north side of the river's estuary (Hallowell 1992, 34, map 3). Hallowell was told, doubtless by Berens, that Cauwαnäs [Zhaawanaash] built it in about 1873. By 1883, the Indian agent reported thirty-three log houses in the settlement (Hallowell, "Pigeon River People," chapter 4, "Housing," 1–2). Zhaawanaash was Jacob Berens's uncle, and the brother of Bear. After Bear died, he was the headman (traditional chief) at Berens River until Jacob Berens became the first treaty chief in 1875. The "MacDonald" who had the other log house nearby was almost certainly Zhaawanaash's son, who took the English name Jim Macdonald; he was close to ninety when he met Hallowell in 1934 (Hallowell 1992, 24). The genealogy is complex as family members adopted different English surnames. Zhaawanaash was baptized Roderick Ross in 1877, but his sons took various surnames: Ross, Felix, and MacDonald (Hallowell 1992, 13); the surname Sawanas(h), variously spelled, also endures at Berens River. Frederick Leach (1973, 12) wrote that on the first list of treaty Indians (1875) at Berens River, MacDonald was the only English name (perhaps he saw Berens as an Ojibwe name).

16　The missionary was Egerton R. Young, who had served at the Methodist mission at Rossville, Norway House, MB, from 1868 to 1873. In summer 1873, he sent his trusted Rossville interpreter, Timothy Bear, to prepare the ground for establishing a mission; see Young 1907, 204–6. The Norway House builders were "Big Tom" Mamanowatum and Martin Papanekis. Both were

Rossville Crees mentioned frequently in Young's writings. Young and several men worked on cutting, squaring, and hauling timber with thirty-two dogs across the ice for the church, schoolhouse, and parsonage (Young 1890, 259–60).

17 The flat-roofed house that Berens recalled may have been the first house that the Youngs and their two children occupied when Young's family joined him in late summer 1874. Young wrote that "its construction was peculiar" and "it failed us most signally in times of rain and wet." The roof was of poplar logs covered thickly with mud and one night huge chunks of mud fell on the children's beds (Young 1890, 262–3). It was probably sloped, shanty-style, with no peak or gable.

18 Hallowell was told that Bear's father, Yellow Legs, had lived on the west side of Lake Winnipeg. The family later moved to Berens River and Bear was the first to take the surname Berens. Bear and his brother, Zhaawanaash, carried on the *Midewiwin* or Grand Medicine ceremony until Bear's death, probably in 1873 (Hallowell 1992, 11–15). William Berens never knew his great-grandfather but his wife, Mistamut, lived long enough to pass on stories about earlier times (see, e.g., Hallowell 1992, 24–5).

19 For many people treaty payments and annuities were the first money they had handled, supplanting the older barter trade. Traders gravitated to treaty sites to sell goods for the cash that was being handed out.

20 Alexander Morris and James McKay arrived at Berens River on the first HBC steamer, the *Colvile* on the morning of 20 September 1875 to conduct the negotiations for Treaty 5. They needed a pilot, "as no steamer had ever before entered the river" (Morris 1880, 147).

21 On Morris and McKay, see Friesen 1982, 608–14; and Turner 1972, 473–5 respectively. The "Indian Agent" would be Thomas Howard who, Morris wrote, "accompanied me as Secretary and Pay Master" (1880, 147). Morris's daughters, Christine and E.C. Morris, signed the treaty as witnesses, as did E.R. Young and his wife Elizabeth, and William McKay, Jacob Berens's father-in-law. Berens signed as the new chief.

22 Morris wrote that the treaty was signed about 11 pm, after some difficulty over the question of reserves. Payments of treaty presents of $5 per person then began and were finished at about 1 am (Morris 1880, 147). The coming of steam transport and commercial fishing, and finds of valuable minerals

and timber in the vicinity of Lake Winnipeg increased the pressures for treaties in the area. David Laird, minister of the Interior, wrote of good land for agriculture on the west shore and added, "with pending Pacific Railway construction west of the Lake ... the Lake and the Saskatchewan River are destined to become the principal thoroughfare of communication between Manitoba and the fertile prairies in the West" (Gray 2006, 3).

23 Earlier, Berens referred to his grandfather (Bear) as "headman." In Ojibwe, he would doubtless have used the term *ogimaa*. Hallowell learned from Berens the term, *atawágani ogimakan* [*adaawaagani-ogimaakaan*] for fur or barter chief (1992, 27n9); this term carries the suffix, *-kan* (*-gan*), which signifies artificial or made-up. Similarly, Ojibwe people style treaty or "Indian Affairs" chiefs as *ogimaaganag*, made-up chiefs. Bear, and Zhaawanaash after Bear's death and before the treaty was signed, were *ogimaag*, real chiefs, or headmen in Berens's usage. Jacob Berens defeated a rival, Peter Stoney, a powerful medicine man from Bloodvein River to the south (Hallowell 1992, 36; see also 1976, 432 ["Ojibwa World View and Disease"] on a subsequent illness that Jacob attributed to Stoney). Morris did not mention a rival claimant, but would have fostered an elective process. Jacob Berens was the son, nephew, and grandson of previous local headmen; consensus would have favoured him, as it later favoured his son William after Jacob died in 1916.

24 Morris wrote that on 4 August 1876, Thomas Howard and J. Lestock Reid, commissioners, met at the Berens River schoolhouse with about thirty Indians "from the Grand Rapids of Berens River" who were "most anxious to accept the Queen's bounty and benevolence." They asked that their "head man," Num-ak-ow-ah-nuk-wape, be recognized as chief, but the commissioners "ultimately prevailed upon them" to accept Jacob Berens as their chief and to "make their head man a Councillor to him." This saved the expense, as they noted, of paying a further chief and two councillors (Morris 1880, 157–8).

25 Semmens from his base at Berens River also visited Little Grand Rapids, Poplar River, Pikangikum (ON), and Fisher River. At Berens River, he held services in the new church and taught in the Methodist day school. He wrote that his congregation of about twenty-five was comprised of well-dressed, orderly people but regretted that the "material ... was so crude." He found

the Ojibwe hard and "full of the viciousness of their heathen ways." Semmens was transferred from Berens River in 1878. He served as Indian agent at Berens River from 1901 to 1903 (Gray 2005, 917).

26 From 1878 to 1884, Berens River had no resident missionary; the Rev. Andrew Ross visited intermittently from Fisher River, across Lake Winnipeg. In 1880–81, William Hope, a Methodist appointee, taught the school. The Rev. Enos Langford served the mission from 1884 to 1888 (Gray 2006, 8, 69).

27 Berens River parents complained frequently in the 1880s about the school. In his 1881 report, Inspector Ebenezer McColl wrote that the children were "very backward" and showed no improvement since his last visit. "The whole band complains of the inefficiency of the Mission school and asks for a Government school. The chief [Jacob Berens] stated that he valued his religion and loved his minister, but that he never yet knew of an instance where any of his people were educated at the Mission schools, as only the most inferior teachers were invariably employed." Report of E. McColl, Inspector of Indian Agencies, 1881, Canada, *Sessional Papers*, 1882, vol. 15, no. 5, 107. In his 1885 report, Indian agent Angus McKay wrote, "the Methodist mission school at Berens River…under the management of Miss Gussie Parkinson [Langford's sister-in-law], has been a complete failure" (Canada, *Sessional Papers*, 1886, vol. 19, no. 4, 67). The same year, McKay wrote to McColl that the mission school was "poorly attended because most parents [wanted] a government school instead." The students included "Willie and Jacob Berens," aged about seventeen and fifteen, who were "reading in the 1st book." The boys wrote and spelled very badly. NAC, RG10, vol. 3715, file 21, 257, Berens River, 25 March 1885, reel C11063.

28 This was probably around Christmas of 1877. McColl was appointed inspector of Indian Agencies and Accounts in the Manitoba Superintendency in the fall of 1877 after his predecessor, J.A.N. Provencher, was dismissed for fraud (McColl 1989, 48). Hallowell in a note identified Mr Clark as William Palmer Clarke. William Clark was a junior chief trader 1875–80 and was in charge of the Manitoba District (HBCA, biographical sheets).

29 James Settee Jr., son of Cree Anglican clergyman James Settee, opened that school in about 1877. On a school for Jack Head, see NAC, RG10, vol. 3617, file 4641, microfilm reel C-10107, J.A.N. Provencher to Minister of the Interior,

Winnipeg, 22 March 1875. Egerton R. Young, while based at Norway House, had visited Jack Head and reported that the Indians there wanted a school. He estimated that about forty children would attend.

30 This is Berens's first reference to his family growing potatoes. The plant had arrived in the southern Manitoba region by the 1820s in the context of the fur trade. Native potato growing was well established between lakes Winnipeg and Manitoba (and probably elsewhere) by the 1850s (Moodie and Kaye, 1986).

31 The name Zhaawanaash, variously spelled, appeared in the HBC Berens River account books through 1882 (B.6/d/7). As the Rev. A.W. Ross reported from Fisher River in 1883 (xxix) that "our oldest member … Sowanas" died at Berens River the previous winter, the winter described in the above text must be that of 1882–83. The reminiscences say almost nothing about Berens's precise activities between 1878 and 1886, and some events may be conflated here or not in chronological order, e.g., the smallpox mentioned in the next paragraph.

32 The Icelanders reached the west side of Lake Winnipeg in summer 1875 and settled in an area where Indian treaty terms had not yet been negotiated. They were hit by smallpox in the winter of 1876–77, but their Ojibwe neighbours around Sandy Bar, already troubled by their displacement, suffered still more severely. See Brydon 2001, 164–90.

33 The Berens River HBC journal of 28 December 1876 noted the arrival of John Lambert with the Red River packet on his way to Norway House (HBCA B.16/a/8, fo. 17). On 14 March 1877, Berens River HBC clerk James Flett wrote that he "went to Jacob Berens tent to vaccinate some of them there." On 4 April 1877, "four [dog] trains of quarantine men arrived" at Berens River; two stayed there and the rest went to other posts (B.16/a/8, fos. 19d, 20d).

34 The first commercial fisheries opened on Lake Winnipeg in 1883, and in the beginning everyone seemed to benefit from the boom. William Berens and many others found new summer jobs while continuing to trap with their families in winter. Indian agent Angus McKay reported in 1887 that at Berens River, with the exception of illness from an epidemic that year, both the hunting and fishing had been excellent (Gray 2006, 4–5). By 1890, however, Aboriginal people had seen rapid depletions of whitefish and sturgeon. At a

council held at Berens River on 12 July 1890, Chief Jacob Berens addressed Lieutenant Governor of Manitoba John Christian Schultz strongly on the issue but to little effect, as noted in Part I. See Schultz 1987 [1890].

35 Fred W. Wilkins, dominion land surveyor, arrived in May 1886 to survey Lake Winnipeg, using a micrometer and a transit theodolite (a surveying instrument for measuring horizontal and vertical angles). The "target" would be the stadia or rod that was held vertically at a set distance for sightings from the theodolite. The position of islands was determined by angles taken from stations on the shore. Wilkins had funds to hire four labourers at $1.25 per day apiece plus 50 cents daily for rations. He completed the survey by November. AM, Department of Interior, 1886, Survey Administration Files, GR289, Field Books, box G402, file 55.

36 The Winnipeg firm Carscaden and Peck was described as dealing "in clothing, furnishing goods, hats, caps, and buffalo robes." It did well in the 1880s but disappeared by 1900. Rostecki, 1972–73.

37 Frank C. Dickson was a Hudson's Bay Company clerk in 1889–93 (HBCA, biographical sheet); possibly if this was the same man, he had another employer before he joined the HBC. Willie Cochran, Simpson, Stevenson, and Foster have not been identified.

38 This would be the summer of 1886. The HBCA biographical sheet for James Flett (B) states that he left Berens River for the Red River District in 1885, but the post journal for summer 1885 shows no break and mentions no transition. There is a break in the journals, however, between 23 July 1886 (B.6/a/9) and 1 November 1887 (B. 16/a 10). Flett was from Birsay, Orkney, and entered HBC service in 1846 as a labourer; from 1854 to 1871 he served at Norway House where he rose to the rank of clerk. He had been at Berens River since 1873.

39 Joe Boucher was likely Joseph Bouchez who served the HBC in various canoe positions and as fisherman, carpenter, etc., in the Norway House district, 1852–72, and then went free. William Everett or Everette, born at Trout Lake (ON), served the company, 1865–86, as labourer, fisherman, storekeeper, etc., in the Norway House and Red River districts, and went free in 1886 (HBCA, biographical sheets). He was the father of Nancy, whom William Berens married in 1899.

40 The name Banfield appears in the Berens River post journal for 27 May 1886,

which noted the arrival from Selkirk of Banfield's schooner with a party of "surveyors" who were going upriver (HBCA B. 16/a/9, fo. 32d). They were geologist A.P. Low and botanist J.M. Macoun. See Low 1887, 5F–16F.

41 Kathleen Monkman wrote of a "John Thomas who built the first house on the island at Loon Straits" on the east side of Lake Winnipeg. Because he raised numerous dogs, he "became known as John Doggie, the name that he became known by permanently." He soon sold the house to Andrew Monkman (son of Joseph) and moved to Matheson Island (2000, 9).

42 This is Berens's first mention of Frederick Augustus Disbrowe (1852–1943), whom he later knew well. Disbrowe, born in England, joined the Hudson's Bay Company in 1903 as a clerk and served at Berens River from 1903 to 1923 (HBCA biographical sheet). He had served on the Canadian side in the Northwest Rebellion shortly after his arrival in Canada. After he left his job as a clerk with the fish company, he became one of the first teachers in the Indian school at Poplar River, up the east coast of Lake Winnipeg. Leach, 1973, 35. The Berens River journal (HBCA B. 16/a/10, fo. 58) mentioned "F.A. Disbrowe school teacher Poplar River" visiting on 1–2 October 1888.

43 As no Berens River journal appears to survive from summer 1886 through October 1887, these activities are not on record. The HBCA Index of Servants' Engagement Registers 1866–1893 (B. 239/u/3 #184) lists William Berens as interpreter, staring on 27 July 1887, but the above description indicates he was casually employed by perhaps March or April, several months earlier. The first entry in B.16/a/10 (fo. 46, 1 November 1887) and numerous later entries make reference to Berens working for the company.

44 "Maud" or "Mod" was Hallowell's effort to transcribe "Moar." John Moar 'A' (senior) was made clerk at Berens River in 1887; he had previously served there for two years as postmaster. In 1888, he was transferred to Little Grand Rapids (HBCA, biographical sheet).

45 A sturgeon pen was also in operation at Berens River when the E.R. Young family was there, 1874–76. E. Ryerson Young in his memoir, "A Missionary and His Son" (typescript, n.d., in possession of J.S.H. Brown), 62, described how the family's helper Kennedy, when supplies ran low, would select a sturgeon in the "fish pond" and "spear it, drag it ashore, and dress it by hanging it tail upwards to the limb of a tree."

46 The Berens River post journal noted the arrival of Mr McLean on 18 June

1888. McLean later chastised William Berens about leaving his HBC job without leave, as mentioned below.

47 On 15 August 1888, surveyor A.W. Ponton arrived at Berens River "on his way to Little Grand Rapid to survey Indian reserve." Three days later, he and his party left on their trip upriver (which also included Pikangikum, some distance beyond). They returned to Berens River on 20 September (HBCA B.16/a/10, fos. 56d, 57d). See also Hallowell 1992, 100.

48 John Moar 'A' Sr. had left Berens River on 26 July 1888 to become HBC clerk at Little Grand Rapids (HBCA B.16/a/10, fo. 55d). He held that position until his retirement after forty-five years of service (1861–1906). His son, J.R. Moar, also served for about fifty years, and J.R. Moar's son served forty-seven years. Leach 1973, 10–11.

49 Sagaski, variously spelled, was a powerful leader and medicine man at Pikangikum. His first marriage was to not only a clan-mate (Sturgeon) but his own sister, following dream instructions from "the master of the beaver" (Hallowell 1967 [1955], 302–3). R.W. Dunning (1959, 112–13) also heard about "Sugguski" or Creeper (d. ca. 1920) during his sojourn at Pikangikum in the early 1950s.

50 For more on the experience of William Berens at and near Pikangikum, see his story in Part III, 94–5.

51 As the HBC was still British, the salary was quoted in pounds. At the exchange rate given, the salary was $162/year, a considerable raise from Berens's previous pay of $125/year. W.J. McLean made a short visit to Berens River on 12 October 1888. Over the following months, William Berens was busy at many jobs: fixing fences, hauling hay, mending nets, hauling fish, making a dog sleigh with his father, and making numerous visits to Indian camps to bring back furs (HBCA B.16/a/10, fo. 58 and following).

52 The Berens River journal recorded on 24 October 1889 that Mr Swain and his family arrived that day from Fisher River. As John Moar had left in July of 1888, it is unclear who was in charge at this point, but the writer noted on 25 October, "Mr. Swain is satisfied that he will not require me any longer as it is getting late in the season" (HBCA B.16/a/10, 70d). The same writer continued making entries until 29 November. A new hand, presumably Swain's, then made two entries, but wrote nothing more after that. There is no HBCA biographical sheet for this man.

53   Alexander S. Barbour (1955–56) cited William Overton as one of several men
     who came from the east with Charles Gauthier who founded the Dominion
     Fish Company in 1882 and became prominent in the fish business.

54   The *Glendevon*, built in 1882, was owned by Charles Gauthier of the Domin-
     ion Fish Company; it burned in 1891. See
     www.mhs.mb.ca/docs/steamboats/index.shtml, "Canadian Prairie Steam-
     boats," accessed 5 December 2007.

55   In his diary entry for 30 January 1901, Angus McKay noted that "Pollock &
     Co." was a branch of the Dominion Fish Company. AM, Nan Shipley Collec-
     tion, McKay Diary, 1901.

56   Donaldson Bogart Dowling of the Geological Survey of Canada was con-
     ducting a survey in the Dauphin River area at the time. His *Report on the
     Geology of the West Shore and Islands of Lake Winnipeg*, submitted in 1899,
     was published in 1900. It described the soils, fisheries, geology and fossils
     of Lake Winnipeg and its islands.

57   Charles Hunt French entered HBC "general service" on Lake Winnipeg in
     1887. From 1891 to 1894, he was a company dog driver, sailor, and fisherman
     based at Lower Fort Garry. Rising from clerk to district manager at various
     posts in British Columbia, he returned to Winnipeg to serve as fur trade
     commissioner from 1927 to 1930 when he retired (HBCA biographical
     sheets). The Pollocks and William Purvis were prominent in the fish business.

58   By 1891, some observers recognized the serious threats posed by overfishing.
     A report by Samuel Wilmot in Canada's parliamentary Sessional Papers that
     year presented the results of a survey of the whitefish fisheries of Lake Win-
     nipeg. Wilmot concluded that "if the improvident system of commercial
     fishing practised by fishing and trading corporations be allowed to prevail
     … the whitefish wealth of the lakes of the North-West will soon become ex-
     hausted." He recommended numerous remedies and restrictions and added,
     "the Indians should have the exclusive right of fishing in their reserves, and
     in all other waters which it may be considered expedient to set apart for
     them. Fish traders or other persons should not be allowed to fish in these
     waters under any pretence whatever" (1891, 62, 61). He may have heard the
     concerns raised by Jacob Berens and others; see Schultz 1987 [1890].

59   The Manitoba Commercial Bank failed in 1893: www.mhs.ca/docs/people/
     brock_jh.shtml, accessed 5 December 2007.

60 This is the surname of a trapper and trader who was often mentioned in
     the Berens River HBC journals in this period, e.g., B.16/a/10.

61 Captain Sandy [Alexander] Vance was active in Lake Winnipeg shipping into
     the 1890s; he ran the fish tug *The Fisherman* in 1893 and was a mate on the
     passenger boat *The City of Selkirk* in 1894.

62 Stefan and Johannes (Steve and Joe) Sigurdson were fishing for pickerel in
     southern Lake Winnipeg in the 1890s (Barbour 1955–56), and family mem-
     bers carried on in the fishing business in later years.

63 If William Berens and Nancy Everett were engaged for three years, the above
     events date to about 1895–96. They were married 16 January 1899. This event
     was foretold to William Berens in a dream he had some years earlier; see
     Part III, 97. The Berens and Everett family trees compiled by Raymond
     Beaumont indicate that she was born in 1879 to William Everett and
     Margaret Boucher.

64 The Dominion Fish Company bought out Reid and Tait in 1894. Commer-
     cial fishing was concentrated around Horse Island in the mid-1890s (Bar-
     bour, 1955–56). James A. McLachlan became the Methodist missionary
     at Berens River during the 1890s. He and six Berens River children were
     drowned on 12 September 1903 when their boat was swamped near Grind-
     stone Point en route to the Brandon Residential School (Gray 2006, 166–67).

65 The surname d'Arcis appears as a Monkman family connection in
     Monkman 2000, 12.

66 Loon Straits was not an Indian reserve. Its main occupants from the late
     1800s onward were people of mixed ancestry, notably the Monkman family
     of Cree, English, and Scottish descent (Monkman, 2000).

67 Mr Flett was probably James Flett, former HBC clerk at Berens River, whom
     Berens had known well. He left HBC service in 1897 and was said to be in the
     Selkirk area in 1897–98 (HBCA biographical sheet).

68 The Louise Bridge, named after Queen Victoria's daughter, Princess Louise,
     was built in 1881. The reference to McColl's two boys being on the trip helps
     to date this trip. McColl's correspondence from his summer tour of duty in
     July 1897 mentioned that his sons Gilbert and Samuel were traveling with
     him (McColl 1989, 133, 135).

69 William McKay died on 13 January 1887 at the age of ninety-four in Parkdale,
     MB, leaving a wife and two sons and a daughter by a former marriage,

according to his obituary in the *Selkirk Record* of 21 January 1887. His first
wife, Julie Chalifoux, died in July 1860 (Pat McCloy, McKay genealogical
table). Their marriage at Norway House on 13 August 1826 is recorded in
the Anglican Red River marriage register (St. John's Cathedral), no. 122.

70 "Dose" is a slang term for a bout of gonorrhea or syphilis (*Canadian Oxford
Dictionary*).

71 Short had succeeded Angus McKay as Indian agent in 1897 and served until
John Semmens replaced him in April 1901. McKay indicated in his Berens
River diary that the change was not of Short's choosing. On 2 April, McKay
recorded a rumour that Short had been dismissed. On 8 April, he noted that
Semmens had arrived, much to the "great disgust" of ex-agent Short. Angus
McKay, 1901, AM, Nan Shipley Collection.

72 Hallowell inserted 1899 in square brackets. The date given in the family tree
compiled by Raymond Beaumont is 16 January 1899.

73 Henry Cochrane was educated in Red River and ordained there in St. John's
Cathedral on 1 August 1858. He later served at St. Peter's Church on the lower
Red River, and at the Pas from 1874 to 1880 (Boon 1952–53).

74 "The girls" were Nancy Everett and Short's daughter Julia, who had joined
him at Berens River soon after he replaced Angus McKay as Indian agent in
the summer of 1897. Since Short was frequently traveling, Julia later wrote,
he "arranged for Nancy Everett, an Indian girl, to keep me company during
his absence. Nancy understood English but did not speak it" and also did not
cook, and their communication was imperfect. On Christmas Day 1898,
Nancy was not there when Julia "had twenty-three Indian callers" that day;
she was probably involved with her family and, as she told William above,
with the church celebration. However, as Berens recalled, she and Julia both
greeted Short and Berens when Short returned, to Julia's "great delight" that
evening (AM, Julia Anna Asher [nee Short] 1951, 4).

75 The person spoken to was clearly Nancy. Hallowell has kept the pronouns
"him" and "he" that Berens doubtless used here. The Ojibwe language has
two genders, animate and inanimate, and Ojibwe people speaking English
commonly interchange "he" and "she," as this pronominal distinction does
not occur in Ojibwe.

76 This would be Fryer of Ewing and Fryer, a sturgeon-fishing company in the
Berens River area that also got into the whitefish business (Barbour, 1955–56).

77 The Dominion Fish Company was founded by Charles Gauthier in 1882 (Barbour, 1955–56). Angus McKay noted in his diary for 27 May 1901that Pollock and Company, mentioned earlier, was a branch of that company (AM, Nan Shipley Collection).

78 Besides the two incidents just related, the others would be the Selkirk incident when Berens suffered his leg injury, and probably, the episode of the conjuror and the rolling head, told in III, 2.

79 Louis Bird, Omushkego Cree scholar and storyteller, tells a legend that offers a parallel to this concept. We-mis-hoosh was a powerful shaman who extended his own life for decades by killing off his sons-in-law (Bird 2005, 107–24).

80 James Green Stewart, Jr., was a clerk from about 1881 to 1886, and again from 1996 to about 1901; in 1900–01, he was in charge of the Berens River post (HBCA biographical sheet). The Berens River post journal, B. 16/a/11, contains numerous references to William Berens traveling between Poplar and Berens rivers. In February 1900, Berens was serving at Poplar River when he had a dream that later appeared as a harbinger of his sister Eliza's death at Berens River on 18 February 1900; see Part III, 103–4. The Boer War in South Africa was intense in 1900–01, the period referred to here.

81 Christy Harding, an Englishman who entered HBC service in 1896, may have served temporarily at Berens River. HBC records list him as a clerk at Norway House 1901–04, whereupon he was sent to Fort Simpson (HBCA, biographical sheet). George Raymond Ray took charge at Berens River on 1 April 1901 (HBCA B.16/a/11, fo. 27). Angus McKay wrote in his diary that day that when Ray arrived to replace Harding, "Indians [are] indignant over the matter" (McKay 1901, AM, Nan Shipley Collection). Clearly William Berens was not happy with Ray, as he soon left HBC employ to return to the fish business. In June 1903, Ray was listed as manager at Churchill (HBCA biographical sheet).

82 This was probably Thomas Monkman of Matheson Island, across Lake Winnipeg. He was a grandson of Joseph Monkman whom Berens mentioned at the start of these reminiscences.

83 Disbrowe was placed in charge of the HBC post at Berens River in 1903 (HBCA B.16/a/11, 8–9 June 1903).

84 William Gibeault is mentioned in the Berens River journals, HBCA B.16/a/11, 5 October 1903 and following. This final story in the Reminiscences parallels

William Berens's earliest memories of his father, Jacob Berens (on the HBC side) trying to get ahead of the free trader William Sinclair in 1870; see the opening passages of these reminiscences.

85 In his research notes under the heading, "Precognition," Hallowell identified this man as "Old Douglas (Bozαmαn)," a Poplar River Indian who "always knew if a stranger was coming." He glossed the nickname in English as "bowsman," which was the standard fur trade term for men hired to serve in the bow of a canoe or York boat, and would be a natural nickname for men who at some time worked in that capacity. That nickname was also applied to William Berens's son, Gordon.

Part III

1 Hallowell 1976, 364–5, "Ojibwa Ontology and World View," reprinted in Hallowell, in press.

2 See Brown 2006, 22–6, for a discussion of the variety of circumstances in which dreams involving powerful personages might or could be told.

3 In August 2007, Percy Berens told Maureen Matthews that his father never talked to him about *memengwesiwag* [*memegweshiwag* (*memegwesiwag*, var.)] (Berens 2007). William would, however, tell stories of *wíndīgo*, the cannibal monster, perhaps because *wíndīgo* was better known and not usually a giver of personal blessings.

4 Louis Bird, Hudson Bay Omushkego storyteller, observed similarly that boys going through dream quests had to "go through severe tests and conditioning." When physical strength is not enough, "you apply your mind to be able to do something that you cannot do, and it's possible." This means also facing and overcoming one's fears (Bird 2005, 41, 43). Berens, growing up in a church-going family, never deliberately went on a traditional dream quest, but he certainly was exposed to the sorts of lessons it taught.

5 One of Hallowell's most cited late articles is his "Ojibwa Ontology, Behavior, and World View" (1960), reprinted in Hallowell 1976.

6 Darnell 2001, 244.

7 Berens told this story to Hallowell in the summer of 1940. This James Bird may have been a son or nephew of the well-known James Bird Jr. ("Jemmy

Jock") (HBCA biographical sheet on James Bird Jr.; John C. Jackson, personal communication, December 2007). The records of the Red River Quarterly Court of Assiniboia do not mention this incident (Dale Gibson, personal communication, December 2007). Since James Bird Senior and Junior were the best-known members of a large family, it is also possible that the victim's given name was misremembered. We do not know where it occurred or if Bird died immediately. See also the Reminiscences (Part II, 41 and 204–5, n. 14) for the Grant-McKay connection.

8   As Mary McKay was born in 1836 (Beaumont, Berens family genealogy), this incident would date to around 1850. As of the 1830s, Grant was having problems with alcohol (MacLeod and Morton 1974 [1963], 115); possibly these continued. From the 1830s onward, the General Quarterly Court of Assiniboia was functioning, even if imperfectly.

9   Berens described seeing two traditional Ojibwe structures on this voyage. The *bikogaan* was a small, conical, tepee-like dwelling, a few of which Hallowell and Berens saw in use at Little Grand Rapids and Pikangikum in 1932. The conjurer's lodge was a huge *zhaaboondawaan* (*cabandawan* in Hallowell's orthography). This type of long lodge, which could hold a man with several wives and their families, had almost disappeared by the 1930s (Hallowell 1992, 102–3, 106, and figs. 19, 21).

10 This story, somewhat rewritten and polished, was published in Hallowell 1967 [1955], 175 ("The Ojibwa Self and Its Behavioral Environment," reprinted in Hallowell, in press); a shorter discussion appears on p. 283. As Berens was about sixteen, the incident probably happened around 1882.

11 Hallowell papers, Series V, research, sibs and totems. Berens told this story while talking with Hallowell about the Pelican clan. See Appendix.

12 The above text is transcribed from Hallowell's handwritten fieldnotes. In an eight-page typescript entitled "Rocks and Stones" (see Hallowell, in press), Hallowell wrote a more polished account, adding that Yellow Legs used the stone in the *Midewiwin* and that it was "about the size of a bowling ball but slightly elongated." William Berens pointed out to Hallowell its mouth and eyes, "but I found them hard to discern, although a rough indentation undoubtedly represented the former." Hallowell added that as of the 1930s, "the stone no longer exhibits its animate traits." The stone passed to William's

son, Percy Berens, and rested next to Percy's house on the Berens River reserve for a long time until some boys rolled it down into the river.

13 "The dreamer first said bull, then corrected himself" [AIH]. A steer is a castrated bull. The story evokes the opening passage of Berens's reminiscences – his early memory of being chased by horned cattle. Hallowell, "Check List of Ojibwa Dream Items," William Berens, 1.3.

14 "He refers to the aboriginal naming custom which also involved a blessing derived from the dreamed power. Since the narrator is a Christian and lives in an acculturated community naturally no such occasion has arisen" [AIH]. On the manuscript page following, Hallowell commented, "The bull is thus one of W.B.'s *pawagan*[*ak*]." That is, Berens could have drawn upon the powers that this dream visitor offered, if he had wished. More generally, Hallowell wrote, "The 'dream pattern' is illustrated by W.B.'s dreams even though he did not, as a boy, undertake a puberty fast. The myth-like quality is apparent."

15 Hallowell's manuscript header to one version of this text noted that Berens had this dream when he was about sixteen years old (that is, in about 1882), and that he had "never fasted in the regular way." As in the other encounters Berens told of, the spirit beings came to him to threaten or challenge and, once he proved his courage, they offered some sort of blessing or gift. Hallowell, "Check List of Ojibwa Dream Items," William Berens, 1.2 ("Invulnerability dream"). This text is the fullest version; phrases added in parentheses are interpolated from another manuscript version.

16 Hallowell in a published comment on this dream (1976, 467, "The Role of Dreams in Ojibwa Culture," in Hallowell, in press), said that Berens linked the red tuque with the red marks on the insect's head. "Tuque" is a Canadian variant of the term "toque," for a knitted, close-fitting winter hat.

17 In Ojibwe belief, if Berens had told the dream to his wife (he married in 1899), he would have lost its gift of invulnerability. In the 1930s, he evidently felt no need to keep it secret. The question of war and bullets may have come up around 1914, as Canadians, both Aboriginal and non-Aboriginal, were being drawn into World War I. In a header to the fullest manuscript version of the dream, Hallowell wrote, "W.B. did not see the creature in its natural form but the "boss" [of these insects]. Bosses have soul and body. [They] have something like human shape; that is why they can talk like people, e.g.,

in the conjuring tent. To dream of natural things as they are is not a dream of the real *pawágan* pattern. W.B. introduced this account into a discussion of this point." Hallowell Papers, Series V, Research, Saulteaux Indians, Dreams; Hallowell 1967 [1955], 179, ("The Ojibwa Self in Its Behavioral Environment," also reprinted in Hallowell, in press), expands upon this point; see also the briefer account in Hallowell 1976, 467.

18 English-speaking fur traders used the term "deer" for caribou for a long time. This is probably a reference to caribou, and the mention of both moose and caribou suggests that this happening may date to the early 1890s when caribou were being supplanted by moose in the Berens River area that was ravaged by fire in 1889 (see Reminiscences, 39).

19 See published versions in Hallowell 1967 [1955], 97, ("The Ojibwa Self and Its Behavioral Environment," reprinted in Hallowell, in press), and 1992, 90. Below the manuscript text, Hallowell added that, "Later on the north bank of the Berens River, [Berens] saw such a place, to prove his dream." Berens's great-grandfather, Yellow Legs, was said to obtain his medicines with the help of these beings and William could have returned to that spot and done likewise if he had wished. As a Christian, he did not accept their help and was hence later able to tell the dream to Hallowell without penalty (cf. Brown, 2006, 26). Hallowell, "Check List of Ojibwa Dream Items," William Berens, 1.1.

20 Hallowell, "Check List of Ojibwa Dream Items," William Berens, 1.13.

21 The head loss motif evokes Berens's story of the conjuror (86). For further discussion of this dream, its context, and the history of the Catholic mission at Berens River, see Gray, 2006, 100–1. Berens probably had the dream in about 1917 judging by the number of children he mentioned. The Catholics had been visiting for some time by then and were settling in. Father Joseph De Grandpré and Brother Frederick Leach established a Catholic day school in 1918 (Gray 2006, 13). Hallowell, "Check List of Ojibwa Dream Items," William Berens, 1.8 ("Struggle with Catholics").

22 The conjuror's lodge in story number 2, above, was a magical, dreamed version of this type of dwelling, of which Berens saw several when he visited Pikangikum on this trip (Hallowell 1992, 106).

23 Hallowell, "Check List of Ojibwa Dream Items," William Berens, 1.13 (Love medicine dream). Compare the much more prosaic account of this trip in Berens's reminiscences, "Surveying Up the River," 54.

24 Hallowell noted that Berens told him this story in 1940. Kesigabau or Kaa-see-ka-pow (John Ross) married Mary Everett sometime in 1889–90; their first child was born in November 1890 (Raymond Beaumont, Everett family genealogy). At the end of his research note on this topic, Hallowell added that he was told, "the danger of love medicine is that when it wears off you will *hate* the person who put it on you. That is why it is bad if people marry under its spell."

25 Hallowell, "Check List of Ojibwa Dream Items," William Berens, 1.7 ("Anticipation of marriage").

26 Hallowell papers, Series V, research notes, kinship terms and relations. Cross-cousins are one's father's sisters' children and mother's brothers' children, who, being in a different descent line, are potential "sweethearts" and marriage mates. Parallel cousins are the children of same-sex siblings and are equated with one's siblings in Ojibwe kinship; they therefore could not marry in the traditional system. The distinction extends to other more remote cousins, and cross-cousins of any age may joke in this manner.

27 This undated story, transcribed from Hallowell's research notes, is headed "Windigo. W.B." and is numbered 9B. The opening line suggests that the windigo was sent by another medicine man The story does not appear to be mentioned in Hallowell's published works. The reference to leaves, and to the following spring, suggests that it happened in the fall. As the following story (16) indicates, *windīgowag* were not expected to be very active or dangerous in summer.

28 The published version of this story is in Hallowell 1992, 64–5. In August 2007, William's son Percy still remembered his father telling him about this event (Percy Berens to Maureen Matthews and Margaret Simmons, recorded and transcribed by Maureen Matthews).

29 Hallowell in *The Role of Conjuring in Saulteaux Society* (1971 [1942]), 36 cites numbers of instances of shaking tents being set up in dwellings in wintertime.

30 Fears of *windīgos* and accounts of *windīgo* executions often receive the most attention in the literature, but cures were attempted too, as in this case. Fur trader George Nelson wrote in 1823 that the Ojibwe he knew along Lake Winnipeg were "in general kind and extremely indulgent to those thus infected … and are desirous of doing all they can to assist" (Brown and Brightman 1988, 93).

31 Told by Berens to Hallowell, 1940. Pagak is a skeletal being, alarming to experience but usually benign as well as powerful; see Part IV, 229, n. 58.

32 See Hallowell 1967 [1955], 253–4 ("Fear and Anxiety," reprinted in Hallowell, in press). William Berens had what Hallowell described as a phobia about frogs and toads; a toad had crawled up his pant leg when he was a boy and he had crushed it (an act that in itself could have carried penalties; see stories 3 and 4 above). Further, Ojibwe people believed that toads would harass those who told myths in summertime and Berens had been telling some of those stories to Hallowell out of season.

33 We have not been able to find a translation for *anickanwakon*, nor can we discern the meaning of "jumper" as it is used here.

34 Hallowell papers, Series V, Dreams. "Check List of Ojibwa Dream Items," William Berens, 1.4. Published in Brown 2006, 29.

35 In another page of notes on William Berens's dreams, Hallowell added that Berens had this dream "a couple of years ago," that is, sometime in the 1930s. The first woman was "moving her feet in front and behind each other (demonstrated) as if she were skating." The fisher skin was worth $85. Hallowell, "Check List of Ojibwa Dream Items," William Berens, 1.5 ("Hunting luck").

36 The year after William Berens told this dream, Hallowell published "Freudian Symbolism in the Dream of a Saulteaux Indian" in the British journal *Man* (1938, 47–8). The article represents Hallowell at the peak of his interest in psychological analysis. Ascribing to the dream a Freudian symbolism that he attempted to explain to Berens, Hallowell wrote, as noted in Part I, that Berens "seemed in no way resistant to the idea." His listener may simply have been polite and bemused; it is hard to know. Hallowell, "Check List of Ojibwa Dream Items," William Berens, 1.9 ("Money [Freudian Symbolism]").

37 William Berens' younger sister Eliza (Elizabeth) married John Everett on 21 November 1892 (Beaumont n.d., Genealogies of Berens and Everett families). The Berens River HBC journal recorded that Berens arrived from Poplar River on 12 February 1900. On 15 February, the writer noted, "John Everette's wife very sick not expected to live." She died the evening of 18 February (HBCA B. 16/a/11, fos. 7, 9).

38 Hallowell, "Check List of Ojibwa Dream Items," William Berens, 1.6 ("Survival of relatives").

39 This could be a reference to the Strait of Belle Isle, the narrow channel that separates Labrador from Newfoundland.

40 Series V, Saulteaux Indians, Myths and Tales, research field notes, file 21. Hallowell later noted (1976, 456–57) that the Western concept of the "natural" is "not indigenous to Ojibwa thought. Consequently, the use of the term 'supernatural' doubly distorts their outlook."

41 Hallowell 1934, 396–97, reprinted in Hallowell, in press.

42 Hallowell 1939, "Some European Folktales of the Berens River Saulteaux."

43 Hallowell 1934, 397.

44 Brown 2006, 34–5; see also Hallowell 1976, 380. The old man evidently told the story after he decided he had no more use for the powers or blessings that the dream visitor had brought him.

45 Jones 1919, 245–9.

46 Hallowell 1976, 364. Hallowell here also quoted William Jones as saying, "Myths are thought of as conscious beings, with powers of thought and action" and, as noted earlier, they are grammatically animate.

Part IV

1 Hallowell's texts for this book manuscript, entitled, "Myth, Tale, and Behavior in Saulteaux Society," are among his papers at the American Philosophical Society, Philadelphia. See especially files 17, 19, 20, 21, 23. Series V, Saulteaux Indians, Myths and Tales, and draft Introduction, file 24. Hereafter this piece will be cited as Introduction. All notes in Part IV that are authored by Hallowell are set in quotation marks and labelled [AIH]. See also Series I, MSS, in Hallowell's papers for manuscript material pertaining to this book project.

2 Series V, Saulteaux Indians Myths and Tales, file 25.

3 Hallowell 1992, 113–14.

4 Series V, Saulteaux Indians, Myths and Tales, draft Preface, file 25. Some of the versions drawn upon for this collection, however, are handwritten and

closer in form to field notes. Their annotations, some of which are lacking in the typed texts, are included here.

5 Similarly, sixty years later when Susan Gray spoke with Ojibwe people living in the Berens River community, they were enthusiastic about her project. Of special appeal was the realization that, with the completion of her work, people from "the wider world," as they liked to put it, would read about them, their culture, and their ideas (Gray 2006, Preface). On a draft version of the Matcikiwis story, below (6), Hallowell added a marginal note about Berens hearing the stories nightly from his father and paternal grandmother.

6 Series V, Saulteaux Indians, Myths and Tales, "Saulteaux Indians Myths and Tales," file 25. Tcakabec was a tiny magical man who possessed great strength and strong powers. He lived with his older sister after the death of their parents and embarked on a series of adventures that included being swallowed by a great fish and snaring the sun. In some stories he ends up living on the moon. See, for example, stories in Bird 2007, 23–37.

7 "Memoirs, 678. Cf. Chamberlain, Nanibozhu, 195 [who] also refers to the same penalty." [AIH] [A.F. Chamberlain, 1906, "Cree and Ojibwa Literary Terms," *Journal of American Folklore*, 19:346–7].

8 Hallowell, draft Preface.

9 Hallowell 1967 [1955], 116, "The Northern Ojibwa," reprinted in Hallowell, in press.

10 Hallowell, draft Introduction.

11 Overholt and Callicott 1982, 27.

12 Jones 1917, and 1919, xi.

13 Smith 1995, 18 (her book is based on her work with Manitoulin Island Ojibwe).

14 Hallowell, draft Introduction.

15 Berens River people, according to Hallowell, used the term *bawaagan(ag)* more often than *manidoo*. As Hallowell wrote to Frank Speck from Fishing Lake Reserve, Saskatchewan on 19 July 1931, "Later when I reached Berens R. I had some fine sessions with the chief [William Berens] … the belief in a high god – *manitu* may well have once been characteristic of the Oj. so far as my impressions are concerned. But he is the creator & owner of everything not only man … The *pawáganak* are central in the active life of man, since they are the spiritual aspects of the concrete forces & objects of nature which

he must use for a living, while *manitu* is remote (cannot be a *pawágan*, by the way) and is only infrequently referred to (e.g. in the *midewin*) directly." And again to Speck from North Battleford, Saskatchewan on 1 August 1931: "And it's strange that aside from David Thompson I have nowhere [in written sources] run across the term *pawágan*. Yet that is the universal term among Cree & Saulteaux for dream-guardian and one of the "keys." <u>Manitu</u> is never used in the plural and cannot be a *pawágan*. Missionary influence or an old High God? In fact I was told by old "Fine Day" a splendid type of old fashioned Indian who fought the whites in the N.W. Rebellion + with whom I had 3 good sessions, that we used that word [*manitu*] more in the course of our conversation than he had heard it in a year. The usual reference is to *katapetcaket* or *katapemiwet* (owner, boss)." APS, Correspondence of Frank Speck, Manuscript coll. 170 (2:F3). Transcribed by Jennifer S.H. Brown.

16 Hallowell, draft Introduction.

17 Hallowell, draft Introduction.

18 The Ojibwe English term "our grandfathers," although often used as a translation for *aadizookaanag* (other-than-human persons such as the Four Winds, Sun, Moon, Thunderbirds, "owners" or "masters" of species of plants and animals, and the characters in myths), was a more inclusive category. The *ätisokának* (Hallowell's version of this term), when collectively spoken of as "our grandfathers," were also to be distinguished from the usual human kin term *nimishoomis*, "my grandfather." Wisɑkedjak is a culture hero character, a trickster/transformer who combines "attributes of great magical power, pathetic helplessness, wisdom, stupidity, altruism, and moral chaos" (Brown and Brightman 1988, 108). Mikīnäk is the Great Turtle, a powerful other-than-human being, always present in the conjuring tent – see Gray 2006, 36.

19 "The same formula is to be found at the close of some of Jones's texts e.g., vol. II, p.148, 149." [AIH] In an unfinished typescript for this book project, entitled "B. Anthropomorphic Characters of Mythology," 8, Hallowell wrote that the closing formula of all the myths was invariable. He added, "I was not able to discover its meaning but one informant said that as a child he used to look upwards in the wigwam to see the partridge gizzard. Then his elders would laugh at him."

20 "Kohl, p. 88, says: 'I have often heard it stated that men are the only story-

tellers, and that men and boys are alone permitted to listen to them. I know
not if this be the case, though it may be with some sort of stories, but it is a
fact that I found many old women equally eloquent and inventive.' I think it
is obvious from the conditions already described that there can be no sexual
segregation of the listeners." [AIH]

21 Hallowell, draft Introduction.

22 Overholt and Callicott 1982, 26.

23 Series V, Saulteaux Indians, Myths and Tales, unpublished paper, "Tcɑkábɛk,"
file 20. (For a Cree example of Tcakabek meeting humans [Europeans], see
Bird 2005, 152–7, "Cha-ka-pesh and the Sailors.")

24 For stories told by William Berens see Series V, Saulteaux Indians, Myths and
Tales, files 17, 19, 20, 21, and 23. For stories told by other people from communities along the Berens River see files 16, 17, 20, 22.

25 Such as, "South Wind Against North Wind," "Wisɑkedjak Discovers
Women," "How Wisɑkedjak Got Married," "*Tawanɑnge* [Thunderbird
Skins]," "*Kamitáwasegwɑt [Gaa-midaawaswegad* ?] [Sleepy Stories],"
"Wisɑkedjak Is a Child for a Day," "Wisɑkedjak and Kaiánwe," "Wolf and
Wolverine," "Big Mosquito," "Wis kedjak and Ruffed Grouse," "A Bewitching
Owl," "The Eleven Brothers," and "Wisɑkedjak and the Cannibal."

26 This story calls to mind the conversations that Hallowell had with Berens
River people on the question of stones being alive (animate), at least in some
instances. See Part III, "The Medicine Stone," 88–90, and Hallowell, "Rocks
and Stones" (Hallowell, in press).

27 Brown and Brightman 1988, 108.

28 Series V, Indian Linguistics, file 2. In real life, as often also in Ojibwe myths,
this pattern of matrilocal residence was common for new husbands.

29 Thistle 1986, 69.

30 Young 1903, 37–8; see also Brown 2008 on Eddie's recollections of their
storytelling. Zhaawanaash, as noted in Part I, was the younger brother of
William Berens's grandfather, Bear.

31 Bird 2007, 29–37.

32 AIH, Series V, Saulteaux Indians, Myths and Tales, file 28.

33 Overholt and Callicott 1982, 141.

34 Jones 1919, 701–7.

35 Overholt and Callicott 1982, xi. See also Mary Black Rogers' comments on this in her Foreword, xv.

36 See Smith 1995, 55; and Overholt and Callicott 1982, 142–3. See also Series V, Saulteaux Indians, "Rocks and Stones," c. 1936 (Hallowell, in press). This paper presents an excellent discussion of the Ojibwe belief in the animate or magical properties believed by Ojibwe to be possessed by some rocks and stones.

37 Overholt and Callicott 1982, 145.

38 Sugarhead 1996, Bird 2005 and 2007, Ellis 1995.

39 "The narrator [William Berens] heard it narrated by his grandmother" [AIH.]. See also "James Settee and His Cree Tradition" for a version of this story written by Cree Anglican clergyman James Settee (Brown 1977, 40–7), which lacks the puberty dream episode, however. The motif of a large, dangerous personage (here, Flint) being defeated and broken into many small pieces that will not threaten humans recurs in other stories, as with the destruction of the monster snake in Aásī (5) and the giant mosquito in story no. 13.

40 "It was explained by the narrator that the woman adopted this means of achieving a magical conception. It must be remembered that a boy undertaking a puberty fast must never have had sexual contact with a woman and that what this woman did was so defiling that no ordinary boy would have received a blessing." [AIH]

41 "He could only have accomplished this and made the request he did if he had already dreamed of the 'boss' of these trees. This implies that he had already been blessed, despite this feminine visitor." [AIH]

42 For Ojibwe versions, see William Jones, "Star of the Fisher" (1919, 469–87); Cecilia Sugarhead, "The Five Moons of Winter" (1996, 39–41). For a Cree version, see Louis Bird, "Creator Talks to the Animals about the Emergence of the Humans" (2005, 78–80).

43 "It was pointed out that the birds mentioned above, such as ducks and geese, do not sit on trees, so that they could not get 'summer'." [AIH]

44 Another version in Hallowell's papers (told by James Bear at Berens River) is much shorter than this one and different in the order of events. The flood occurs at the end of the story after Wisɑkedjak has succeeded in killing the

Lynx, and it is a crow who finally determines the satisfactory size of the earth. James Bear told this story to Dorothy Spencer in 1934. Series V, Saulteaux Indians, Myths and Tales, file 19.

  William Jones recorded several Ojibwe versions: "Nänabushu and the Wolves," "Nänabushu and the Wolves Continued," "Death of Nänabushu's Nephew," "Nänabushu Slays Toad-Woman" (1917, 73–85, 85–9, 89–101, 145–59, 145–59); "Nänabushu and the Wolves," "Death of Nänabushu's Nephew," "Nänabushu Slays Toad-Woman" (1917, 235–49, 251–61, 261–79); "Nänabushu and the Wolves," "The Death of Nänabushu's Nephew," "Nänabushu Slays Toad-Woman," "The Scattering of the Animals and the Regulation of Nature" (1917, 373–89, 389–99, 399–407, 407–9). For a Cree version, see Ellis, "The legend of Weesakechahk and the Flood." This story begins with Weesakechahk already on the raft in the flood, and it is the wolverine who finally determines the satisfactory size of the earth (1996, 35–9). Fur trader George Nelson recorded another version in 1823, "The Battle of Weesuckajock and the Water Lynxes" (Brown and Brightman 1988, 45–8).

45 "An incident not found in this version but told to me by my informant A[rthur] F[elix] is the following: When Wisαkedjak was running with the wolves he heard something jingling as they travelled along. So he stopped and said, 'Listen, do you hear anything?' 'No,' said his little brother (the wolf). So they went on. But Wisαkedjak heard the noise again. So he stopped to listen once more. 'I think it's something on you,' said the wolf. So Wisαkedjak felt his balls. They were frozen and knocked together as he ran. That's what made the sound." [AIH]

46 "I.e., killed the wolf, who was not, of course, drowned in the ordinary sense of the term." [AIH]

47 "One arm-stretch (fathom) is termed *pezïgonik.*" [AIH]

48 In the version told by James Bear, various other animals joined Wisαkedjak on the raft as the world filled with water. Series V, Saulteaux Indians, Myths and Tales, file 19

49 "The narrator explained that every time Wisαkedjak pulled up one of the drowned animals he put the breath of life into each of them." [AIH]

50 In James Bear's version, Wisαkedjak brought the muskrat back to life at this point. Series V, Saulteaux Indians, Myths and Tales, file 19.

51 In 1930, Hallowell recorded another version of this story, very similar to the

above except in small details and titled "Hahäs." The teller, Willie Cret, was a Nelson House Cree who was born at Poplar River in the 1880s. Series V, Saulteaux Indians, Myths and Tales, file 21. Ojibwe versions include William Jones, "Filcher of Meat" (1919, 381–99); and Cecilia Sugarhead, "The Legend of Aayaash" (1996, 71–91), which also contains part of the Rolling Head story that William Berens told Hallowell. For a Cree version, see C. Douglas Ellis, "The Legend of Ayas" (1995, 45–61).

52 "If hit in the head a partridge will act much like a chicken with its head cut off." [AIH]

53 "Formerly the women wore no underclothes." [AIH]

54 "This kinship term is always employed by *pawáganak* (guardian spirits) in addressing beneficiaries." [AIH]

55 "The narrator later explained that the boy was afraid the snake would dive and never take him to land if he knew that a thunderstorm was coming up." [AIH]

56 "Because it was too shallow so close to shore to allow the snake to dive and escape *pinési*." [AIH] See Appendix.

57 "[My] sister-in-law, cross cousin (woman speaking)." [AIH]

58 Several Berens River stories besides those of William Berens relate to this theme: "Wisɑkedjak Brings 'Sickness,'" "An Old Woman Begs the Moon to Look after her Orphan Granddaughter," "Wisɑkedjak Discovers Women," "Dung Man," "How Wisɑkedjak Got Married," "*Tawanɑnge* (Thunderbird Skins)," "*Kamitáwasegwɑt* [Sleepy Stories]," "Mikīnäk," "Wisɑkedjak Is a Child for a Day," "Wisɑkedjak and Kaiánwe," "Pagak," and the Tcakabek stories. AIH, Series V, Saulteaux Indians, Myths and Tales, files 16, 17, 20, 22.

59 For another Ojibwe version, see William Jones, "The First-Born Son" (1919, 133–49).

60 "The narrator used the English term 'witch' (wizard). The Indian term refers to those who practice various forms of magic. The practice of magic is so much feared that even one's own relatives are not supposed to know anything about it." [AIH]

61 "Because the women cut and haul wood for the camp and build the fire and replenish it." [AIH]

62 See Hallowell's essay on Thunderbirds – Appendix; also Gray 2006, 31–2. Thanks to John Nichols for help on the Ojibwe phrase used here.

63 "Narrator forgot the name of the other contestant." [AIH]

64 "One at either end of the hole which the "beavers" (snakes) entered and left their dwelling place." [AIH]

65 For another Ojibwe version, see William Jones, "Snapping Turtle" (1919, 737–45).

66 "When stories in which Mikīnäk appears are narrated, every time he speaks the *raconteur* adopts the throaty nasal tone which is characteristic of Mikīnäk when he speaks in the conjuring lodge." [AIH]

67 See William Jones, "The Origin of Dogs" (1919, 171–5) for another Ojibwe version.

68 For two other Ojibwe versions, see William Jones, "Nänabushu Flies with Geese" (1917, 127–31), and "Nänabushu Flies with the Geese" (1917, 433–5). C. Douglas Ellis provides a Cree version, "Weesakechahk Flies with the Waveys" (1995, 139–43).

69 For two Cree versions, see Louis Bird, "Wisɑkedjak Goes West and Grants Two Wishes" (2007, 193–7); and C. Douglas Ellis, "The Legend of Weesakechahk and the Flood." The latter, which deals with the flooding and recreation of the earth, ends with Wisɑkedjak walking out upon his newly formed earth and encountering the first two Indians. One asks that he may live forever and Wisɑkedjak turns him to stone (Ellis 1995, 35–9); see also "Weesakechahk Creates an Immortal" (Ellis 1995, 171).

70 Given the Ojibwe belief that some rocks and stones were alive, Wisɑkedjak might well have granted this man's wishes in a literal way. See Hallowell, "Rocks and Stones," in press.

71 "Coming from the region of the earth they had left." [AIH]

72 Several other stories that Hallowell collected relate to this theme: "Big Skunk," "The Man Who Married a Beaver," "The Man with Animal Wives," "Fisher's Revenge," "Cingɑbis" [Zhingibis, grebe, hell-diver], "Crawfish and Otter," "A Bewitching Owl," "Mink," "Mikīnäk and the Mud Turtles," "Wisɑkedjak and Ruffed Grouse," "Wisɑkedjak as the Bungling Host," "Wisɑkedjak Becomes Encased in a Bear Skull," and "Wisɑkedjak Tricks the Birds." See AIH, Series V, Saulteaux Indians, Myths and Tales, files 16, 17, 20, 22.

73 John Keeper at Little Grand Rapids told Hallowell another version of this story in 1934. His was similar except the magic objects are a stone (which

becomes a wall) and a beaver tooth (which becomes a palisade). In this version, it is the young man who tricks the wizard into a series of trials and prevails; the wizard turns into a caribou in the end. AIH, Series V, Saulteaux Indians, Myths and Tales, file 22. William Jones recorded three other Ojibwe versions: "The Orphans and Mashōs" (1919, 45–103); "Old Man Mashōs" (1919, 179–89); and "The Rolling Skull" (1919, 405–14). Cree versions include Louis Bird, "The Legend of We-mis-shoosh" (2005, 107–123) and C. Douglas Ellis, "Memishoosh the Conjuror" (1995, 69–89).

74 "I was told that this event is sometimes bowdlerized when there are women in the audience." [AIH]

75 "As elsewhere among the northern Indians it was part of a woman's task to bring in the meat to camp. The man sometimes built a small fire, the smoke from which was sufficient to keep the wolves away even if the carcass was left overnight. If it was not likely that the meat would be brought back within three or four days, a stage was built in a tree and the carcass placed upon it. Besides verbal instructions as to location the hunter would hang moss on trees here and there, break a few branches or blaze trees, so that the woman could easily find the place. This custom is only found today among certain families of the Pekangikum band." [AIH]

76 "The ordinary term for which is *cacage*. In this narrative the term employed is *cete*. I was told that this is the term used across the lake. Perhaps the fact that W.B.'s grandfather [Bear] came from there accounts for the occurrence of the term in this story, a narrative which is of course known both east and west of Lake Winnipeg." [AIH]

77 "The narrator commented that bells are mentioned in several 'old' stories. 'That is why the Indians think a lot of bells,' he said." [AIH]

78 "I.e., the 'boss' of the sturgeon was one of his 'guardian spirits' (*pawáganak*). It is unusual for a 'guardian spirit' to be addressed by this [kinship] term." [AIH]

79 "The whooping crane. The long legs of this bird suggest at once the particular reason why it was called upon for help in this crisis." AIH)

80 "From opposing horizontal limbs of two poplars at a convenient distance from each other there were suspended two long poles which formed the sides of the swing. These side poles were trimmed, save for a short branch left near the end of each one. In the natural 'crutch' thus left intact were

caught the horizontal limbs overhead and suspension from them achieved
by this means. The side poles were joined together by a cord at the bottom."
[AIH]

81   "The generic term for the two [species of?] spruces and balsam is *cingubik*,
     -igen is a suffix denoting a dwelling or shelter of some kind. The structure in
     question is for temporary use only. Trimmed young trees are arranged in a
     tipi-like formation and covered with 'brush' of spruce or balsam, and on the
     outside, sticks are laid to hold the brush in place." [AIH]

82   "I.e., guardian spirits or helpers." [AIH]

83   The style of this story is rather telegraphic because it is transcribed directly
     from Hallowell's field notes. Hallowell edited and adapted it for publication
     in *The Beaver*, December 1933, 22, under the title, "The Giant Mosquitoes,"
     but as his published prose is considerably embellished, this text relies on the
     original notes. Nonetheless, the published text clarifies a few details that are
     unclear in the notes.

84   In 1938, Alec Keeper at Little Grand Rapids told Hallowell a much shorter
     version, in which Hare kills and eats a baby bear and manages to escape its
     mother's vengeance (AIH, Series V, Saulteaux Indians, Myths and Tales, file
     19). This story is in file 17.

85   "The comparison implied is with the tail of the beaver which is considered a
     delicacy by the Indians." [AIH]

86   "If you get mad because you cannot kill something, you sometimes call it a
     '*djíbai.*' It is a kind of abjuration." [AIH] The term refers to spirits of the
     dead; see Hallowell 1967 [1955], chapter 7, reprinted in Hallowell, in press.

87   "The narrator commented that the story showed that the Wolverine could
     not be trusted. "He is a bad one," he said, "even if he is a *pawágan!*" [AIH]

88   William Everett told Hallowell another story about cannibals (*windīgos*) in
     1934: "Wisɑkedjak is saved by a weasel" (Series V, Saulteaux Indians, Myths
     and Tales, file 20). Although William Berens told Hallowell only one myth
     (17) that specifically mentioned *windīgos*, he also told of his real-life experi-
     ences of hearing and seeing these beings and of encountering a human being
     at risk of becoming *windīgo* (see III, 98–100). There were different types of
     windīgos – cannibalistic beings who struck terror into the hearts of Cree and
     Ojibwe people. A starving human could be driven to eat human flesh and

would become insane. Persons subjected to sustained cruelty reach a point when they could not tolerate any more abuse and might become *wíndïgo*. Some *wíndïgos* were giants and others looked perfectly human, eating people at irregular intervals and going undetected for periods of time (see, for example, "Anway and the Cannibals" in Bird 2007, 116–22). Their hearts were said to be made of ice and cannibal exterminators knew that the hearts must be burned. If powerful shamans became *wíndïgos*, they could pose a great threat, as they possessed formidable powers. Particularly difficult to destroy were those who stored their hearts in a nest of feathers (or, as in the story of the Eleven Brothers, of human hair) in a high place away from their bodies. To extinguish these beings, one had to locate their hearts pulsing in the nest and spear them, as this story recounts. For further stories and discussions of *wíndïgos* see "Wihtigos and Cannibal Hearts" (in Bird 2007, 112–26); and Brown and Brightman 1988, 88–94 and 158–71, which recount the detailed observations of fur trader George Nelson, who showed enormous understanding of these beings in their various forms.

89 "Bits of tin fastened to the ends of a fringe of leather thongs." [AIH]

90 "A dwelling constructed of two series of poles resting at an angle of about 45 degrees against either side of a ridge pole. The covering was of birch-bark. Usually it was a multiple-family dwelling, with several fires built along the main axis or was occupied by a polygynous family. Such shelters are no longer built. Cf. [Frances] Densmore B[ulletin] BAE. 86 [1929], p. 26 for details of construction." [AIH] Such a structure also figures in the story in III (11), this volume. For a rare early photograph, see Hallowell 1992, 106.

91 John Keeper at Little Grand Rapids told Hallowell two other versions of this story in 1934. "Kaiánwe and the Cannibals" does not include the beginning of this story but begins with the protagonist tricking and killing the cannibals. In Keeper's other version, "Sóbatɑm," the old cannibal gets his supply of human meat by eating his daughters-in-law. One of these women manages to escape and runs to a village of humans. The old cannibal and his son follow her but both are killed by the people (AIH, Series V, Saulteaux Indians, Myths and Tales, file 21). For a Cree version, see Louis Bird, "Anway and the Cannibals" (2007, 116–22). Although the plot is very different, Anway and Wemtigóze use the same strategy to kill cannibal families.

92 "I.e., each brother and each sister of otter-girl was to alternate between
the siblings of the other family, walking single file on the trail. Note sexual
segregation here, the men in front, the women behind." [AIH]

93 "This means a sure fall to a person walking on snowshoes." [AIH]

94 See Hallowell, "Temporal Orientation in Western Civilization and in a
Preliterate Society" (1955, chapter 11, reprinted in Hallowell, in press) for his
discussion of the twelve phases in the Berens River Ojibwe lunar calendar,
three of which were named for birds (eagle, goose, and loon) that regularly
appeared in a certain "moon" or month as spring approached.

95 "This house does not figure in the plot and I was not able to grasp the exact
details of its construction." [AIH]

96 "I.e., so much bent that there would be hardly enough spring in it to project
an arrow." [AIH]

Appendix

1 This text is transcribed from an essay of eleven handwritten pages that Hallowell wrote probably in 1934 (Hallowell papers, Series V, Saulteaux Indians).
It stands out as his most focused and detailed study of a topic central to
Ojibwe worldview and mythology. It is lightly edited: usage has been standardized, punctuation added, abbreviations expanded, and current Ojibwe
orthography added in brackets where possible, as elsewhere in this volume.

2 "Truman Michelson, Bureau of American Ethnology Bulletin 95 [*Contributions to Fox Ethnology – II*, 1930], 51, has cited the references in the ethnological literature of North America." [AIH] Hallowell's use here of the term
"Pigeon River" (a translation of the older Ojibwe river name) suggests he
may have written it at the time when he was drafting an ethnography,
"Pigeon River People," which was never published. His use of the same term
in his *American Anthropologist* article "Some Empirical Aspects of Northern
Saulteaux Religion" (1934) and some other parallels with that article suggest
a 1934 date for this text.

3 "See the Bird Calendar compiled from the Records of the Natural History
Society of Manitoba." [AIH]

4 "Cf. Thunder Cape [at Thunder Bay, ON] – Lake Superior and the legends
concerning it." [AIH]

5   William Berens visited Thunder Lake once while trading (see Part III, 3, for his story of an incident there). In his research notes (Series V) Hallowell recorded Berens's account of his visit to the nest on "Manitu Island" and sketched, from his description, the pattern of the boulders that formed it. In the 1990s, Charlie George Owen of Pauingassi gave a vivid description of this site in a radio program that is rich in contemporary Ojibwe and Cree accounts of Thunder Birds, their characteristics, behaviour, and significance. See Maureen Matthews, " Thunderbirds," *Ideas*, CBC Radio, Toronto, broadcast May 1995.

6   The only Peter Berens in the Berens family tree at hand was a son of Jim (James Flett) Berens. He was born 20 November 1887 (Berens genealogy prepared by Raymond Shirritt Beaumont), so the story may date to the late 1890s. Jim Berens was a brother of Jacob and Albert, either of whom may have been the uncle in question. All are mentioned elsewhere in this volume; see index. In publishing this anecdote (e.g., in "Some Empirical Aspects of Northern Saulteaux Religion" (1934, 395, 398); see also Hallowell 1976, 370), Hallowell stated that it was a man, not a woman, whose dream verified Peter's description.

7   "Among other North American peoples the Thunder Bird is associated with quite different avian species. Cf. Michelson, Bureau of American Ethnology Bulletin 95 [*Contributions to Fox Ethnology – II*, 1930], p. 54." [AIH]

8   "Why the swan is associated with the Thunder Birds, I do not know." [AIH]

9   "See the story of Aasī [Part IV, 5] in which there is an etiological episode with reference to the disappearance of giant snakes from the earth as a result of the pursuit and destruction of one of them by *pinèsï*." [AIH]

10 "The oldest man in Pigeon River." [AIH] The eyewitness was John James Everett of Berens River, who recounted this episode to Hallowell while they were visiting Little Grand Rapids in July 1932 (Hallowell, Fieldnotes, July 1932). A marginal note in the fieldnotes adds that this happened "21 years ago," i.e., in 1911). On Fair Wind's life, his big drum ceremony, and his ceremonial practices including the *wabanówīwin*, see Brown and Matthews, "Fair Wind: Medicine and Consolation on the Berens River," 1994, and Matthews and Roulette, "Fair Wind's Dream: *Naamiwan Obawaajigewin*," 1996.

11 "Tinder secured from the excrescences of the birch. It is inevitably placed on top of the tobacco in ceremonial smoking. The pipe can then be lighted

by a *skabéwis* (servant) and passed to the smoker. The tinder will ignite the tobacco and so the *skabéwis* does not have to puff on it first." [AIH]

12   The Waabano ceremony usually lasted all night until dawn; *waabano* refers to dawn or "what is represented by the east"; see Matthews and Roulette (1996, "Fair Wind's Dream," 330) who also note that Ojibwe people held it "in the spring and summer to celebrate rebirth and revitalization or healing."

13   Angus [Aangish] was Fair Wind's son and his wife was Red Bird; in English, the family surname was and is Owen. Hallowell in "Spirits of the Dead in Saulteaux Life and Thought," 1955 [1940] (reprinted in Hallowell, in press), recounted the important ceremonial roles played by Angus.

14   John Duck (Machkajence) conducted *Waabano*, big drum, and shaking tent ceremonies that Hallowell witnessed (see Hallowell 1992, *The Ojibwa of Berens River*, 84, fig. 16). In 1938, however, he gave his big drum to United Church missionary Luther Schuetze (Schuetze, *Mission to Little Grand Rapids*, 157–8).

15   Hallowell met Asagesi at Little Duck (Barton) Lake, which connects with the upper Berens River near Poplar Hill. Although his fieldnotes for 14–15 July 1932 are too telegraphic, it must have been on that occasion that they had the conversation about religious matters and the *Waabano*, which Hallowell recorded in his research notes on Saulteaux religion. Asagesi told him of *k'tci anang* [*gichi anang*] or a great star, implied to be a source of his powers: "When Asagesi dreamed of his *wabanowigamik* there was a brilliant star above the tent which flooded it with light. This is why the young people who dance in the wabano can conceal nothing from him. Everything is (to him) always flooded with light." He also told Hallowell that *k'tci anang* was "seen only in dreams" and "was 'beyond' the 'real' stars and much brighter than any of them." The celestial symbolism of the great star, of the pole reaching to the sky, and of the Thunder Bird made for a powerful combination (Series V, Research, Saulteaux Indians, Religion).

16   "Of which I have a sample." [AIH] This bird figure became part of the Hallowell collection in the Museum of the American Indian MAI (Heye Foundation) in New York City and is illustrated in the frontispiece of Hallowell, 1992, *The Ojibwa of Berens River, Manitoba*; the MAI collections are now in the National Museum of the American Indian, Washington, DC. A similar

bird figure appears on a post in Hallowell's photograph of Fair Wind and family members in front of his *Waabano* pavilion at Pauingassi (see Matthews and Roulette, 1996, "Fair Wind's Dream," 332, figure 1).

17 In the margin of his field notes for 10 July 1932 at Little Grand Rapids, Hallowell translated this name as "When *pinesi* calls there is always rain"; but in respectful usage, a speaker would not state the name. For full accounts of Fair Wind and this big drum ceremony and its connections to the Dream Dance that originated in Minnesota and Wisconsin in the late 1800s, see Matthews, "The Search for Fair Wind's Drum," 1993; Brown and Matthews, Fair Wind," 1994, 63; and Matthews and Roulette, "Fair Wind's Dream," 1996, 357.

References

Archival Sources

American Philosophical Society (APS), Philadelphia
Alfred Irving Hallowell Papers, 1892–1981. Ms. Coll. 26
> Berens, William. Letters to A.I. Hallowell, 11 July 1935; 22 August 1936;
> 10 July 1941; 31 July 1945; 3 January 1947.

> Hallowell, A. Irving. Field notebooks, July–August 1930; June–August 1931;
> June–July 1932; June–August 1933.
>> Folklore: Berens River, 1932–33.
>> Berens, Boucher and Everett genealogies, n.d.
>> "III. Introduction." Unpublished typescript on oral narrative and
>> behavioral world. "Folklore: Berens River." 1932–33.
>> "Pigeon River People." Unpublished typescript.
>> "Rocks and Stones." Unpublished typescript, ca. 1936.
>> Series V. Indian Linguistics, file 2.

Series V. Research. Kinship terms and relations.

Series V. Research. Sibs and totems.

Series V. Research. Saulteaux Indians. Religion.

Series V. Research. Saulteaux Indians. Dreams; Check list of dream items.

Series V. Saulteaux Indians, Myths and Tales, files 16, 17, 19, 20, 21, 22, 23, 24, 25, 28.

Series V. Saulteaux Indians, "Thunder Bird," ca. 1934–35

Frank G. Speck Papers, 1903–1950. Ms. Coll. 126

Series II. Circumboreal. F. Ojibwa. 2F3, Box 2. Hallowell to Frank G. Speck, 1931.

Archives of the Diocese of Rupert's Land (Anglican), Winnipeg

Dynevor. Baptismal register.

Archives of Manitoba (AM), Winnipeg

Julia Anna Asher [nee Short]. 1951. "Life in the North 1897–1900." MG8 B10.

George Duncan MacVicar Papers. MG3 B9.

A.E. McEwan. "Four Years at Berens River." MG8 B52.

Angus McKay Diary. Nan Shipley Collection. P268, 1901.

Department of Interior. 1886. Survey Administration Files, GR289, Field Books, box G402, file 55.

Hudson's Bay Company Archives (HBCA), Archives of Manitoba, Winnipeg

B.16/a/5–12. Berens River post journals, 1863–1914.

Biographical Sheets [employees]: *http://www.gov.mb.ca/chc/archives/hbca/biographical/index.html*

Index of Servants' Engagement Registers 1866–1893 (B. 239/u/3 #184)

National Archives of Canada (NAC), Ottawa

RG10, vol. 3617, file 4641, J.A.N. Provencher to Minister of the Interior, Winnipeg, 22 March 1875 (reel C-10107).

RG10, vol. 3715, file 21,257, Berens River, 25 March 1885 (reel C11063.)

Other Unpublished Sources

Beaumont, Raymond Shirritt. N.d. Genealogies of Berens and Everett Families.

Berens, Maurice. 1985. "Chief William Berens, 1866–1947." Unpublished paper, University of Winnipeg. Copy in possession of Jennifer S.H. Brown.

Berens, Gordon. 1992. Interview with Jennifer S.H. Brown and Maureen Matthews, transcribed by Maureen Matthews.

Berens, Percy, 1994. Interview with Jennifer S.H. Brown and Susan Elaine Gray: notes taken by Jennifer S. H. Brown.

– 2007. Interview with Maureen Matthews, transcribed by Maureen Matthews.

– 2008. Interview with Susan Elaine Gray and David G. McCrady: notes taken by David G. McCrady.

Bittern, Antoine. 1992. Interview with Jennifer S.H. Brown and Maureen Matthews, transcribed by Maureen Matthews.

Dueck [Gray], Susan Elaine. 1986. "Methodist Indian Day Schools and Indian Communities in Northern Manitoba, 1890–1925." Masters thesis, University of Manitoba.

McCloy, Pat. William McKay genealogy, "table." Glenbow Archives, Calgary. Copy supplied by Mary Black Rogers.

Young, E. Ryerson. Ca. 1950s. "A Missionary and his Son." Copy of unpublished typescript in possession of Jennifer S.H. Brown.

Published Sources

Barbour, Alexander S. 1955–56. "A Brief History of the Manitoba Fisheries." Manitoba Historical Society. *Transactions*. Series 3.

Bird, Louis. 2005. *Telling Our Stories: Omushkego Legends and Histories from Hudson Bay*. Ed. Jennifer S.H. Brown, Paul W. DePasquale, and Mark F. Ruml. Peterborough, ON: Broadview Press.

– 2007. *The Spirit Lives in the Mind: Omushkego Stories, Lives, and Dreams*. Compiled and edited by Susan Elaine Gray. Montreal: McGill-Queen's University Press.

Bishop, Charles A. 1974. *The Northern Ojibwa and the Fur Trade: An Historical and Ecological Study*. Toronto: Holt, Rinehart and Winston of Canada.

– 1981. "Territorial Groups Before 1821: Cree and Ojibwa." In June Helm, ed. *Handbook of North American Indians*. Vol. 6, *Subarctic*, 244–55. Washington, DC: Smithsonian Institution.

Boon, T.C.B. 1952–53. "St. Peter's Dynevor, the Original Indian Settlement of Western Canada." Manitoba Historical Society. *Transactions*. Series 3(9).

Boulanger, Tom. 1971. *An Indian Remembers: My Life as a Trapper in Northern Manitoba*. Winnipeg: Peguis Publishers.

Brown, Jennifer S.H. 1977. "James Settee and His Cree Tradition: An Indian Camp at the Mouth of Nelson River Hudson's Bay." In William Cowan, ed. *Actes du huitième congrés des algonquinistes*, Ottawa: Carleton University.

– 1980. *Strangers in Blood: Fur Trade Company Families in Indian Country*. Vancouver: University of British Columbia Press.

– 1982. "The Track to Heaven: The Hudson Bay Cree Religious Movement of 1842–43." In William Cowan, ed., *Papers of the Thirteenth Algonquian Conference*, 53–64. Ottawa: Carleton University. 53–64.

– 1987a. "A Cree Nurse in a Cradle of Methodism: Little Mary and the E.R. Youngs at Norway House and Berens River." In Mary Kinnear, ed., *First Days, Fighting Days: Women in Manitoba History*, 19–40. Regina: Canadian Plains Research Center.

– 1987b. "'I Wish to Be as I see you': An Ojibwa-Methodist Encounter in the Fur Trade Country, Rainy Lake, 1854–55." *Arctic Anthropology* 24(1): 19–31.

– 1989. "'A Place in Your Mind for Them All': Chief William Berens." In James A. Clifton, ed. *Being and Becoming Indian: Biographical Studies of North American Frontiers*, 204–25. Chicago: Dorsey Press.

– 1998. "Jacob Berens." *Dictionary of Canadian Biography*, 14: 63–4. Toronto: University of Toronto Press.

– 2006. "Fields of Dreams: Revisiting A.I. Hallowell and the Berens River Ojibwe." In Sergei Kan and Pauline Turner Strong, eds., *New Perspectives on Native North America: Cultures, Histories, and Representations*, 17–41. Lincoln: University of Nebraska Press.

– 2008. "Growing Up Algonquian: A Missionary's Son in Cree-Ojibwe Country, 1869–1876." In Karl S. Hele and Regna Darnell, eds, *Papers of the Thirty-ninth Algonquian Conference*. London: University of Western Ontario.

– and Robert Brightman. 1988. *"The Orders of the Dreamed": George Nelson* on *Cree and Northern Ojibwa Religion and Myth, 1823.* Winnipeg: University of Manitoba Press.

– and Maureen Matthews. 1994. "Fair Wind: Medicine and Consolation on the Berens River." *Journal of the Canadian Historical Association,* new series, 4: 55–74.

Brumble, H. David III. 1988. *American Indian Autobiography.* Berkeley: University of California Press.

Brydon, Anne. 2001. "Dreams and Claims: Icelandic-Aboriginal Interactions in the Manitoba Interlake." *Journal of Canadian Studies* 36(2): 164–90.

Canada. *Sessional Papers.* 1882: Report of E. McColl, Inspector of Indian Agencies, 1881, vol. 15, no. 5, 107. 1886: Report of A. MacKay, Indian Agent, 1885, vol. 19, no. 4, 67.

Chamberlain, A. F. 1906. "Cree and Ojibwa Literary Terms." *Journal of American Folklore* 19: 346–47.

Clark, Lovell. 1990. "John Christian Schultz." *Dictionary of Canadian Biography* 12: 949–54. Toronto: University of Toronto Press.

Clifton, James A., ed. 1989. *Being and Becoming Indian: Biographical Studies of North American Frontiers.* Chicago: Dorsey Press.

Darnell, Regna. 2001. *Invisible Genealogies: A History of Americanist Anthropology.* Lincoln: University of Nebraska Press.

DeMallie, Raymond J., ed. 1984. *The Sixth Grandfather: Black Elk's Teachings Given to John G. Neihardt.* Lincoln: University of Nebraska Press.

Densmore, Frances. 1979 [1929] *Chippewa Customs.* St. Paul, Minnesota Historical Society Press.

Dowling, Donaldson Bogart. 1900. *Report on the Geology of the West Shore and Islands of Lake Winnipeg.* Geological Survey of Canada, *Annual Report.* New series, 11. Ottawa.

Dunning, R.W. 1959. *Social and Economic Change among the Northern Ojibwa.* Toronto: University of Toronto Press.

Ellis, C. Douglas. 1995. *Âtalôhkâna nêsta tipâcimôwina/ Cree Legends and Narratives from the West Coast of James Bay.* Winnipeg: University of Manitoba Press.

Friesen, Jean. 1982. "Alexander Morris." *Dictionary of Canadian Biography* 11: 608–14. Toronto: University of Toronto Press.

Gray, Susan Elaine. 1995. "Methodist Indian Day Schools and Indian Communities in Northern Manitoba, 1890–1925." *Manitoba History* 30: 2–16.

– 1999. "They Fought Just Like a Cat and a Dog!": Oblate-Methodist Relations at Berens River, Manitoba, 1920–1940." *Prairie Forum* 24(1): 51–64.

– 2005. "John Semmens." *Dictionary of Canadian Biography* 15: 917–18. Toronto: University of Toronto Press.

– 2006. *"I Will Fear No Evil": Ojibwa-Missionary Encounters Along the Berens River, 1875–1940.* Calgary: University of Calgary Press.

Hallowell, A. Irving. 1934.* "Some Empirical Aspects of Northern Saulteaux Religion." *American Anthropologist* 36(3): 389–404.

– 1935.* "Notes on the Northern Range of *Zizania* [wild rice] in Manitoba. *Rhodora* 37: 302–4.

– 1938.* "Freudian Symbolism in the Dream of a Saulteaux Indian. *Man* 38: 47–8.

– 1939. "Some European Folk Tales of the Berens River Saulteaux." *Journal of American Folklore* 52: 155–79.

– 1940.* "Spirits of the Dead in Saulteaux Life and Thought." *Journal of the Royal Anthropological Institute* 70: 29–51.

– 1967 [1955]. *Culture and Experience.* New York: Schocken Books.

– 1971 [1942]. *The Role of Conjuring in Saulteaux Society.* New York: Octagon Books.

– 1976. *Contributions to Anthropology.* Chicago: University of Chicago Press.

– 1992. *The Ojibwa of Berens River, Manitoba: Ethnography into History.* Fort Worth: Harcourt Brace Jovanovich.

– In press, 2010. *Contributions to Ojibwe Studies, 1934–1972.* Jennifer S.H. Brown and Susan Elaine Gray, eds. Lincoln: University of Nebraska Press. [*Articles by Hallowell marked with an asterisk are reprinted in this publication.]

Harvey, Graham. 2006. *Animism: Respecting the Living World.* New York: Columbia University Press.

Hewson, L.C. 1960. "A History of the Lake Winnipeg Fishery for Whitefish, *Coregonus clupeaformis,* with Some Reference to Its Economics." *Journal of the Fisheries Research Board of Canada* 17: 625–39.

Holzkamm, Tim E., Victor P. Lytwyn, and Leo G. Waisberg. 1991. "Rainy River Sturgeon: An Ojibway Resource in the Fur Trade Economy." In Kerry Abel and Jean Friesen, eds., *Aboriginal Resource Use in Canada: Historical and Legal Aspects,* 119–39. Winnipeg: University of Manitoba Press.

Ingold, Tim. 2000. "A Circumpolar Night's Dream." In Tim Ingold, ed., *The Perception of the Environment: Essays in Livelihood, Dwelling and Skill*, 89–110. London: Routledge.

Jones, Percy E. 1917. "Our Indian Mission at Berens River, Lake Winnipeg," 2 February 1917. *Missionary Bulletin* 13(2): 299–300.

Jones, William. 1917. *Ojibwa Texts, Part 1*. Truman Michelson, ed. Leyden, NY: Publications of the American Ethnological Society 7.

– 1919. *Ojibwa Texts, Part 2*. Truman Michelson, ed. Leyden, NY: Publications of the American Ethnological Society 7.

Leach, Frederick. 1966. "Indian Medicine Men and Their Remedies." *The Moccasin Telegraph*. (Winter): 1–3.

– 1973. *55 Years With Indians and Settlers on Lake Winnipeg*. St. Boniface, MB: Oblates of Mary Immaculate.

Low, A.P. 1887. "Preliminary Report on an Exploration of Country from Lake Winnipeg to Hudson Bay." Geological and Natural History Survey of Canada, *Annual Report* (new series) 2: 5F-16F, Montreal.

Lytwyn, Victor P. 1986. *The Fur Trade of the Little North: Indians, Pedlars, and Englishmen East of Lake Winnipeg, 1760–1821*. Winnipeg: Rupert's Land Research Centre, University of Winnipeg.

Maclean, John. 1918. *Vanguards of Canada*. Toronto: Mission Society of the Methodist Church.

MacLeod, Margaret, and W.L. Morton. 1974 [1963]. *Cuthbert Grant of Grantown: Warden of the Plains of Red River*. Toronto: McClelland and Stewart.

Manson, William C. 1986. "Abram Kardiner and the Neo-Freudian Alternative in Culture and Personality." In George W. Stocking, Jr. ed., *Malinowski, Rivers, Benedict and Others: Essays on Culture and Personality*. Madison, WI: University of Wisconsin Press.

Matthews, Maureen, with Jennifer S.H. Brown, Margaret Simmons, and Roger Roulette. 1993. "The Search for Fair Wind's Drum." *Ideas*. Toronto: CBC Radio.

– with Roger Roulette and Margaret Simmons. 1995. " Thunderbirds." *Ideas*. Toronto: CBC Radio.

– and Roger Roulette. 1996. "Fair Wind's Dream: *Naamiwan Obawaajigewin*." In Jennifer S.H. Brown and Elizabeth Vibert, eds., *Reading beyond Words: Contexts for Native History*, 130–60. Peterborough, ON: Broadview Press.

McColl, Frances. 1989. *Ebenezer McColl: "Friend to the Indians."* Winnipeg: Hignell Printing.

Mochoruk, James David. 1994 "Walter Robert Bown." *Dictionary of Canadian Biography* 13: 103–4. Toronto: University of Toronto Press.

Monkman, Kathleen. 2000. *Loon Straits through the Years: The Monkman Ancestry.* Winnipeg: privately printed.

Moodie, D. Wayne. 1991. "Manomin: Historical-Geographical Perspectives on the Ojibwa Production of Wild Rice." In Kerry Abel and Jean Friesen, eds., *Aboriginal Resource Use in Canada: Historical and Legal Aspects*, 71–9. Winnipeg: University of Manitoba Press.

– and Barry Kaye. 1986. "Indian Agriculture in the Fur Trade Northwest." *Prairie Forum* 11(2): 171–84.

Morantz, Toby. 1984. "Oral and Recorded History in James Bay." In William Cowan, ed., *Papers of the Fifteenth Algonquian Conference*, 171–92. Ottawa: Carleton University.

Morris, Alexander. 1880. *The Treaties of Canada with the Indians of Manitoba and the North-West Territories.* Toronto: Belfords, Clarke.

Morton, W.L., ed. 1956. *Alexander Begg's Red River Journal.* Toronto: Champlain Society.

Neihardt, John G. 1932. *Black Elk Speaks, Being the Life Story of a Holy Man of the Oglala Sioux as Told to John G. Neihardt* . New York: William Morrow.

Nichols, John D., and Earl Nyholm. 1995. *A Concise Dictionary of Minnesota Ojibwe.* Minneapolis: University of Minnesota Press.

Overholt, Thomas W., and J. Baird Callicott. 1982. *Clothed-In-Fur and Other Tales: An Introduction to an Ojibwa World View.* London: University of America Press.

Peers, Laura. 1994. *The Ojibwa of Western Canada 1780–1870.* Winnipeg: University of Manitoba Press.

Pentland, David H. 1981. Synonymy [of Saulteaux and Its Variants]. In June Helm, ed., *Handbook of North American Indians.* Vol. 6, *Subarctic*, 254–5. Washington, DC: Smithsonian Institution.

Rogers, Edward S., and Mary Black Rogers. 1978. "Method for Reconstructing Patterns of Change: Surname Adoption by the Weagamow Ojibwa, 1870–1950." *Ethnohistory* 25: 319–45.

Rogers, Mary Black. 1977. "Ojibwa Power Belief System." In Raymond D. Fogelson and Richard N. Adams, eds. *The Anthropology of Power: Ethnographic Studies From Asia, Oceania and the New World, 141–51*. New York: Academic Press, 1977.

– 1988. "Ojibwa Power Interactions: Creating Contexts for 'Respectful Talk.'" In Regna Darnell and M. Foster, eds., *Native North American Interaction Patterns*, 44–68. Ottawa: National Museums of Canada, Mercury Series, 112.

Ross, A.W. 1885. Report from Fisher River. *59th Annual Report of the Missionary Society of the Methodist Church of Canada*. Toronto.

Rostecki, Randy R. 1972–73. "Some Old Winnipeg Buildings." Manitoba Historical Society *Transactions* 3 (29).

Schuetze, Luther L. 2001. *Mission to Little Grand Rapids: Life with the Anishinabe 1927 to 1938*. Vancouver: Creative Connections.

Schultz, John Christian. 1987 [1890]. "Notes on Indian Council at Treaty Rock, Berens River, Lake Winnipeg, Man. 12th July 1890." Introduction and notes by Frank Tough. *Native Studies Review* 3(1): 117–27.

Semmens, John. 1884. *The Field and the Work: Sketches of Missionary Life in the Far North*. Toronto: Methodist Mission Rooms.

Smith, Theresa S. 1995. *The Island of the Anishnaabeg: Thunderers and Water Monsters in the Traditional Ojibwe Life-World*. Moscow, Idaho: University of Idaho Press.

Steinbring, Jack H. 1981. "Saulteaux of Lake Winnipeg." In June Helm, ed., *Handbook of North American Indians*. Vol. 6, *Subarctic*, 244–55. Washington, DC: Smithsonian Institution.

Stocking, George W., Jr. 2004. "A.I. Hallowell's Boasian Evolutionism: Human Ir/rationality in Cross-Cultural, Evolutionary, and Personal Context." In Richard Handler, ed., *Significant Others: Interpersonal and Professional Commitments in Anthropology, 196–260*. Madison: University of Wisconsin Press.

Sugarhead, Cecilia. 1996. *Nonoontaan/I Can Hear It: Ojibwe Stories from Lansdowne House*. Edited, translated, and with a glossary by John O'Meara. Winnipeg: Algonquian and Iroquoian Linguistics, Memoir 14.

Thistle, Paul. 1986. *Indian-European Trade Relations in the Lower Saskatchewan River Region to 1840*. Winnipeg: University of Manitoba Press.

Tough, Frank. 1996. *"As Their Natural Resources Fail": Native Peoples and the Economic History of Northern Manitoba, 1870–1930*. Vancouver: University of British Columbia Press.

Turner, Allan R. 1972. "James McKay." *Dictionary of Canadian Biography* 10: 473–5. Toronto: University of Toronto Press.

Vennum, Thomas. 2007. *Lacrosse Legends of the First Americans*. Baltimore: Johns Hopkins University Press.

Wallace, Anthony F.C. 1980. "Alfred Irving Hallowell December 28, 1892–October 10, 1974." *Biographical Memoirs*, 195–213. Washington, DC: National Academy of Sciences, vol. 51.

Wilkinson, L., and J.T. Fisher. 2005. "The Response of Mammals to Forest Fire and Timber Harvest in the North American Boreal Forest." *Mammal Review* 35(1): 51–81.

Wilmot, Samuel. 1891. "Special Report of Mr. S. Wilmot Relative to the Preservation of the Whitefish Fisheries of Lake Winnipeg." Canada. Sessional Papers, No. 8, Appendix 3. Ottawa.

Winnipeg Telegram. 1899. Obituary of Joseph Monkman, 9 June.

Winnipeg Tribune. 1947. Obituary of Chief William Berens. 2 September.

Young, Egerton Ryerson. 1890. *By Canoe and Dog-Train among the Cree and Salteaux Indians*. New York: Hunt and Eaton.

– 1903. *Algonquin Indian Tales*. London: Fleming H. Revell.

– 1907. *The Battle of the Bears*. Boston: W.A. Wilde.

Index